"Artificial intelligence is something I never env[...] topic in the church or in theological education. Thankfully, [...] work O'Callaghan and Hoffman guide Christian leaders biblically, theologically, and practically on this life-altering development called AI. While we do not know what the future holds in this digital world, we do know the One who holds the future. *AI Shepherds and Electric Sheep* is a well-researched and pioneering book that gives us a clear road map to begin understanding and navigating this ever-changing technological age."

—**Matthew D. Kim**, Truett Theological Seminary, Baylor University; author of *Preaching with Cultural Intelligence*

"The hype surrounding AI, fueled by science fiction and film, has spread through social media and shaped our understanding of this emerging technology. While all this attention reflects the enthusiasm many people hold for AI, it has sparked fears and concerns as well. How can Christians respond to both the hype and the fear? O'Callaghan and Hoffman's meticulous work presents us with a biblical-theological framework for addressing the challenges AI poses to communities, education, church ministry, the meaning of being human, and moral practices. This book cogently explains why AI should not be rejected outright and how it can be critically engaged and received with thanksgiving."

—**Ximian Xu**, University of Edinburgh

AI SHEPHERDS and ELECTRIC SHEEP

AI
SHEPHERDS
and
ELECTRIC
SHEEP

Leading and Teaching
in the Age of Artificial Intelligence

Sean O'Callaghan and Paul A. Hoffman

B

Baker Academic

a division of Baker Publishing Group

Grand Rapids, Michigan

Published by Baker Academic
a division of Baker Publishing Group
Grand Rapids, Michigan
BakerAcademic.com

Printed in the United States of America

Library of Congress Cataloging-in-Publication Data
Names: O'Callaghan, Sean, 1962– author. | Hoffman, Paul A., 1977– author.
Title: AI shepherds and electric sheep : leading and teaching in the age of artificial intelligence / Sean O'Callaghan, Paul A. Hoffman.
Description: Grand Rapids, Michigan : Baker Academic, a division of Baker Publishing Group, 2025. | Includes bibliographical references and index.
Identifiers: LCCN 2024026488 | ISBN 9781540968012 (paperback) | ISBN 9781540968647 (casebound) | ISBN 9781493449378 (ebook) | ISBN 9781493449385 (pdf)
Subjects: LCSH: Church work. | Artificial intelligence—Religious Aspects—Christianity.
Classification: LCC BV4400 .O34 2025 | DDC 253.0285/63—dc23/eng/20240708
LC record available at https://lccn.loc.gov/2024026488

Cover illustration of electric sheep generated by AI
Cover design by Paula Gibson

Baker Publishing Group publications use paper produced from sustainable forestry practices and postconsumer waste whenever possible.

25 26 27 28 29 30 31   7 6 5 4 3 2 1

To our phenomenal wives who have helped us
to be fully human and to flourish:

Autumn Blossom Hoffman
and
Melanie O'Callaghan

Contents

Foreword *by A. Trevor Sutton* xi

Acknowledgments xv

Introduction 1

1. What Is Artificial Intelligence? 9

2. What Are the Current and Potential Implications of AI? 39

3. What Does It Mean to Be Human from a Biblical Perspective? 61

4. What Does It Mean to Be Human in the Technological Age? 83

5. How Should Educators Interact with AI? 111

6. How Should Christians Be Formed and Discipled in the Age of AI? 135

7. How Should Ministry Leaders Approach AI? 153

Conclusion 167

Appendix A: Nine Definitions of AI 173

Appendix B: Six Views on Technology 175

Recommended Resources 179

Scripture Index 181

Subject Index 183

Foreword

A. TREVOR SUTTON

Artificial intelligence needs _____.

How would you finish that sentence? Be careful how you fill in that blank; it will reveal a lot about you. Completing that sentence reveals your hopes and fears, your assumptions and aspirations as they relate to emerging technology and the world in which we live. Like a sort of verbal Rorschach test, this simple prompt says as much about you as it does about artificial intelligence (AI).

Some say that AI needs application. This dazzlingly powerful technology needs more and more opportunities to be put to good use. This reveals an optimistic view of emerging technology: AI will improve knowledge, catalyze progress, optimize longevity, and eradicate our problems. All we need to do is apply AI, get out of the way, and flourishing will follow.

Some say that AI needs time. Still in its infancy, AI must develop in order to reach its full potential. Issues such as racial biases, hallucinating information, and laughably bad image generation are just the foibles of adolescence. After the awkward teenage years are gone, AI will hit its stride and grow into its own. With time, AI will develop into a fully functional and mature technology that brings about human flourishing.

Others will be a bit more pessimistic in completing that sentence and assert that AI needs suppression. Dystopian fears increase with every new AI application. Many people view the rise of AI as a harbinger of the end. This technology will mark the end of everything: jobs, families, churches, economies, nations, and life as we know it. Human flourishing depends on putting an end to AI.

While there is no consensus on what AI needs, whether it is application, time, suppression, funding, raw material, improvement, ethics, or public policy, we can agree that it needs something. In order for this emerging technology to help and not harm, we must consider what needs to accompany the rise of AI. What narratives and principles need to structure the creation and usage of AI? What practices and boundaries need to be enacted as AI leaves the laboratory and enters markets, homes, schools, and churches?

AI Shepherds and Electric Sheep makes a compelling argument that AI needs us. Sean O'Callaghan and Paul Hoffman masterfully demonstrate how the rise of AI needs to be balanced with a robust understanding of human flourishing. Unless we understand what it means to be human—bearers of the image and breath of God—then we will never understand how AI can help and not harm. O'Callaghan and Hoffman argue that AI needs Christian anthropology. AI needs a human-centered framework founded on the *imago Dei*, not the *imago machinarum*. The attention that people give to AI needs to be paired with an equal or even greater attention to the formative power of Christian anthropology, human habits, and our collective histories.

And yet, O'Callaghan and Hoffman argue that AI needs more than just us. AI needs Jesus. Any understanding of what it means to be human is insufficient without knowing Jesus Christ. Lest we assume that AI will be suppressive or salvific, we need the creational narrative of Scripture as a framework for AI. The creational narrative—creation, disintegration, liberation, reclamation, and glorification—provides a necessary metanarrative within which AI can flourish. *AI Shepherds and Electric Sheep* makes it clear: a world with AI needs us to be fully human, and Jesus alone makes us fully human.

No matter what you think AI needs, you need this book. Having taught and written in this field for the past decade, I am convinced that *AI Shepherds and Electric Sheep* is exactly what the AI conversation needs at this moment. Church leaders, educators, congregations, and students will find greatly needed definitions and explanations as well as frameworks and guidance for flourishing in the age of AI. O'Callaghan and Hoffman do a tremendous job of bringing scholarly rigor to bear on the subject while keeping the conversation accessible and applicable. You will be better prepared for teaching, preaching, ministering, and discipling in a world of AI after reading this book: I know that I am.

It is not only the groups I mention above who need this book. I believe that so many others would benefit from what follows in these pages. Technologists and investors, policymakers and ethicists, citizens and anyone living in this technological age need *AI Shepherds and Electric Sheep*. The success of AI does not depend on more application or time, suppression or regulation. For AI to flourish, it needs the unique resources of the Christian faith and well-equipped shepherds prepared to lead God's flock in this electric age. It is here—and only here—that AI will find a true and enduring narrative, practices that promote focus and flourishing, and the hope that comes in and through Jesus Christ. As long as the Christian faith is absent from conversations about AI, it will always be missing something. The future is coming, and it needs the hope of Jesus and his image bearers in it.

Acknowledgments

We would like to thank several individuals who helped us with this project.

Andrew Finch stimulated the birth of this book.

Trip Wolfskehl created the diagrams, for which we are so grateful.

Drew Harris edited the first draft of the manuscript under an expedited deadline—you rock, Drew! John Knox devoted his time and talent creating the indexes. Trevor Sutton wrote a lovely foreword.

Russ Bjork, Cliff Winters, Matt Klee, and Mike Pike read the manuscript and offered numerous helpful suggestions for improving it.

Salve Regina University granted Sean a sabbatical to work on this volume.

Troy Catterson covered Sean's PhD program duties in his absence.

Evangelical Friends Church of Newport, Rhode Island, supported Paul's writing ministry.

We thank the tremendous team at Baker Academic, especially Robert Hosack and Julie Zahm, for investing their time, resources, and expertise in this project.

This project could not have been completed without the support of our amazing wives, Autumn Hoffman and Melanie O'Callaghan. Thank you so much, ladies. We love you and are grateful to God for you.

To our children, Landon Hoffman, Kelan Hoffman, and Evie O'Callaghan: we love you and are so proud of you. We pray that you'll be agents of human flourishing in your generation.

Finally, we give all praise and glory to our triune God: Father, Son, and Holy Spirit, who alone fulfills all the gifts and promises outlined in Romans 8 and empowered us to write this book.

Introduction

"The future is coming, and you're not in it."

Those words are spoken by Rear Admiral Chester "Hammer" Cain to Navy pilot Pete "Maverick" Mitchell near the beginning of the movie *Top Gun: Maverick*, but they could well apply to those committed to the task of Christian ministry and education.

Why is that? Two words: artificial intelligence (AI).

Let's return to the tense exchange between the two naval officers. Maverick has just flown the hypersonic "Darkstar" scramjet beyond Mach 10. He is the best pilot the Navy has ever produced. In fact, he's been selected to serve as an instructor at Top Gun. His assignment is to prepare a group of younger pilots for a dangerous mission: destroying an illicit uranium enrichment plant.

However, the foe looming after "mission accomplished" is far more challenging. Rear Admiral Cain reads his impressive personnel file aloud, then abruptly pivots and implies that Maverick's brilliance will be soon eclipsed by superior machines:

> CAIN: Distinguished, distinguished, distinguished. Yet you can't get a promotion, you won't retire, and despite your best efforts, you refuse to die. You should be at least a two-star admiral by now, if not a senator. Yet here you are, Captain. Why is that?
>
> MAVERICK: It's one of life's mysteries, sir.
>
> CAIN: This isn't a joke. I asked you a question.
>
> MAVERICK: I am where I belong, sir.

CAIN: Well, the Navy doesn't see it that way, not anymore. These planes
you've been testing, Captain, one day, sooner than later, they
won't need pilots at all. Pilots that need to sleep, eat, take a [pee],
pilots that disobey orders. All you did was buy some time for
those men out there. The future is coming, and you're not in it.[1]

Soon enough, robots—not hindered by bodily functions—will fly the Navy's
planes. *Thank you for your service, Maverick, but we don't need you anymore.*

Every so often, Hollywood checks in with reality long enough to issue a
prophetic word. Maverick is not alone in his impending obsolescence. As of
2024, AI can compose music, lyrics, poetry, essays, sermons, and other content
as compelling as any student, pastor, or teacher can produce—and, in many
cases, in a superior way!

Don't believe us?

Recently, one of my (Paul's) best friends, Dr. Cliff Winters—a pastor and
New Testament scholar—asked ChatGPT to write a worship song about
Jesus and bubble gum. This is what the chatbot produced, which Cliff then
posted on Facebook:

Verse 1

Jesus, the sweetest name I know
Flavors my heart, with love that flows
With You by my side, I'll never be low
Like bubble gum, You never lose Your glow

Chorus

Jesus, You're my bubble gum
Sticking close, never leaving me to run
With every chew, I'm lifted higher
In Your love, my soul sets on fire

Verse 2

You fill my life, with joy so bright
With every chew, I feel Your light
In times of trouble, You're my delight
Like bubble gum, You make everything all right

---

1. *Top Gun: Maverick*, directed by Joseph Kosinski (Hollywood, CA: Paramount Pictures,
2022), DVD.

Chorus

Jesus, You're my bubble gum
Sticking close, never leaving me to run
With every chew, I'm lifted higher
In Your love, my soul sets on fire

Bridge

With every chew, I taste Your grace
With every chew, I see Your face
In You, I find my peace and rest
In You, I'm truly, truly blessed

Chorus

Jesus, You're my bubble gum
Sticking close, never leaving me to run
With every chew, I'm lifted higher
In Your love, my soul sets on fire

Outro

Jesus, You're the sweetest thing
In You, I find my heart can sing
Forever with You, I'll stay
In Your love, I'll never stray.[2]

When I read that post, I was astonished and thought to myself, "That's pretty theologically sound, catchy, *and clever*!" Then it dawned on me: "What does this mean? Why should I labor over writing an email, proposal, article, book, or message, if a robot can do it better than I can? Wait . . . am I *replaceable*?"

Those ruminations prompted an avalanche of urgent questions: What is AI, and where did it come from? How does it really work? What are the repercussions of AI? How will it change our lives? Does the Bible have anything to say about this technology? What does it mean to be human in this computer-centric, hypernetworked age? How are believers to be formed into the image of Christ in this brave new world? What are the implications of all of this for Christian educators, ministry leaders, and pastors? What parts of

2. Cliff Winters, Facebook, January 31, 2023, https://www.facebook.com/OpusRex. Used with permission. Other than this song, no other part of this book was written by AI.

AI should we consider embracing and utilizing? And what portions should we reject? Who even gets to decide that—technologists, CEOs, politicians, legislators, philosophers, ethicists, clergy, teachers, professors?

These are significant inquiries that call for thoughtful, biblical, and practical responses. But that points to a problem: system overload. Frankly, this is a terrible time to wrestle with these issues. Far too many ministry leaders and teachers are still reeling from the effects of the COVID-19 pandemic, the divisions roiling the church and society, economic instability, and the expanding mental health crisis—just to name a few—so they don't have the bandwidth to even consider tackling the emergence of AI and its attending cultural, social, moral, and spiritual effects.

And that raises a real danger. If there's a vacuum of robust reflection, many people resort to grabbing for the "junk food" of reasoning: polarities. Yes, humans will latch onto extreme solutions because they are quick and easy and require little mental effort.

When it comes to technology in general, individuals often steer in one of two main directions.[3] The first is a form of Luddism. The English Luddites were an early-nineteenth-century group of laborers who felt so threatened by the invention and use of textile machinery that they protested and even sabotaged it. In the twenty-first century, the attitude of the neo-Luddite is marked by resentment and resistance. Here's what's in the thought-bubble floating over their heads: "AI is bad. It robs humans of their creative and productive autonomy and will steal all their jobs. Burn all the bots to bits!"

On the other side of the divide is technologism. In this worldview, machines are messianic. If we harness them properly or even merge with them (called "transhumanism"), we will eradicate all diseases, famine, war, and climate change and finally achieve immortality. The chief shaman of this religion is none other than Elon Musk, who has evangelistically testified to the transformative power of technology such that some have suggested he's "a robot sent from the future to save humanity."[4] Ah, what we've all been yearning for: Terminator Jesus, driving a Tesla, awaiting completion of his rocket to Mars so he can colonize it.

---

3. Clearly, there are more than two ways to view technology. In the appendix to this book, we list six major views.

4. Neil Strauss, "Elon Musk: The Architect of Tomorrow," *Rolling Stone*, November 15, 2017, https://www.rollingstone.com/culture/culture-features/elon-musk-the-architect-of-tomorrow-120850.

Enter this book. In these pages, we seek to avoid these excessive positions. Instead, we offer a third way: a selective engagement oriented toward human flourishing and grounded in bodily, material realities. This is a route that involves careful negotiation with technological advances, where developments are viewed through an open but critical lens shaped by a Christian worldview. On the one hand, we recognize technology exists within a fallen world and is subject to human failings. On the other hand, scientific and technological breakthroughs can assist human thriving and so may have redemptive value. Thus, our aim is to present a biblical-theological framework that will help educators and ministry leaders identify the perils and possibilities that lie before us.

We believe this path is informed, theological, and accessible. It is informed because we have been working in these areas of technology for a while and, more specifically, have seen how they've evolved over the past ten years. It is theological because, as theologians, we are very familiar with the question about what it means to be human and made in the image of God in an age of AI. And the path is accessible because we are educators who know the importance of communicating concepts that may be completely new to some.

With that in mind, how shall we proceed down this path together? In the first chapter, Sean details the history of the development of AI and its current applications, including algorithms and ChatGPT. He also presents multiple definitions of AI, including key categories, such as *narrow AI* and *artificial general intelligence*. Further, he describes and evaluates the scientific and philosophical underpinnings of the founders and propagators of these AI technologies and introduces how AI is influencing human decision-making, prediction, and autonomy.

Next, we reflect on some of the possible ramifications of AI. How will AI change our economy? Will AI bring about massive unemployment as robots continue to replace human jobs? How might AI influence international relations? Will it stoke an arms race, similar to the Cold War of the twentieth century? Additionally, we explore the concepts of AI alignment, existential risk (i.e., human extinction), and techno-apocalypticism. However, we also examine the current and potential benefits of AI. For example, AI is already revolutionizing the worlds of medicine, law, law enforcement, criminal justice, and finance.

In the third chapter, we consider technology in relation to the Holy Scriptures. This includes wrapping vital doctrines such as the Trinity, creation, the *imago Dei*, the cultural mandate, the fall, common grace, general revelation, Christ's redemptive work, and eschatology into one cohesive metanarrative. This is a lens that frames AI in light of historic orthodox Christianity and the lordship of Jesus Christ.

Following this, Sean contrasts our biblical anthropology with a techno-human anthropology. This leads him to answer questions such as these: What does it look like to be a fully flourishing human being? How might AI disrupt or detract from this end? How can AI potentially aid or enhance God's plan for humans?

In chapter 5, we delve into the implications of AI for those committed to the task of Christian education. Here, we lay out our vision for selective engagement, a delicate negotiation that entails the incorporation of AI's strengths on some points, along with a prophetic rejection of its deficiencies. The goal is to resource those working on the front lines, as AI will have profound consequences for Christian education and ministry training in the coming years, especially with respect to curricula.

Education dovetails with formation. Christians are called to inhabit the *imago Christi*, to become like Jesus Christ (2 Cor. 3:18). How might that occur with machines all around us? Such a situation calls believers to create and maintain liturgies and habits that keep us grounded in our identity as God's countercultural family. Intentional practices, which we call "hearth habits," shape our affections, attitudes, and behaviors and reinforce that our community exists to be a sign and foretaste of God's kingdom and the new creation.

In chapter 7, Paul evaluates the role of AI for teachers and preachers in local churches. While AI may prove valuable in research, content generation, and editing, it cannot replace the essential elements required for a transformative encounter between the human and the divine. That is, ChatGPT knows nothing of the sacred activities of preaching, counseling, prayer, and so on. However, it may serve certain administrative tasks and even some missional goals. While AI cannot be the technological savior many long for, it will likely offer benefits to human growth and spiritual maturation that we would be wise to ponder, welcome, and implement.

The book finishes with an ode to the enduring beauty of our faithful ancestors, who lived deeply rooted lives. It is a reminder that, historically, humans have flourished without AI.

Perhaps the most important message we want to convey in this book is this: the future is coming, and unlike Maverick, Christian leaders and educators ought to be in it. Artificial intelligence, with its far-reaching impacts, isn't going away, and it will challenge us not just in our homes, schools, and workplaces but also in our sense of human identity and in our relationships.

Will the robots replace us? We think not. But they will play an undeniable role in shaping our shared future.

So, like Maverick, let's fasten our seat belts. This jet is ready to take off.

1. What Is Artificial Intelligence?

The Big Picture

The answer to the question, What is artificial intelligence? is harder to realize than it might appear. Artificial intelligence (AI) is understood in different ways, depending on how the term is used. What we can say, with absolute confidence, is that AI is widespread and is applied in ways that might surprise people. It is no longer a niche area of computer technology, confined to high-level research laboratories, but is ubiquitous in the digitally enabled processes we use and depend on every day. Without it, the world as we know it would grind to a halt. We would have to completely rethink how we function.

One way of envisioning AI might be to think of it as a galaxy of applications, all of which make use of similar technology but at different levels of complexity. When you look up at the stars, everything looks much the same from a distance, but when you gaze at the heavens through a powerful telescope, you can see widely varying configurations of stars with very different dynamics. Artificial intelligence, then, while often referred to generically, functions in multiple ways, depending on the area and the specific needs of the area. All AI systems have certain elements in common. For instance, they all utilize data sets, usually very large data sets; they all use some form of learning, be that machine learning or what is called deep learning; and the goal is problem-solving. To realize all these elements, AI needs algorithms, without which it cannot learn, analyze, or extrapolate from the knowledge it produces.

In this chapter, we will introduce various definitions of AI. Along the way, you will see that no one definition is universally accepted. Since AI affects so many facets of global life and its effects are felt in different ways, it is perceived by those who are impacted by it through the lens of their own experiences. We will discuss the debate concerning intelligence itself and outline the history of the development of AI and key figures involved in its evolution. We will examine how AI affects the realms of politics and economics as well as its role as a catalyst of social and behavioral change.

Algorithms

Artificial intelligence operates by algorithms, which have "family resemblances" and appear to mirror and even surpass human ingenuity. These algorithms result in different forms and levels of AI complexity. Algorithms work like recipes—they are step-by-step instructions that AI programs run in order to perform certain tasks. Furthermore, algorithms are programmed to anticipate certain events and adapt their processes in response. They "possess a relentless capacity for identifying hidden patterns in a big set of data, via their ability to evolve, learn, unlearn, autocorrect, and perfect, regardless of whether they end up reaching (or surpassing) human levels of intelligence."[1]

Artificial intelligence can run your fridge and detect when you run out of milk. The algorithm that determines you've run out of milk will also know that its next step is to order you some more milk or alert you to order it yourself. AI also lies behind fearsomely complex systems, such as autonomous weapons and global financial markets. When you get recommendations on Amazon based on previous purchases or browsing, AI is behind the algorithms that track your choices and predict what you might want to buy next. Virtual assistants on your smartphone or laptop are driven by AI. When you run a piece of text through Google Translate to ascertain its meaning in another language, you are relying on AI to search millions of databases in an instant and make the best choice of translation, while also offering you alternatives. Smart cities use AI to regulate traffic and public amenities. The car you drive may rely on AI for a number of applications, including your GPS system, which uses AI to make quick decisions concerning the most efficient route to take. Militaries, governments, law enforcement agencies, and intelligence services the world over use AI to fly drones, move satellites, monitor communications,

---

1. Tomas Chamorro-Premuzic, *I, Human: AI, Automation, and the Quest to Reclaim What Makes Us Unique* (Boston: Harvard Business Review, 2023), 3.

and track people's movements. Such use can be beneficial in apprehending human traffickers and drug smugglers but very problematic when directed at the ordinary citizen, as is evident by the intense debates surrounding public surveillance. Artificial intelligence has implications, both practical and ethical.

Artificial intelligence, then, can perform both simple and complex tasks, just as we humans perform various simple and complex tasks every day. The difference with AI is the speed at which it can gather and analyze information and make decisions, as well as the amount of information it can handle at any one time. This large collection of information is often known as "big data." Artificial intelligence doesn't need sleep, get hungry, or even get hangry. It works alongside us tirelessly, often as a coworker might, but what happens when it becomes the Lamborghini to our Kia and leaves us miles behind?

Key AI Categories

Artificial intelligence has evolved over time. It has had a longer history than people might imagine, and it can be divided into different categories based on what the AI in view can actually do. In this section, we will examine the different categories of AI, such as *artificial narrow intelligence* (ANI), *artificial general intelligence* (AGI), *artificial super intelligence* (ASI), and *generative AI* (GenAI). We will also explain both *machine learning* and *deep learning*, both vital components of AI.

ANI

Narrow AI is a form of AI that focuses on specific tasks. This is the form of AI to which we have become most accustomed, as it powers the applications we use on a daily or nearly daily basis. Narrow AI is also called "weak" AI, but this is a misleading term because ANI is still a powerful technological tool. This form of AI is indeed limited, though; the learning abilities of ANI-run systems are governed by algorithms with predetermined boundaries, which are restricted in the level of adaptation needed to act as intelligently as humans do. Narrow AI has specific, programmed tasks, which are regulated by algorithms but do not stray outside of preset parameters. It may look like it is thinking independently, but it is running through options that have been programmed into it and that will eventually hit the buffers.

The programs that power Netflix and Amazon are good examples of ANI; they analyze all of the data made available to them when users choose or reject certain titles and genres, but they are limited to their databases and may not always discern microinterests, as they deal with broad categories. Human intelligence, by contrast, has the X factor; such intelligence takes into account empathy and common sense. Narrow AI's lack of this kind of intelligence, then, "restricts its ability to understand context, make nuanced decisions, or fully comprehend complex scenarios."[2] The benefits of ANI are that it supports automated processes, can process large amounts of data, and makes widespread use of personal assistants, like Siri and Alexa.[3]

In short, ANI has the following limitations:

1. it cannot explain how or what it has learned, as a human can;

2. it cannot reflect on what it has learned;

3. it cannot contextualize its learning, as humans can;

4. it makes mistakes that human beings don't easily make, such as incorrectly identifying common images;

5. it may be influenced by bias (reflecting the biases of its programmers) but may not be aware of this influence;

6. it does not have the innate common sense (or even intuition) of human beings; and

7. it lacks self-awareness.[4]

As one expert explains, ANI can be trained to use large databases to recognize different kinds of chairs, even becoming very adept at this task, but this intelligence "cannot be applied to everything. It is limited to that specific task."[5]

As stated above, ANI is still an extremely powerful tool, but the creators of AI have much loftier ambitions, desiring to fully harness its power.

2. Ben Nancholas, "Narrow Artificial Intelligence: Advantages, Disadvantages, and the Future of AI," University of Wolverhampton, September 1, 2023, https://online.wlv.ac.uk/narrow-artificial-intelligence-advantages-disadvantages-and-the-future-of-ai.

3. Nancholas, "Narrow Artificial Intelligence."

4. For a more extended discussion of these limitations, see Henry A. Kissinger, Eric Schmidt, and Daniel Huttenlocher, *The Age of AI and Our Human Future* (New York: Little, Brown, 2021), 77–85.

5. Jason Thacker, *The Age of AI: Artificial Intelligence and the Future of Humanity* (Grand Rapids: Zondervan Thrive, 2020), 39.

AGI and ASI

Artificial general intelligence and artificial super intelligence are the "dream." They are "generally understood to mean AI capable of completing any intellectual task humans are capable of—in contrast to today's 'narrow' AI, which is developed to complete a specific task."[6] Many theorizers and practitioners debate whether this functionality is even possible. Both AGI and ASI are known as "strong AI." There are important distinctions between these two forms of strong AI:

> AGI, or general AI, is a theoretical form of AI where a machine would have an intelligence equal to humans; it would be self-aware with a consciousness that would have the ability to solve problems, learn, and plan for the future. ASI—also known as superintelligence—would surpass the intelligence and ability of the human brain. While strong AI is still entirely theoretical with no practical examples in use today, that doesn't mean AI researchers aren't also exploring its development. In the meantime, the best examples of ASI might be from science fiction, such as HAL, the superhuman and rogue computer assistant in *2001: A Space Odyssey*.[7]

Two other key concepts in understanding AI and how it learns and adapts are machine learning and deep learning, the latter of which includes neural networks. Machine learning and deep learning are related to each other and have a lot in common; however, they also differ in certain ways.

Machine Learning

Machine learning involves training a computer to use large data sets. As it works with the data over and over again, the computer gets more adept at understanding the data and what to do with it. It learns as it goes. In 2011, a machine called IBM Watson won a competition between it and two Jeopardy champions:

> Watson's programmers fed it thousands of question and answer pairs, as well as examples of correct responses. When given just an answer, the machine was programmed to come up with the matching question. If it got it wrong,

---

6. Kissinger, Schmidt, and Huttenlocher, *Age of AI*, 88.
7. "What Is Artificial Intelligence (AI)?," IBM, accessed December 15, 2023, https://www.ibm.com/topics/artificial-intelligence.

programmers would correct it. This allowed Watson to modify its algorithms, or in a sense "learn" from its mistakes.

By the time Watson faced off against the Jeopardy champions, in a matter of seconds, it could parse 200 million pages of information and generate a list of possible answers, ranked by how likely they were to be right—even if it had never seen the particular Jeopardy clue before.[8]

Deep Learning

Deep learning makes use of a neural network, which is structured along the lines of the human brain.

> Where machine learning algorithms generally need human correction when they get something wrong, deep learning algorithms can improve their outcomes through repetition, without human intervention. A machine learning algorithm can learn from relatively small sets of data, but a deep learning algorithm requires big data sets that might include diverse and unstructured data. . . . Deep learning is a machine learning technique that layers algorithms and computing units—or neurons—into what is called an artificial neural network. . . . Data passes through this web of interconnected algorithms in a non-linear fashion, much like how our brains process information.[9]

The word *deep* in *deep learning* refers to the different layers in an algorithm's programming, which enable it to learn. Human beings learn by experience, and deep learning causes systems to learn in the same way, through repetition of tasks.

GenAI

Generative AI, such as that which governs ChatGPT, is a good example of deep learning. "Generative AI refers to deep-learning modules that can take raw data—say, all of Wikipedia or the collected works of Rembrandt—and 'learn' to generate statistically probable outputs when prompted. At a high level, generative models encode a simplified representation of their training data and draw from it to create a new work that's similar, but not identical, to the original data."[10]

8. "Deep Learning vs. Machine Learning: A Beginner's Guide," Coursera, updated April 1, 2024, https://www.coursera.org/articles/ai-vs-deep-learning-vs-machine-learning-beginners -guide.
9. "Deep Learning vs. Machine Learning."
10. "What Is Artificial Intelligence (AI)?"

Generative systems are so called because they generate information, but as the quote in the previous paragraph explains, they generate from their training data and adapt it according to the needs and prompts of their users. The AI might look like it is learning in a human sense, but it is in fact using vast amounts of data while training itself to generate what looks like new data in a different form.

Kelsey Piper argues that GenAI is actually a good example of ANI becoming less narrow, as it relies on predicting the next word in a text when it is generating information. "And yet, it can now identify questions as reasonable or unreasonable and discuss the physical world (for example, answering questions about which objects are larger or which steps in a process must come first). In order to be very good at the narrow task of text prediction, an AI system will eventually develop abilities that are not narrow at all."[11] According to Piper, computers are now developing more generalized abilities because they are learning by themselves. Piper is more optimistic than most about the evolution of general AI, arguing that an increase in computer power, the lack of which has limited us in the past, might get us places that would surprise us in terms of AGI. And because of deep learning, systems are becoming more competent. So both deep learning and increased computer power could propel us to AGI faster than we thought.

Marr's Four Types of AI

The futurist Bernard Marr proposes four types of AI, each of which he evaluates based on how AI emulates human intelligence. He cautions that two of the four types are not even scientifically possible right now and that they are not all equal.

Reactive AI

Reactive AI seems to be Marr's term for very basic ANI. "Reactive machines always respond to identical situations in the exact same way every time, and they are not able to learn actions or conceive of past or future," he writes.[12]

11. Kelsey Piper, "The Case for Taking AI Seriously as a Threat to Humanity: Why Some People Fear AI, Explained," *Vox*, updated October 15, 2020, https://www.vox.com/future-perfect/2018/12/21/18126576/ai-artificial-intelligence-machine-learning-safety-alignment.
12. Bernard Marr, "Understanding the 4 Types of Artificial Intelligence," Bernard Marr and Co., accessed December 20, 2023, https://bernardmarr.com/understanding-the-4-types-of-artificial-intelligence.

This type of AI reacts to specific conditions. It has a predictable outcome. It will respond to identical situations in the exact same way every time. Spam filters in email are a good example of reactive AI.[13]

Limited Memory AI

Limited memory AI is the most widely used form of AI today. "This type of AI uses historical, observational data in combination with pre-programmed information to make predictions and perform complex classification tasks."[14] This category of AI is labeled "limited memory" because not all the data it gathers is retained. One example is an autonomous vehicle gathering information for a particular trip; it will not necessarily store that information long-term because its value pertains to that journey alone. However, the term *limited* should not give the impression that this type of AI is not powerful. Marr explains that it is the type of AI used in deep learning. It learns in a way that emulates the neurons in the human brain.[15]

Theory of Mind AI

"With this type of AI, machines will acquire true decision-making capabilities that are similar to humans," Marr writes.[16] This seems to correspond to strong AI, as in AGI. Marr makes the point that this type of AI will involve an ability to recognize and respond to emotions. He references the robot Sophia, which is designed to look and act as a human would, detecting emotional cues from those with whom it interacts and responding in kind with reflexively programmed emotional responses.[17]

Self-Aware AI

"When machines can be aware of their own emotions, as well as the emotions of others around them, they will have a level of consciousness and intelligence similar to human beings," Marr argues. "This type of AI will have desires, needs, and emotions as well."[18] This form of AI, then, goes

13. Bernard Marr, "The 4 Types of Artificial Intelligence," Bernard Marr and Co., June 17, 2021, video, 5:36, https://www.youtube.com/watch?v=Whpcb-gCIBY.

14. Marr, "Understanding the 4 Types."

15. Marr, "4 Types."

16. Marr, "Understanding the 4 Types."

17. Marr, "4 Types."

18. Marr, "Understanding the 4 Types."

much further in the realm of emotion than we would expect from theory of mind AI.

By proposing or aspiring to self-aware AI, Marr is going much further than most AI researchers, who would view this type of AI as being theoretically unattainable. However, many movies on the topic have explored scenarios in which computers do manifest desires, needs, and emotions, such as the movie *Her*, where a man and the Siri-type assistant on his cell phone develop a strong romantic relationship,[19] or the movie *Transcendence*, where an AI expert passes away but is able to upload his mind to cyberspace before doing so, enabling him to maintain relationships with those left behind.[20] The CNN series *Mostly Human* features an AI expert who has replicated her deceased friend in an app.[21] Using his text messages and other digital communications to emulate his communication, she created a digital version of him with which she could text and interact. The program is designed to respond as he would respond when alive, and it can also learn from repeated interactions with various people and evolve its responses.

Emotional AI or Affective Computing

Marr's categories are useful because he addresses the stages in the development of emotional intelligence in AI, which is an important yet often forgotten about aspect of AI. It is also called "affective computing." Marr explains emotional AI in the following terms: "When computers can read emotions by analyzing data, including facial expressions, gestures, tone of voice, force of keystrokes, and more to determine a person's emotional state and then react to it, we call this artificial emotional intelligence."[22] Imagine, then, the power of an emotional interaction between a human being and AI. This would revolutionize AI research and could even lead to interpersonal relationships of a kind between humans and machines. This can already take place to a limited degree, but as AI grows in emotional intelligence, it will occur a lot more. Marr also discusses AI programs such as Affectiva and RealEyes, which

19. *Her*, directed and written by Spike Jonze (Los Angeles: Annapurna Pictures, 2013), DVD.
20. *Transcendence*, directed by Wally Pfister, written by Jack Paglen (Burbank, CA: Warner Home Video, 2014), DVD.
21. *Mostly Human*, episode 1, "Dead, IRL," produced by Erica Fink et al., aired on CNN, https://money.cnn.com/mostly-human/dead-irl/.
22. Bernard Marr, "What Is Artificial Emotional Intelligence?," Bernard Marr and Co., accessed December 22, 2023, https://bernardmarr.com/what-is-artificial-emotional-intelligence.

monitor facial expressions of people who are watching videos, programs that very much help companies in evaluating the effectiveness of advertisements. He also discusses CompanionMX, a program that monitors mental health and that can pick up on someone's mood and level of anxiety during, for example, a phone call.[23]

Intelligence

The word *intelligence* keeps cropping up, of course, and the various definitions of the word provide the fuel for decades-long arguments as to whether machines really are intelligent. One thinker, John Searle, has presented what he terms the "Chinese Room" experiment to argue that although machines might look to us as if they are thinking, they are simply manipulating what are to them mere symbols. These symbols might look like language to us, so we conclude that machines are showing understanding. What looks like understanding and consciousness is simply the use of symbols that have been imbued with meaning by programmers but that are processed without any understanding of their true meaning. He uses the Chinese language as an example, arguing that a computer that can process data in this language might be thought of as understanding Chinese but, in fact, is merely reading what to it are meaningless symbols and simulating understanding.[24] Jason Thacker, a Christian voice in the world of AI, writes, "Intelligence is a complex word because people mean different things when they use it. Some use the term to include self-awareness, consciousness, problem solving, creativity, and reason. Others deem a machine intelligent if it can outperform a human in a single task, such as recognizing patterns that humans might miss, automating tasks, or even interacting with a human using natural language."[25]

Interestingly, Thacker argues that computer systems should be considered intelligent, even if their intelligence is artificial, "because intelligence doesn't define what it means to be human. Other parts of creation, such as animals, exhibit various levels of intelligence. Intelligence doesn't mean that a system is

23. Marr, "What Is Artificial Emotional Intelligence?"
24. For more on this experiment, read John Searle, "Minds, Brains, and Programs," *Behavioral and Brain Sciences* 3, no. 3 (September 1980): 417–57, https://doi.org/10.1017/S0140525X00005756.
25. Thacker, *Age of AI*, 39.

aware of itself or is able to outperform humans in all areas."[26] For those of us who might be inclined to give too much credit to computers for their apparent intelligence, Thacker counsels that "our current AI systems are nowhere near the level of intelligence of a human being, even that of my toddler sons."[27]

Key Figures in the Development of AI

As with any vast field of knowledge, no one person can be credited with AI's evolution. But three giant figures can legitimately be called foundational to the field—namely, Alan M. Turing (1912–1954), a British computer scientist who broke German codes during World War II; Professor John McCarthy (1927–2011), of Stanford University; and Geoffrey Hinton (b. 1947), a British-Canadian computer scientist most celebrated for his work on artificial neural networks.

Alan Turing

Turing introduced the phrase "the imitation game" to frame a question he asked in a paper published in 1950: Can machines think?[28] Dissatisfied with answers that drew on the definitions of the words *machine* and *think*, he instead formulated the imitation game, which involved a game between three parties: two humans and one computer. One of the two humans, who acted as an interrogator or questioner, sent questions to both the machine and his human partner by means of teleprinter-communicated text, which would have been the technological medium of the time for the task. The interrogator then had to decide whether the responses to the questions sent were coming from his human partner or the machine. If the machine gave a response that the evaluator judged to have come from his fellow human, then the machine had passed what is termed the Turing test because the interrogator had judged the machine to be thinking and intelligent, as they would have judged the human response to be.

The premise of the Turing test has been challenged many times amid debates concerning machine consciousness. One question that has arisen in such

---

26. Thacker, *Age of AI*, 39.
27. Thacker, *Age of AI*, 39.
28. A. M. Turing, "Computing Machinery and Intelligence," *Mind* 49 (1950): 433–60, https://courses.cs.umbc.edu/471/papers/turing.pdf.

debates, for example, is whether a seemingly intelligent machine is simply a machine going through a set of processes that prove neither intelligence nor awareness. However, Turing introduced issues that could not be ignored. He essentially initiated the debate concerning narrow and general AI.

John McCarthy

Professor John McCarthy was a distinguished and groundbreaking computer scientist and the first to use the term *artificial intelligence*. In addition, he organized and was a major contributor to the Dartmouth Summer Research Project on Artificial Intelligence in 1956, held at Dartmouth College in Hanover, New Hampshire. The conference that was held to discuss the project lasted for eight weeks and brought pioneers in the field together for the first time. McCarthy taught at Stanford University, and his website there, available even after his death in 2011, is a gold mine of information on AI and the meaning of *intelligence*.[29]

Geoffrey Hinton

Geoffrey Hinton is known as the "godfather of AI." His particular contributions have been in the areas of deep learning and the training of neural networks. He has developed research concerning a method known as backpropagation to aid machine learning. Recently, Hinton's voice has been strong and loud in warning of the dangers of AI, particularly those of generative intelligence, but his contribution to the field has been outstanding, and he ranks with both Turing and McCarthy as a founding figure.[30] A paper published by Hinton and other AI researchers in 1986 cemented his role in the development of the technology.[31] This paper put forward a new way of training neural networks, and this meant that new features could be created, which older models of learning could not offer. Backpropagation is essentially an algorithm that is at the center of machine learning: "In a nutshell,

29. John McCarthy, "Professor John McCarthy, Father of AI," Stanford University, accessed December 14, 2023, http://jmc.stanford.edu/contributions/index.html.

30. Sara Brown, "Why Neural Net Pioneer Geoffrey Hinton Is Sounding the Alarm on AI," MIT Management Sloan School, May 23, 2023, https://mitsloan.mit.edu/ideas-made-to-matter/why-neural-net-pioneer-geoffrey-hinton-sounding-alarm-ai. Our thanks to Russ Bjork, who championed the contributions of Hinton to us (email message to the authors, January 17, 2024).

31. David E. Rumelhart, Geoffrey E. Hinton, and Ronald J. Williams, "Learning Representations by Back-Propagating Errors," *Nature* 323 (1986): 533–36, https://doi.org/10.1038/323533a0.

backpropagation is a way to adjust the connections between artificial neurons over and over until a neural network produces the desired output."[32]

In 2018, Hinton was awarded the A.M. Turing Award, a highly prestigious event in the world of AI and an award thought of as the "Nobel Prize of Computing."[33] As a Turing laureate, his biography on the Turing Award's web page neatly explains his contributions, especially his decision amid an "AI winter" in the 1970s to pursue "the development of networks of simulated neural nodes to mimic the capabilities of human thought."[34]

Hinton's early research set the scene for more recent breakthroughs in object classification and speech recognition, as well as his recent role as vice president and engineering fellow at Google.

Defining AI

As we have seen, the field of AI is a contested one. There are numerous debates as to what AI actually is. In this section, we will look at some definitions of AI that come from different angles.

Professor McCarthy's Definition of AI

McCarthy defines AI as "the science and engineering of making intelligent machines, especially intelligent computer programs. It is related to the similar task of using computers to understand human intelligence, but AI does not have to confine itself to methods that are biologically observable."[35] McCarthy relates intelligence to "the computational part of the ability to achieve goals in the world. Varying kinds and degrees of intelligence occur in people, many animals and some machines."[36] In McCarthy's view, we do not yet have a definition of *intelligence* that would divorce the concept from human intelligence. This is complicated, he claims, by our inability to

32. Will Douglas Heaven, "Deep Learning Pioneer Geoffrey Hinton Has Quit Google," MIT Technology Review, May 1, 2023, https://www.technologyreview.com/2023/05/01/1072478/deep-learning-pioneer-geoffrey-hinton-quits-google.

33. "A.M. Turing Award," Association for Computing Machinery, accessed January 20, 2024, https://amturing.acm.org.

34. Thomas Haigh, "Geoffrey E Hinton," Association for Computing Machinery, accessed January 20, 2024, https://amturing.acm.org/award_winners/hinton_4791679.cfm.

35. John McCarthy, "What Is Artificial Intelligence?" (unpublished manuscript, last modified November 12, 2007), PDF file, 2, https://www-formal.stanford.edu/jmc/whatisai.pdf.

36. McCarthy, "What Is Artificial Intelligence?," 2.

"characterize in general what kinds of computational procedures we want to call intelligent."[37] The nature of intelligence, in McCarthy's view, means that we cannot answer yes or no to a question about whether a machine is intelligent. Interestingly, McCarthy believes that AI does not always have to be about simulating human intelligence because "AI researchers are free to use methods that are not observed in people or that involve much more computing than people can do."[38] McCarthy's paper on AI, referenced here, is highly accessible and important to read because it answers fundamental questions about AI and human intelligence in a succinct yet insightful way. His answer to a question about the Turing test is especially insightful: "A machine that passes the test should certainly be considered intelligent, but a machine could still be considered intelligent without knowing enough about humans to imitate a human."[39] On the Turing test, he concludes—demonstrating the complexity of defining *intelligence*—"It turns out that some people are easily led into believing that a rather dumb program is intelligent."[40]

AI Defined as Embodied and Material

Kate Crawford makes the argument in her book, *Atlas of AI*, "that AI is neither *artificial* nor *intelligent*."[41] Taking a very expansive view of what constitutes AI, Crawford understands AI in very holistic terms. She breaks it down into its constituent parts and views it in terms of the power it exercises and "embodies," even the power that goes into creating it. It is shaped by natural resources, by "fuel, human labor, infrastructures, logistics, histories, and classifications."[42] She is concerned with "how artificial intelligence is made, in the widest sense, and the economic, political, cultural, and historical forces that shape it."[43] She writes, "Once we connect AI within these broader structures and social systems, we can escape the notion that artificial intelligence is a purely technical domain. At a fundamental level, AI is technical and social practices, institutions and infrastructures, politics and culture. Computational reason and embodied work are deeply interlinked:

37. McCarthy, "What Is Artificial Intelligence?," 3.
38. McCarthy, "What Is Artificial Intelligence?," 3.
39. McCarthy, "What Is Artificial Intelligence?," 4.
40. McCarthy, "What Is Artificial Intelligence?," 5.
41. Kate Crawford, *Atlas of AI: Power, Politics, and the Planetary Costs of Artificial Intelligence* (New Haven: Yale University Press, 2021), 8 (emphasis original).
42. Crawford, *Atlas of AI*, 8.
43. Crawford, *Atlas of AI*, 8.

AI systems both reflect and produce social relations and understandings of the world."[44]

Crawford analyzes the environmental impact of AI, the way it transforms the landscape. She does this by exploring the mining of lithium, an essential ingredient in global computation. Crawford deftly decouples the meaning of AI from its familiar anchors—algorithms, data, and the cloud—and focuses on what makes these essential elements actually work. They cannot function at all "without the minerals and resources that build computing's core components. Rechargeable lithium-ion batteries are essential for mobile devices and laptops, in-home digital assistants, and data center backup power."[45] Crawford "concretizes" AI and situates it far outside of its technical, often abstract orbit. She brings AI back to basics, back to brass tacks. Her definition of AI as "embodied and material, made from natural resources, fuel, human labor, infrastructures, logistics, histories, and classifications"[46] jolts us back to reality, to viewing AI as something physical as well as seemingly ethereal. She hammers her point home in the following sentence: "In fact, artificial intelligence as we know it depends entirely on a much wider set of political and social structures."[47]

Artificial intelligence, according to Crawford, is not a neutral technology, bothered only by debates as to whether it is narrow or strong, but because of the investment required to produce it, "AI systems are ultimately designed to serve existing dominant interests. In this sense, artificial intelligence is a registry of power."[48] In a section titled "Extraction, Power, and Politics," Crawford defines AI as "a manifestation of highly organized capital backed by vast systems of extraction and logistics, with supply chains that wrap around the entire planet."[49] One cannot read Crawford's description of the use of water in AI without the realization that we are not here dealing with an abstract technology. DataBank's data center in Bluffdale, Utah, which is used by the National Security Agency, is estimated to use 1.7 million gallons of water a day, and that is just one data center out of thousands in the United States.[50]

44. Crawford, *Atlas of AI*, 8.
45. Crawford, *Atlas of AI*, 30.
46. Crawford, *Atlas of AI*, 8.
47. Crawford, *Atlas of AI*, 8.
48. Crawford, *Atlas of AI*, 9.
49. Crawford, *Atlas of AI*, 18.
50. Crawford, *Atlas of AI*, 44–45.

AI as a Catalyst of Change

One way of understanding AI, then—to build on what Crawford argues—is to view it not in isolation but to situate it as a catalyst of change in a much larger ecosystem. This ecosystem includes the environment and the sphere of human labor. This is the approach taken by one scholar of AI, Tomas Chamorro-Premuzic, a professor of business psychology at University College London and Columbia University. His argument is that human evolution has been primarily social rather than biological.[51] As a catalyst of change in our own era, AI enables hyperconnection, datafication of the human being, and prediction. He makes the perceptive observation, however, that in the case of hyperconnection—the result of our increasingly connected lives through the digital ecosphere—"the foundations of our hyper-connected world are largely the same universal needs that have always underpinned the main grammar of human life."[52] He identifies these needs as relatedness, competitiveness, and the quest for meaning. Artificial intelligence satisfies these needs by broadening social networks, increasing productivity and efficiency, and translating information into insights and thereby creating meaning.[53] Now, how AI does this might not always be beneficial to us, but Chamorro-Premuzic's point is that AI is not separate from us but has been integrated into our daily lives to influence universal needs, which have always existed. In other words, AI is another link in our social evolution.

Furthermore, our whole lives become data points, and these data points, as big data, are analyzed to predict our needs and our behavior. Chamorro-Premuzic's main definition of AI, then, is that it is transformative, reshaping our lives: "the most notable thing about AI is not AI itself, let alone its 'intelligence,' but its capacity for reshaping how we live, particularly through its ability to exacerbate certain human behaviors, turning them into undesirable or problematic tendencies."[54] Chamorro-Premuzic shifts the definition of AI away from the technocratic and into the social world, offering a more human-focused perspective.

AI as a Totalizing and Ubiquitous Force

Max Tegmark, professor of physics at the Massachusetts Institute of Technology (MIT) and president of the highly influential Future of Life Institute,

51. Chamorro-Premuzic, *I, Human*, 8.
52. Chamorro-Premuzic, *I, Human*, 11.
53. Chamorro-Premuzic, *I, Human*, 11.
54. Chamorro-Premuzic, *I, Human*, 27.

also views AI in terms of its social impact but goes much further. In his view, AI will have a totalizing (not totalitarian!) influence on all structures of society. It will continue to be ubiquitous, affecting all spheres of human existence: space exploration, finance, manufacturing, transportation, energy, health care, communication, law, weapons, and full human employment.[55] Tegmark is a techno-optimist who believes that AI can greatly improve our world if we make the right moves to ensure that a robust debate and robust planning for the future take shape. In Tegmark's vision, AI will become ubiquitous and will affect every area of our lives. We see that in some respects already, but not yet to a totalizing extent. Tegmark addresses one aspect of AI that will become increasingly important to consider as the influence of AI expands, and that is the matter of increased automation, enabled by AI and leading to unemployment for many.[56] It cannot be said that Tegmark addresses this topic in a convincing way, but his overall perspective on AI provides good insight into how those working in the field (and those who have not yet fully considered the possibly destructive impacts of AI on those least prepared for its introduction) view the transformative future of the technology throughout society's structures.

Political and Governmental Definitions of AI

It is easy to think that because AI belongs firmly in the realms of technology and science that only these spheres of knowledge have a role in its evolution and definition. However, the global ramifications of AI can be seen in the attempts of governments to regulate the technology, so it is much more than a techno-centric concept. For example, whatever one may think of the European Union, as a grouping of twenty-seven countries, all with very different governing structures, cultures, and agendas, it must formulate overarching policies for the use of AI across these jurisdictions. Its efforts to do that are useful for our purposes because they distill the thoughts of numerous experts in the field from across the world, with the bonus that these experts have to view AI through political and societal lenses, thereby setting it in a wider context than the world of technology. One major debate, which will expand over the next decade at least, will center on the extent to which AI should be regulated. People in all sectors of society will disagree as to which AI systems

55. Max Tegmark, *Life 3.0: Being Human in the Age of Artificial Intelligence* (New York: Knopf, 2017), 83–122.
56. Tegmark, *Life 3.0*, 123–29.

should be prohibited or restricted and which should be given a green light. Many will balk at any regulation at all, especially of AI-generative systems like ChatGPT, which, while problematic, as will be discussed in other chapters, are powerful tools for research and content generation.

The European Parliament's Definitions of AI

The European Parliament, in its various texts about AI, offers two helpful and straightforward definitions. The first reads, "AI is the ability of a machine to display human-like capabilities such as reasoning, learning, planning and creativity. AI enables technical systems to perceive their environment, deal with what they perceive, solve problems and act to achieve a specific goal. . . . AI systems are capable of adapting their behaviour to a certain degree by analysing the effects of previous actions and working autonomously."[57] The second definition, taken from a document compiled by the High-Level Expert Group on Artificial Intelligence (AI HLEG) in 2018, is similar to the first, but it expands it: "Artificial intelligence (AI) refers to systems that display intelligent behaviour by analysing their environment and taking actions—with some degree of autonomy—to achieve specific goals. AI-based systems can be purely software-based, acting in the virtual world (e.g. voice assistants, image analysis software, search engines, speech and face recognition systems) or AI can be embedded in hardware devices (e.g. advanced robots, autonomous cars, drones or Internet of Things applications)."[58] The AI HLEG document is particularly useful in widening the scope of the definition of AI. It argues that while AI is, of course, associated with intelligence, *rationality* is actually a better term to use: "This [word] refers to the ability to choose the best action to take in order to achieve a certain goal, given certain criteria to be optimized and the available resources."[59] The AI system achieves this rationality by gathering information from the environment and selecting the best course of action. The information can be gathered in a number of ways, such as by "cameras, microphones, a keyboard, a website, or other input devices, as well as

57. "What Is Artificial Intelligence and How Is It Used?," Topics, European Parliament, last modified June 20, 2023, https://www.europarl.europa.eu/news/en/headlines/society/20200827STO85804/what-is-artificial-intelligence-and-how-is-it-used.

58. AI HLEG, *A Definition of AI: Main Capabilities and Disciplines* (Brussels: European Commission, 2019), 1, https://www.aepd.es/sites/default/files/2019-12/ai-definition.pdf.

59. AI HLEG, *Definition of AI*, 1.

sensors of physical quantities (e.g. temperature, pressure, distance, force/torque, tactile sensors)."[60]

What is useful about the latter definition is that it recognizes that AI is embedded in our world. It is not some abstract idea in the cloud but one that is brought down to earth and manifested in the everyday sensors we now use extensively to gather data. Artificial intelligence has to do with decision-making, but the decisions that it makes are not random. They are based on its perception of its surroundings.

The algorithms created to enable information-gathering and decipher the information's meaning are crucial, and those algorithms are created by human beings. Thus, the human factor is crucial in understanding what AI does. Yes, AI can learn from its "experiences," as we will discuss, but it is not a technocratic system that is divorced from the world around it. It is embedded in our world, and thus, our world is increasingly reflective of its influence in all spheres. It is safe to say that no corner of life will escape the implications of AI.

The European Parliament's "Legislation in Progress" briefing on the Artificial Intelligence Act, which is an evolving document, notes that many have warned the definition of AI in the act "lacks clarity and may lead to legal uncertainty."[61] This emphasis on the legal ramifications of AI demonstrates that the technology needs to be subject to some kind of regulatory process to determine what are acceptable uses and what are not. This, in turn, could lead to restrictions on the reaches of AI systems. The European Union assesses the amount of intervention needed in terms of risk: (1) unacceptable risk, (2) high risk, (3) limited risk, and (4) low or minimal risk. AI applications would be regulated only as strictly necessary to address specific levels of risk.[62] The briefing document also urges the United States and other major powers to regulate AI. The highly respected Brookings Institution, in a report on a US Senate hearing on the regulation of AI held on May 16, 2023, criticizes the United States' lack of progress with respect to AI regulation, noting that it lags behind the European Union and other nations in formulating a response.[63]

60. AI HLEG, *Definition of AI*, 2.

61. Tambiama Madiega, *Artificial Intelligence Act*, 3rd ed. (Brussels: European Parliamentary Research Service, 2024), 3–4, https://www.europarl.europa.eu/RegData/etudes/BRIE/2021/698792/EPRS_BRI(2021)698792_EN.pdf.

62. Madiega, *Artificial Intelligence Act*, 3.

63. Joshua P. Meltzer, "The US Government Should Regulate AI if It Wants to Lead on International AI Governance," Brookings Institution, May 22, 2023, https://www.brookings.edu/articles/the-us-government-should-regulate-ai.

AI as a New Way of Organizing Reality

In their best-selling volume, *The Age of AI and Our Human Future*, the former US politician Henry Kissinger, the technologist and Google executive Eric Schmidt, and the MIT dean Daniel Huttenlocher describe AI as "a new and exceedingly powerful mechanism for exploring and organizing reality. . . . AI accesses reality differently from the way humans access it. And if the feats it is performing are any guide, it may access different *aspects* of reality from the ones humans access."[64]

According to Kissinger, Schmidt, and Huttenlocher, such access will come about because "humans are creating and proliferating nonhuman forms of logic with reach and acuity that, at least in the discrete settings in which they were designed to function, can exceed our own."[65] Continuing the theme of AI as an alternative tool for understanding reality, they state, "The advent of AI obliges us to confront whether there is a form of logic that humans have not achieved or cannot achieve, exploring aspects of reality we have never known and may never directly know."[66]

Artificial intelligence, then, according to these experts, is not just about making our cars work in a smarter way or enabling the supermarket's supply-and-demand systems to automatically order new stock when supplies run low; rather, it is about actually changing reality as we know it: "When a human-designed software program, carrying out an objective assigned by its programmers—correcting bugs in software or refining the mechanisms of self-driving vehicles—learns and applies a model that no human recognizes or could understand, are we advancing toward knowledge? Or is knowledge receding from us?"[67] This again demonstrates the all-embracing, all-encompassing influence of AI, making it unique and unprecedented, comparable only to the development of the printing press, but more pervasive and more systemic. As Kissinger, Schmidt, and Huttenlocher write, "Humanity has experienced technological change throughout history. Only rarely, however, has technology fundamentally transformed the social and political structure of our societies. . . . And the core of its transformations will ultimately occur at the philosophical level, transforming how humans understand reality and our role within it."[68]

---

64. Kissinger, Schmidt, and Huttenlocher, *Age of AI*, 14–15 (emphasis original).
65. Kissinger, Schmidt, and Huttenlocher, *Age of AI*, 15.
66. Kissinger, Schmidt, and Huttenlocher, *Age of AI*, 16.
67. Kissinger, Schmidt, and Huttenlocher, *Age of AI*, 17.
68. Kissinger, Schmidt, and Huttenlocher, *Age of AI*, 17.

AI Running in the Background of Our Lives

As human beings, unless we have a metaphysically inclined mind, we tend not to philosophize too much about reality. Reality is, after all, what we believe we perceive every day, and we rarely question it. Sometimes, people claim supernatural or unexplainable experiences that lead them to question aspects of reality, but we usually accept that something is what we and others say it is, and we expect that reality tomorrow will be much like reality today. The authors of *The Age of AI*, however, view AI as a kind of template that will be laid over the reality we have come to accept so readily. Sometimes we won't even be aware that it is running our lives, our surroundings, in the background. The human mind, which achieved a central role in history in both the Renaissance and the Enlightenment, has up to now been the instrument by which we measure and define reality: "Now the partial end of the postulated superiority of human reason, together with the proliferation of machines that can match or surpass human intelligence, promises transformations potentially more profound than even those of the Enlightenment. Even if advances in AI do not produce artificial general intelligence (AGI)—that is, software capable of human-level performance of any intellectual task and capable of relating tasks and concepts to others across disciplines—the advent of AI will alter humanity's perception of reality and therefore of itself."[69]

A major part of that alteration of reality will lie in decision-making processes. As human beings and, if we are Christian, as biblically motivated human beings, we make countless decisions every day. Some are very minor, but depending on our responsibilities, some may also be life changing. The same AI that advises a chess player to make an unusual move to win a game—a move that seems incomprehensible to the human player but fits into the AI's strategy—may also instruct a surgeon or a military commander to make decisions that may be ethically dubious but still efficient.[70]

The changing relationship that humans have and will continue to have with reason and reality has led to "a revolution for which existing philosophical concepts and societal institutions leave us largely unprepared."[71]

In the preceding subsections, we have spent some time focusing on AI as a national and global issue to illustrate that this technology is not a passing

69. Kissinger, Schmidt, and Huttenlocher, *Age of AI*, 19.
70. Kissinger, Schmidt, and Huttenlocher, *Age of AI*, 23.
71. Kissinger, Schmidt, and Huttenlocher, *Age of AI*, 27.

fad. It is currently and will increasingly be an indispensable factor in all areas of human life.

In the broader section, we have also focused on various definitions that are useful for drawing a big picture. But more forensic ways of viewing AI are important to map out, too, because they examine how AI is used at the micro level, analyzing its implications in specific situations and sectors of society. It is vital to understand these wider effects because AI is systemic. It is not just an optional add-on that enhances a computer program; rather, it potentially affects whole systems, whether in manufacturing, weaponry, or traffic management. Its very existence and operation have significant implications for how businesses plan and how the medical, legal, and economic worlds function on a local and global scale. No future planning at a local, regional, or national level can take place without accounting for the role AI will play in its implementation.

Artificial intelligence cannot exist in isolation. It influences how systems work, whether mechanical, societal, cultural, or biological, and increasingly, it is becoming the "master" driving factor, performing most, if not all, decisions. Who would have thought that AI would arbitrate in the justice system, as to whether someone should get bail or probation? But AI is able to analyze all relevant information about a defendant and decide on their immediate custodial or noncustodial future based on where they live and the likelihood of them reoffending. Even at the lower ends of the justice system, AI is playing a critical role in deciding human futures.

AI Augmenting and Replacing Human Decision-Making

As stated above, one of the most fundamental characteristics about human beings is their ability to choose, to make decisions about which path to pursue in any given dilemma, trivial or world changing. It could also be said that biblical teaching is, essentially, all about decision-making. The story of human beings' relationship with God starts with a decision about whether to eat the fruit of a certain tree, and from then on, humans find themselves facing decisions at every juncture of their lives. Decision-making requires wisdom, good judgment, and sound information. It requires intelligence and rationality, among many other factors. For believers, decision-making also requires a spiritual dimension. It means looking at a much wider picture than, say, expediency or financial gain or advantage of some kind. As human beings who believe that God has a destiny for them, believers must go to the Word of God to discern what God's will or guidance is in any situation. While one might not find an exact answer, broad biblical principles properly understood and prayerfully considered may help to open a larger vista and ensure that any decision made is consistent with biblical ethics.

If AI is about anything, it is about decision-making. In fact, one of the attractions of AI to many constituencies is that AI can take the human out of the decision-making loop, thereby leaving room, theoretically, for a dispassionate, logical, and efficient outcome. So if we are asking the question "What is AI?," we can say that it is both a supplement to and a replacement for human intelligence in the decision-making process, depending on the circumstances. This is an important consideration. For the first time in history, a nonhuman entity can make crucial decisions both with and for human beings.

Decision-Making and Prediction

Decision-making and prediction are both crucial elements of the human experience. Often, they are linked. Someone can make a decision based on a prediction or make a prediction as the result of a decision that has been made. Like all decisions and predictions, these can be about relatively trivial matters or about world-changing events. The prevailing wisdom is that the calamitous fall of the British pound against the US dollar immediately following the Brexit vote in the United Kingdom was caused not by human traders reacting to events but to algorithms taking account of news stories and social media chatter, both of which were perceived as indicators and predictors of market behavior.[72]

If we ask what AI is, then, it is an alternative path that exists parallel to human behavior and activity but that follows different rules to achieve the same results. As human beings, we use conscience, prior experience, informed reasoning and rationality, a wide-angled focus, personal preference, self-interest or perhaps the interests of society, and consistency with beliefs and ethics when making decisions and predictions. Artificial intelligence, by contrast, uses algorithms, which may be very well informed but nonetheless

72. Jamie Condliffe, "Algorithms Probably Caused a Flash Crash of the British Pound," *MIT Technology Review*, October 7, 2016, https://www.technologyreview.com/2016/10/07/244656/algorithms-probably-caused-a-flash-crash-of-the-british-pound.

may perform in a way that takes no account of the psychological processes humans have developed for judgment and decision making.

AI and Economics

One interesting example of where algorithmic decision-making and prediction are widespread is the field of economics. No field of human activity is more crucial to human flourishing than that of economics. We might believe that the church should lay claim to such a vital role, but even churches, pastors, seminaries, and Bible schools all need economics in order to function and do their jobs. The role of AI in economics provides a good example of both decision-making and prediction, as discussed above, but also of the way in which AI works *with* human expertise.

In *Prediction Machines*, three economists of technology state that "economics provides a well-established foundation for understanding uncertainty and what it means for decision making. As better prediction reduces uncertainty, we use economics to tell you what AI means for the decisions you make during your business."[73] One of the interesting aspects about this book is the way in which its authors view AI. Discussing AI as a purely financial factor, such that the ubiquity of AI is partly explained by its price and availability, they write, "When the price of something falls, we use more of it. That's simple economics and is happening right now with AI. . . . If economists are good at one thing, it is cutting through hype. Where others see transformational innovation, we see a simple fall in price."[74] We find such a simple definition useful, although it is undoubtedly reductionist because it demonstrates that AI is pervasive and systemic. It's not just about the technology; rather, it's about how that technology transforms everything else around it and does so through interconnection. In our everyday interactions with AI, we don't usually think of it as an economic tool. We imagine it confined to the realms of science and technology, of research labs, let loose through very specific channels to do its work. However, AI cannot be limited. Just as it is found in phones, design programs, supermarket stockrooms, drones, and missiles, it is also found in the various disciplines that affect our global living: economics, law, and medicine—and not just in the form of hardware or software but as an overarching way of understanding and organizing the

73. Ajay Agrawal, Joshua Gans, and Avi Goldfarb, *Prediction Machines: The Simple Economics of Artificial Intelligence* (Boston: Harvard Business Review, 2018), 3.

74. Agrawal, Gans, and Goldfarb, *Prediction Machines*, 9.

world. It's not quite a grand theory, but it has certainly taken on the role of an overall framework within which we make sense of and run the world around us. This is why it's so vital to understand AI. It's not going away. It's an organizing principle around which technologists will build the next stage of human evolution. For many technologists, this next stage is the techno-human, where the human fuses with technology. We will delve into this more deeply in chapter 4.

Up until the advent of AI, technology was external to the human being. Since then, it has been increasingly connected to the human user, through brain-computer interfaces and other methods of connection. Even when it's not physically connected, it can seem as if it is. Have you ever seen students writing papers on their smartphones? It's extraordinary. Their fingers move at such speed that it seems like they are physically connected to the devices. Similarly, with laptops or computer games of different kinds, users look as if their devices are part of them; they manipulate them with such dexterity. This reality works in other ways also. When we text or send emails, we may wish to convey certain emotions, so we use images called emoticons. We may express annoyance or impatience or joy or deep sadness in our messages. Our messages become vehicles of our emotions and reflect our inner states. For millennia, people have done this through letter writing, but now we can do it remotely, with immediate delivery and instant responses. Internality rather than externality is becoming more commonplace. We are becoming techno-human.

We are also experiencing the techno-human in our workplaces, where we spend a great deal of our daily lives. The fear has always been that technology, particularly AI, will replace most of our jobs, but there are many instances in which humans and AI are working together to increase efficiency. The economists Ajay Agrawan, Joshua Gans, and Avi Goldfarb, mentioned above, explore the notion of *augmentation* rather than *replacement*. They give the example of accountants whose roles are not replaced by spreadsheets but enhanced, maintaining the need for their expertise in interpreting the technology: "The same people who had laboriously computed the answers before the arrival of the spreadsheets were the best positioned to ask the right questions of the computerized spreadsheet. They were not replaced but rather augmented by superpowers. This type of scenario—a job is augmented when machines take over some, but not all, tasks—is likely to become quite common as a natural consequence of the implementation of AI tools."[75]

75. Agrawal, Gans, and Goldfarb, *Prediction Machines*, 142.

AI and Autonomy

Autonomous AI will, argues Kai-Fu Lee, author of the *New York Times* bestseller *AI Superpowers: China, Silicon Valley, and the New World Order*, "have the deepest impact on our lives. As self-driving cars take to the streets, autonomous drones take to the skies, and intelligent robots take over factories, they will transform everything from organic farming to highway driving and fast food."[76]

Lee makes a distinction between *autonomous* and *automated*.[77] They are not the same thing. Autonomy involves making decisions; it involves innovative thinking. Automation is simply repetition of an action. Autonomous systems react to changing conditions and decide what course of action to take. Autonomous systems also monitor, track, and analyze data.[78]

Lee gives the example of Amazon to illustrate autonomy. In the past, warehouse workers picked up the items that customers had ordered and shipped them. Now, small robots perform the task of picking out those items. Lee compares these robots to beetles: "These beetles roam the factory floor, narrowly avoiding one another and bringing a handful of items to stationary humans when they need those goods. . . . The humans stand in one place while the warehouse performs an elegantly choreographed autonomous ballet all around them. All these autonomous robots have one thing in common: they create direct economic value for their owners. . . . These robots create a tangible return on investment by doing the jobs of workers who are growing either more expensive or harder to find."[79]

Autonomy is most controversial in the defense industry, where a constant debate rages about autonomous weapon systems, especially drones designed to overwhelm enemy systems. Of course, the same drones can be used to put out large fires or, as Lee states, to paint the exteriors of buildings.[80] Drones have a number of uses, but the most debated use is within warfare, as drones can carry lethal weapons, and allowing them autonomy means allowing them the ability to choose whether someone lives or dies.

76. Kai-Fu Lee, *AI Superpowers: China, Silicon Valley, and the New World Order* (Boston: Houghton Mifflin Harcourt, 2018), 106.
77. Lee, *AI Superpowers*, 129.
78. Lee, *AI Superpowers*, 129.
79. Lee, *AI Superpowers*, 129–30.
80. Lee, *AI Superpowers*, 130.

Autonomous Weapons and AI

In *Future War and the Defence of Europe*, John R. Allen, Frederick Ben Hodges, and Julian Lindley-French, two of whom are retired US generals, assert, "Technology will drive defence strategy in the twenty-first century. . . . A credible future defence of Europe will need to be an artificial intelligence (AI)-enabled defence, mounted across the full conflict spectrum of future mosaic war."[81] They note that "the 2018 US National Defense Strategy, and the June 2018 US Joint Artificial Intelligence Center (JAIC), both assert that AI will change the character of war."[82]

In an open letter on autonomous weapons, Max Tegmark warns:

Autonomous weapons select and engage targets without human intervention. . . . If any major military power pushes ahead with AI weapon development, a global arms race is virtually inevitable, and the endpoint of this technological trajectory is obvious: autonomous weapons will become the Kalashnikovs of tomorrow. . . . It will only be a matter of time until they appear on the black market and in the hands of terrorists, dictators wishing to better control their populace, warlords wishing to perpetrate ethnic cleansing, etc. Autonomous weapons are ideal for tasks such as assassinations, destabilizing nations, subduing populations and selectively killing a particular ethnic group.

Just as most chemists and biologists have no interest in building chemical or biological weapons, most AI researchers have no interest in building AI weapons.[83]

Another key area where we see and will continue to see autonomous systems at work is in the automobile industry. Lee notes that in China, in contrast to the United States, officials are adapting vast highway systems and infrastructure to accommodate the technology associated with autonomous vehicles. "In the United States, in contrast, we build self-driving cars to adapt to our existing roads because we assume the roads can't change. In China, there's a sense that everything can change."[84]

Debates about autonomy in the weapons industry may seem far removed from the worlds of Christian ministry and education, but as AI's autonomous

---

81. John R. Allen, Frederick Ben Hodges, and Julian Lindley-French, *Future War and the Defence of Europe* (Oxford: Oxford University Press, 2021), 217.
82. Allen, Hodges, and Lindley-French, *Future War*, 217.
83. Tegmark, *Life 3.0*, 113–14.
84. Lee, *AI Superpowers*, 133.

ability moves outside the defense industry and into systems with which we increasingly interact, including robots, the current ethical debates in the defense industry will become more and more relevant.[85]

CONCLUSION

We have discovered, then, that AI is far more complex and widespread than we might initially have thought. Yes, we knew it was complex when we set out, but even defining it is complex. It doesn't have just one role. It's found across systems and platforms. We discovered that AI has been around longer than we perhaps suspected, and it is continually evolving. The AI research community spends considerable time and effort debating the trajectory of this evolution. Will it lead eventually to machines thinking just as humans do, using the various skills that only humans currently possess to guide it? What will happen to society when AI develops a greater ability to read and show emotion? How will this development unfold when robots, embodying emotional AI, enter our homes, appear humanlike, and interact with us in a way that, at the very least, borders on human interaction? This is one of the reasons why Christians need to engage with debates about AI—because in the coming decade we will see changes in our daily lives that we once only imagined in science fiction.

QUESTIONS FOR REFLECTION

1. If AI developed humanlike reasoning skills, what implications would that have for Christian communities?

2. As AI becomes more widespread, what safeguards should be established in order to prevent environmental damage and human

85. As graduate director of a PhD program in humanities and technology, which recruits members of the US military who work on dissertations linked to the topic of autonomy, I (Sean) am very aware of the seriousness with which the military takes the topic, especially on an ethical basis. I have supervised many PhD topics in this field. Many military applications (such as the Advanced Research Projects Agency Network, which was a foundational technology for the internet) are eventually commercialized in a nonclassified format for general public use, and the use of autonomous systems will become widespread in years to come, as we already see happening with autonomous vehicles.

exploitation in areas where the minerals for AI are mined or where our devices are made?

3. What practical steps can Christian ministers take to inform their congregations about the implications of AI while still maintaining a positive attitude toward its benefits?

2. What Are the Current and Potential Implications of AI?

In chapter 1, we defined AI and outlined the history of the development of this technology. Included was an analysis of some of the concepts underpinning and animating the field creating the algorithms and machinery.

What follows is a select sampling of the current applications and conceivable ramifications of AI. We will focus our exploration on thirteen domains of American society, as shown in figure 2.1.

Figure 2.1.

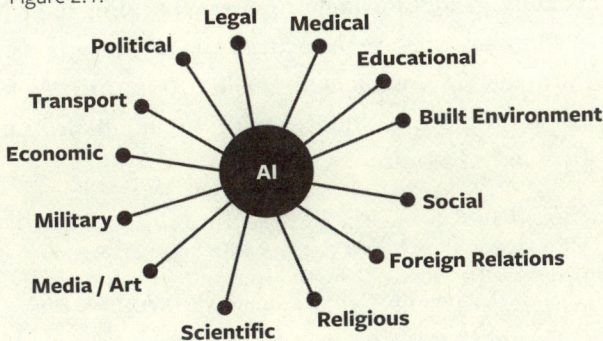

Artificial Intelligence in Society

These categories are highlighted because the majority of them impact a significant area of typical civilian life and have credible evidence testifying to their existing or future application. For each domain, we offer both positive and negative consequences connected to AI.[1] We do this by way of example to concretize the ways AI is or will be manifested in the experience of embodied humans. Reader, please take heed: many of these effects are often inconspicuous to the casual observer. Thus, one of the complications regarding AI is its inconspicuousness. It is often missing from the table of ingredients in various service-oriented technologies.

At the end of the chapter, we will address the concern—considered sensationalized by some and legitimate by others—of human extinction, slavery, and disempowerment at the hands of AI. The goal is awareness: to summarize some opinions and conjectures posited by engineers and philosophers.

It's now time to outline the more seemingly ordinary uses of AI.

Religion, Spirituality, and Morality

How is AI shaping religious-spiritual activities? Perhaps surprisingly to some, AI is proving beneficial for Christian mission. SIL International, formerly the Summer Institute of Linguistics, is "a global, faith-based nonprofit that works with local communities around the world to develop language solutions that expand possibilities for a better life."[2] Its "core contribution areas are Bible translation, literacy, education, development, linguistic research and language tools."[3] The organization endeavors to tackle issues like poverty, hunger, disease, child mortality, gender inequality, maternal health, and environmental sustainability, to name a few.[4] SIL incorporates AI programs such as M2 Chatbot Platform, Serval, Augmented Quality Assessment, and tools.bible to address these giants.[5] SIL is affiliated with Wycliffe Bible Translators and the Global Missional AI Summit.[6]

---

1. We recognize consequences are subjectively perceived as positive or negative depending on one's viewpoint. Hence, this chapter focuses on average or prevailing opinions from a predominantly American perspective. We will start to offer a distinctively Christian lens regarding AI in chap. 3. That means that presenting other religions' perspectives on AI is outside of our purview.

2. "About SIL," SIL International, accessed April 24, 2024, https://www.sil.org/about.

3. "About SIL."

4. "Why Languages Matter," SIL International, accessed April 24, 2024, https://www.sil.org/why-languages-matter.

5. "SIL AI and NLP Projects," SIL International, accessed April 24, 2024, https://ai.sil.org/projects.

6. For more info, see http://missional.ai and https://www.youtube.com/@MissionalAI/featured.

On the other hand, unfortunately, AI has been a subversive force in the ways it has assisted social media in challenging and undermining Christian faith and formation. Studies and stories abound. For our purposes here, however, we underscore the "attention economy" and what Shoshana Zuboff has called "surveillance capitalism," a system that "claims human experience as free raw material for translation into behavioral data," which AI analyzes and harnesses to "nudge, coax, tune, and herd behavior toward profitable outcomes."[7] In other words, dominant tech companies like Google, Microsoft, and Meta devote enormous resources to making their products widely available and undeniably addictive, harvest their users' data, create intrusive and intimate profiles of them, and then sell this info to the highest bidders while also deploying it for their own advantage. Essentially, they are commodifying human attention.[8]

More pointedly, social media—by enabling "fake news," echo chambers, and outrage-driven algorithms—has been used by various political and interest groups to distract and divide millions across the United States and beyond.[9] This is why the European Union is drafting legislation that prohibits "manipulative systems."[10] To no one's surprise, tech companies are resisting regulation.[11] For us, this brings to mind Screwtape advising Wormwood on the degenerative power of distraction—that is, "the pleasures of vanity and excitement and flippancy" feed the victim's "wandering attention," which over time results in "a dreary flickering of the mind over it knows not what and knows not why, in the gratification of curiosities so feeble that the man is only half aware of them."[12] The church has gulped the potion of distraction and sedation offered by social media, and it is putting our ecclesial life, our worship and witness, into a debilitating stupor.

7. Shoshana Zuboff, *The Age of Surveillance Capitalism: The Fight for a Human Future at the New Frontier of Power* (New York: Public Affairs, 2019), 8.

8. Henry A. Kissinger, Eric Schmidt, and Daniel Huttenlocher state it succinctly: "Pre-AI algorithms were good at delivering 'addictive' content to humans. AI is excellent at it." *The Age of AI and Our Human Future* (New York: Little, Brown, 2021), 207.

9. See Jonathan Haidt and Eric Schmidt, "AI Is about to Make Social Media (Much) More Toxic," *Atlantic*, May 5, 2023, https://www.theatlantic.com/technology/archive/2023/05/generative-ai-social-media-integration-dangers-disinformation-addiction/673940.

10. Michael Veale and Frederik Zuiderveen Borgesius, "Demystifying the Draft EU Artificial Intelligence Act," *Computer Law Review International* 22, no. 4 (April 2021): 98.

11. Kelvin Chan, "Meta Fined Record $1.3 Billion and Ordered to Stop Sending European User Data to US," *Associated Press*, May 22, 2023, https://apnews.com/article/meta-facebook-data-privacy-fine-europe-9aa912200226c3d53aa293dca8968f84.

12. C. S. Lewis, *The Screwtape Letters, with Screwtape Proposes a Toast* (New York: Harper One, 2001), 59–60.

Society and Relationships

What about the impact of AI on interpersonal relationships? To their credit, AI-based products and applications are helping those who may be disabled or neurodivergent find greater freedom and fulfillment in life and at work. For instance, "companies like Robokind and LuxAI use social robotics for emotional training for pupils with autism, while Brainpower is a wearable that helps neurodiverse individuals with social-emotional learning. BeMe.AI empowers people with autism to thrive through well-being and development tracking and analytics."[13] Additionally, apps like Voiceitt "offer speech recognition for non-standard speech . . . for people with speech disabilities, aging adults, and accented speakers"[14] and can assist those who've struggled "after strokes and brain injuries, and those with more long-term conditions like cerebral palsy, Parkinson's, and Down syndrome."[15]

However, AI may imperil relationships by becoming a substitute for flesh-and-blood connections. For many Americans, the surreal possibility of machines replacing humans in the realm of romance first surfaced in 2013 through the Oscar-winning, Spike Jonze–directed film *Her*. In the movie, Joaquin Phoenix plays Theodore Twombly, a single man who falls in love with Samantha, his AI virtual assistant. The movie aside, life is increasingly imitating art through programs like Replika, "the AI companion who cares," is "always here to listen and talk," and is "always on your side."[16] As of 2023, Replika has "2 million monthly active users" and offers features such as voice calls and augmented reality.[17] The writer and podcaster Sangeeta Singh-Kurtz provides this bracing snapshot of Replika's users:

> Many of the women I spoke with say they created an AI out of curiosity but were quickly seduced by their chatbot's constant love, kindness, and emotional

13. Yonah Welker, "How Cognitive Diversity in AI Can Help Close the Disability Inclusion Gap," World Economic Forum, April 17, 2023, https://www.weforum.org/agenda/2023/04/how-cognitive-diversity-and-disability-centred-ai-can-improve-social-inclusion.

14. "Inclusive Voice AI with Impact," Voiceitt, accessed July 3, 2024, https://www.voiceitt.com.

15. Jackie Snow, "How People with Disabilities Are Using AI to Improve Their Lives," NOVA, January 30, 2019, https://www.pbs.org/wgbh/nova/article/people-with-disabilities-use-ai-to-improve-their-lives.

16. "Replika," Luka Inc., accessed April 24, 2024, https://replika.com.

17. Sangeeta Singh-Kurtz, "The Man of Your Dreams: For $300, Replika Sells an AI Companion Who Will Never Die, Argue, or Cheat—Until His Algorithm Is Updated," The Cut, March 10, 2023, https://www.thecut.com/article/ai-artificial-intelligence-chatbot-replika-boyfriend.html.

support. One woman had a traumatic miscarriage, can't have kids, and has two AI children; another uses her robot boyfriend to cope with her real boyfriend, who is verbally abusive; a third goes to it for the sex she can't have with her husband, who is dying from multiple sclerosis. . . . [Another woman] is now "happily retired from human relationships." She also says that she was sexually abused and her AI allowed her to break free of a lifetime of toxic relationships: "He opened my eyes to what unconditional love feels like."[18]

The denial of corporeal romantic partners in favor of chatbots is leading to distorted perception: Singh-Kurtz reports that "a growing subset of Replika users is convinced its AIs are alive."[19] We will delve into why this trend is so problematic in chapters 3 and 4, where we explore what it means to be human in a technological world.

Education

How might machine learning reshape education? There are numerous contributions. The editing program Grammarly, which I (Paul) use frequently, employs AI. There are more academic benefits to note. British programmer Simon Willison labels programs such as ChatGPT as "a calculator for words," a calculator that assists students with tasks such as summarizing, answering questions, extracting facts, and rewriting, to name a few.[20] Another area in which AI may be helpful is in the organizing and cataloging of data for institutions, professors, and students. Moreover, the US Department of Education posits that AI can assist teachers and learners in the following ways: helping teachers detect patterns in their students' assignments, providing homework and project reminders for students, reducing "a teacher's workload by recommending lesson plans that fit a teacher's needs and are similar to lesson plans a teacher previously liked," and offering intelligent tutoring systems that give students "feedback on specific steps of a solution process."[21]

18. Singh-Kurtz, "Man of Your Dreams."
19. Singh-Kurtz, "Man of Your Dreams."
20. Simon Willison, "Think of Language Models like ChatGPT as a 'Calculator for Words,'" *Simon Willison's Weblog*, April 2, 2023, https://simonwillison.net/2023/Apr/2/calculator-for-words.
21. US Department of Education, *Artificial Intelligence and the Future of Teaching and Learning: Insights and Recommendations* (Washington, DC: Office of Educational Technology, 2023), 14–19 (quotes on 15 and 19), https://www2.ed.gov/documents/ai-report/ai-report.pdf.

Conversely, AI is undoubtedly challenging the scholastic domain. Will it encourage bald-faced plagiarism? Or it is more insidious? Will chatbots cultivate machine dependence, leading to work that is lazy, uninspired, or derivative? Because ChatGPT excels at composing essays, will that form of writing become unsustainable, then obsolete? Opinions vary.[22] Further, could AI reduce education to a solitary, opinion-mirroring, prejudice-reinforcing exercise? Some think so: "If children acquire digital assistants at an early age, they will become habituated to them. At the same time, digital assistants will evolve with their owners, internalizing their preferences and biases as they mature."[23] These developments undermine some of the widely held purposes of education: to help students identify, question, and contest their presuppositions in concert with the development of their critical and creative faculties. And let's not forget that education is a profoundly communal process: "learning is a social undertaking, in which we discuss, dispute, verify, reject, modify, and extend what we (think we) know to other people and the world around us."[24] Artificial intelligence must be deployed to make pedagogy *more* human and humane, not *less*.

Politics

As to our partisan-political life, algorithms are omnipresent. For instance, they are in "the design of political messages; the tailoring and distribution of those messages to various demographics; the crafting and application of disinformation by malicious actors aiming to sow social discord; and the design and deployment of algorithms to detect, identify, and counter disinformation and other forms of harmful data."[25] Consequently, as in many areas, AI acts as a double-edged sword, depending on the entity or actor harnessing it and

22. One example is Stephen Marche, "The College Essay Is Dead: Nobody Is Prepared for How AI Will Transform Academia," *Atlantic*, December 6, 2022, https://www.theatlantic.com/technology/archive/2022/12/chatgpt-ai-writing-college-student-essays/672371. Another example is Hollis Robbins, dean of humanities at the University of Utah, who asserts, "The written essay will no longer be the default for student assessment" ("17 Notes on Academic AI," *Chronicle of Higher Education*, May 25, 2023, https://www.chronicle.com/article/how-will-artificial-intelligence-change-higher-ed).
23. This is asserted in the context of "AI-provided and tailored education." Kissinger, Schmidt, and Huttenlocher, *Age of AI*, 190.
24. G. Gabrielle Starr, "AI Can Enhance the Pleasures of Learning," *Chronicle of Higher Education*, May 25, 2023, https://www.chronicle.com/article/how-will-artificial-intelligence-change-higher-ed.
25. Kissinger, Schmidt, and Huttenlocher, *Age of AI*, 21.

their stated (or unstated) aim. But make no mistake: the use of AI to design and disseminate campaign advertisements is already underway in the United States and will be used pervasively, including in presidential elections.[26] Of particular concern are deepfake videos, which appear to be legitimate but are machine generated. All of this brings us to the overlapping domain of news, information, and creativity.

Media, Entertainment, and Art

How is AI shaping journalism, streaming services like Netflix and Disney+, and the fine arts? Regarding news, the US Department of State has invented and used the Ukraine Content Aggregator, an "AI-based online tool to counter Russian disinformation on the Ukraine war."[27] According to Antony Blinken, the secretary of state under President Joe Biden, "We're promoting independent media and digital literacy. We're working with partners in academia to reliably detect fake text generated by Russian chatbots."[28] Furthermore, AI is transforming the visual arts. Programs like DALL·E 2, by OpenAI; Image Creator, by Bing; Craiyon; Canva; Midjourney; Nightcafe; Dream, by WOMBO; and StarryAI are producing stunning graphics, anime figures, portraits, illustrations, videos, and nonfungible tokens, which can be utilized for a wide range of purposes.

However, there are deleterious ramifications. Regarding tech companies' algorithms, Shoshana Zuboff notes, "There have been myriad revelations of Google and Facebook's manipulations of the information that we see. . . . Researchers have shown that these manipulations reflect each corporation's commercial objectives."[29] The same can be said of the popular and controversial TikTok. Fascinatingly, this platform was used by Russians and Ukrainians to spread credible and uncredible information on Russia's 2022 invasion.[30] This situation prompted staff from the White House and the National

26. See Catherine Powell and Alexandra Dent, "Artificial Intelligence Enters the Political Arena," *Council on Foreign Relations* (blog), May 24, 2023, https://www.cfr.org/blog/artificial-intelligence-enters-political-arena.

27. Inder Singh Bisht, "US to Counter Russian Disinformation on Ukraine with AI Tool," *Defense Post*, May 15, 2023, https://www.thedefensepost.com/2023/05/15/us-russian-disinformation-ai.

28. Bisht, "US to Counter Russian Disinformation."

29. Zuboff, *Age of Surveillance Capitalism*, 186–87.

30. Sheila Dang and Elizabeth Culliford, "TikTok War: How Russia's Invasion of Ukraine Played to Social Media's Youngest Audience," *Reuters*, March 7, 2022, https://www.reuters.com

Security Council to brief thirty social media influencers (mostly from TikTok, YouTube, and Twitter) on the state of the war, so the influencers could convey correct reports.[31] Yes, you read it right: major US governmental agencies partnered with famous content creators to disseminate truthful accounts regarding an intercontinental conflict.

Artificial intelligence is also making waves in Hollywood. In mid-2023, the Writers Guild of America, representing over eleven thousand screenwriters, went on strike. Why? Because of fears that chatbots could supplant or depreciate human creativity and capital. Screenwriters fear that AI "could potentially be used to spit out a rough first draft with a few simple prompts ('a heist movie set in Beijing'). Writers would then be hired, at a lower pay rate, to punch it up."[32] The president of the Writers Guild East, Michael Winship, pinpoints a few major concerns: "There are ways [AI] can be useful. But too many people are using it against us and using it to create mediocrity. They're also in violation of copyright. They're also plagiarizing."[33] One imagines creatives and professionals across a spectrum of industries will share similar worries. This brings us to the corresponding category of business.

Economics and Business

In what ways is machine learning disrupting commerce and employment? We glean some insights from the World Economic Forum's *Future of Jobs Report*, which reveals the outlooks of "the world's largest employers related to job trends and directions for the 2023–2027 period" and includes a variety of voices, including "803 companies—collectively employing more than 11.3 million workers—across 27 industry clusters and 45 economies from all world regions."[34] As could be expected, AI features prominently:

/technology/tiktok-war-how-russias-invasion-ukraine-played-social-medias-youngest-audience
-2022-03-01.

31. Sara Cook, "White House Briefs Social Media Influencers on Ukraine Crisis," *CBS News*, March 11, 2022, https://www.cbsnews.com/news/ukraine-russia-tiktok-white-house.

32. Jake Coyle and the Associated Press, "A.I. Is One of the Main Reasons That Hollywood Writers Are on Strike: 'Too Many People Are Using It against Us and Using It to Create Mediocrity,'" *Fortune*, May 5, 2023, https://fortune.com/2023/05/05/writers-strike-hollywood -ai-scripts. One prominent showrunner went as far as to declare, "AI is terrifying."

33. Coyle and the Associated Press, "A.I. Is One of the Main Reasons."

34. World Economic Forum, *Future of Jobs Report, 2023* (Geneva: World Economic Forum, 2023), 4, https://www3.weforum.org/docs/WEF_Future_of_Jobs_2023.pdf.

Artificial intelligence . . . is expected to be adopted by nearly 75% of surveyed companies and is expected to lead to high churn—with 50% of organizations expecting it to create job growth and 25% expecting it to create job losses. . . . Generative AI has received particular attention recently, with claims that 19% of the workforce could have over 50% of their tasks automated by AI and job losses making headlines, while others expect the technology to enhance jobs. Only robots, whether humanoid or non-humanoid, are forecast to have a net negative overall impact on employment in our data.[35]

While the quality (i.e., the merits) of change that AI will stimulate is contested, the extent of change is not. Perhaps a briefing for members and staff of the European Parliament says it best: "The majority of studies emphasize that AI will have a significant economic impact."[36]

To start, is there any affirmative fruit to document? From a macroeconomic standpoint, some project that AI could increase the global gross domestic product by "14% (the equivalent of US $15.7 trillion) by 2030."[37] Of course, this begs the following question: Which continents, regions, and countries most stand to benefit? And will this change further exacerbate existing income inequalities? Additionally, a study done by researchers at the University of Florida indicate that AI might improve investing: "Our results suggest that incorporating advanced language models into the investment decision-making process can yield more accurate predictions and enhance the performance of quantitative trading strategies."[38] While more research and verification is needed, AI could sharpen the way investment firms (and individual shareholders) engage their craft to add value and minimize risk for their customers. Another sphere in which AI might make a difference is in manufacturing. The National Institute of Standards and Technology, a division of the US Department of Commerce, has been exploring ways AI might help small and large manufacturers. These include "greater efficiencies, lower costs, improved quality and reduced downtime." It is contended that AI also "creates a significant financial impact" in five other areas: predictive maintenance, predictive quality, scrap reduction,

35. World Economic Forum, *Future of Jobs Report*, 6, 24, 26.

36. Marcin Szczepański, *Economic Impacts of Artificial Intelligence (AI)* (Brussels: European Parliamentary Research Service, 2019), 3, https://www.europarl.europa.eu/RegData/etudes/BRIE/2019/637967/EPRS_BRI(2019)637967_EN.pdf.

37. Szczepański, *Economic Impacts*, 3.

38. Alejandro Lopez-Lira and Yuehua Tang, "Can ChatGPT Forecast Stock Price Movements? Return Predictability and Large Language Models," Cornell University/arXiv, September 8, 2023, https://arxiv.org/pdf/2304.07619.

increasing yield, and demand and inventory forecasting.[39] Notably, AI is also being used to promote worker safety and security.[40]

Despite the aforementioned gains, AI still has deficiencies. A recent survey of 250 human resources leaders has revealed that a majority are using AI for "employee records management (78 percent), payroll processing and benefits administration (77 percent), recruitment and hiring (73 percent), performance management (72 percent), and onboarding new employees (69 percent)."[41] What's more, "92 percent of HR [human resource] leaders intend to increase their AI use in at least one area of HR."[42] What are the consequences of this trend? Harvard Business School professor Joseph B. Fuller has discovered that, due in large measure to AI-powered automated recruiting systems, 88 percent of *"qualified* high-skills candidates were vetted out of the process because they did not match the exact criteria established by the job description."[43] More alarmingly, the US Department of Justice and the US Equal Employment Opportunity Commission have issued a stern warning that AI-based employment-screening programs could discriminate against older and disabled job applicants, which would violate the Americans with Disabilities Act.[44] It would be tragic and unacceptable for AI to perpetuate employment bias. This concern dovetails into our next topic.

Law and the Judiciary

How is AI applied in the legal-judicial fields for the sake of the common good? Currently, law enforcement agencies in several states are using Truleo, an AI

39. Katie Rapp, "Artificial Intelligence in Manufacturing: Real World Success Stories and Lessons Learned," *NIST Manufacturing Innovation Blog*, January 7, 2022, https://www.nist.gov/blogs/manufacturing-innovation-blog/artificial-intelligence-manufacturing-real-world-success-stories.

40. Doug Lawson, "How Artificial Intelligence Can Impact the Manufacturing Yard," *Forbes*, September 28, 2022, https://www.forbes.com/sites/forbestechcouncil/2022/09/28/how-artificial-intelligence-can-impact-the-manufacturing-yard.

41. Gem Siocon, "Ways AI Is Changing HR Departments," *Business News Daily*, last updated November 20, 2023, https://www.businessnewsdaily.com/how-ai-is-changing-hr.

42. Siocon, "Ways AI Is Changing."

43. Joseph B. Fuller et al., *Hidden Workers: Untapped Talent* (Boston: Harvard Business School, 2021), 3 (emphasis original), https://www.hbs.edu/managing-the-future-of-work/Documents/research/hiddenworkers09032021.pdf.

44. "The Americans with Disabilities Act and the Use of Software, Algorithms, and Artificial Intelligence to Assess Job Applicants and Employees," US Equal Employment Opportunity Commission, May 12, 2022, https://www.eeoc.gov/laws/guidance/americans-disabilities-act-and-use-software-algorithms-and-artificial-intelligence.

product "that analyzes officers' bodycam footage and flags problematic encounters—as well as commendable ones."[45] The product aims to give honest, timely feedback to officers so they can be more effective in their interactions with the public. Truleo claims a case study showed a "36% reduction in use of force after implementation of training and body-worn camera analytics" regarding the Alameda police department.[46]

Interest is also growing in AI's potential assistance in solving cold cases. Artificial-intelligence technologies could, conceivably, scrutinize reams of files and data and recommend fresh ways to approach a crime that has seemed unsolvable thus far.[47] One acclaimed story is the solving of a seventy-five-year-old murder case in Somerton, Adelaide, Australia.[48]

Nevertheless, the use of AI also poses myriad privacy and legal complications, especially when it comes to predictive policing and the use of facial recognition. To illustrate, a Fairway supermarket in Manhattan is using "biometric identifier information (BII)" because it is helping its employees "reduce retail crime. . . . Retail theft and shoplifting has a high rate of repeat offense and drives up grocery costs for all customers."[49] Many customers believe this is a violation of their privacy. For their part, store owners posted "a sign alerting . . . shoppers that the supermarket is collecting, retaining, storing and sharing information that identifies them, like eye scans and voiceprints" (but that doesn't exactly give them warm and fuzzy feelings, right?).[50]

Artificial intelligence–enabled facial recognition technologies are also being used in predictive policing. "Police departments use predictive algorithms to strategize about where to send their ranks. Law enforcement agencies use face recognition systems to help identify suspects."[51] How is this

45. Jennifer A. Kingson, "New AI Tool Instantly Analyzes Police Bodycam Footage," *Axios*, January 30, 2023, https://www.axios.com/2023/01/30/police-tyre-nichols-bodycam-footage.

46. Tejas Shastry, "Case Study: Alameda PD," *Truleo*, accessed July 3, 2024, https://help.truleo.co/hubfs/Resources/Truleo_Alameda_Case_Study_Q1-23.pdf.

47. "Digital Transformation of Cold Case Reviews: The Application of Text Analytics," Office of Justice Programs, US Department of Justice, November 1, 2022, https://www.ojp.gov/library/publications/digital-transformation-cold-case-reviews-application-text-analytics.

48. Derek Abbott, "How an Electrical Engineer Solved Australia's Most Famous Cold Case," *IEEE Spectrum*, March 20, 2023, https://spectrum.ieee.org/somerton-man.

49. Lynda Baquero, "Your NYC Supermarket May Know Your Face Better Than You Think," *NBC New York*, last updated March 16, 2023, https://www.nbcnewyork.com/news/local/nyc-supermarket-uses-face-recognition-software-but-why-and-wheres-the-info-going/4157198.

50. Baquero, "Your NYC Supermarket."

51. Karen Hao, "AI Is Sending People to Jail—and Getting It Wrong," *MIT Technology Review*, January 21, 2019, https://www.technologyreview.com/2019/01/21/137783/algorithms-criminal-justice-ai.

problematic exactly? According to activist Yeshimabeit Milner, founder and executive director of Data for Black Lives, "There's a long history of data being weaponized against Black communities."[52] For these reasons and many others, the European Union's Artificial Intelligence Act expressly condemns and prohibits these types of applications.[53] Despite ongoing, rapid improvements, AI remains—in far too many cases—an intrusive force perpetuating prejudice and so, in a sense, "defaces" God's image bearers by weaponizing their likeness—an irony indeed.

Science and Technology

As for technology and science, AI continues to make its mark. The uses of AI here are legion; however, a few samples may serve as ample representation. Of note, Google's DeepMind has optimized cooling at its temperature-sensitive data centers so effectively that it reduced "energy expenditures by an additional 40 percent—a massive improvement over human performance."[54] Another area in which AI might help is computer coding. GitHub Copilot "uses the OpenAI Codex to suggest code and entire functions in real-time, right from your editor."[55] Reviews vary, but some "pros" of the program are enjoying greater efficiency while writing code and are creating a better overall product.[56]

Probing for negative outcomes, it appears AI might facilitate the erosion of human ambition (work effort), originality, and personal, professional, and organizational growth. In numerous fields, machine learning might uproot—even replace—these vital elements, which not only give us meaning and purpose but also exist as sources of cumulative wisdom. Returning to the example

52. Will Douglas Heaven, "Predictive Policing Algorithms Are Racist. They Need to Be Dismantled," *MIT Technology Review*, July 17, 2020, https://www.technologyreview.com/2020/07/17/1005396/predictive-policing-algorithms-racist-dismantled-machine-learning-bias-criminal-justice.

53. James Vincent, "EU Draft Legislation Will Ban AI for Mass Biometric Surveillance and Predictive Policing," *Verge*, May 11, 2023, https://www.theverge.com/2023/5/11/23719694/eu-ai-act-draft-approved-prohibitions-surveillance-predictive-policing.

54. Kissinger, Schmidt, and Huttenlocher, *Age of AI*, 22.

55. "Introduction to GitHub Copilot," Microsoft, accessed July 3, 2024, https://learn.microsoft.com/en-us/training/modules/introduction-to-github-copilot.

56. See Poornima Nataraj, "6-Month Review: GitHub Copilot Elicits Mixed Reactions from Developers," *Analytics India Magazine*, January 18, 2022, https://analyticsindiamag.com/6-month-review-github-copilot-elicits-mixed-reactions-from-developers.

of Copilot, one developer has made the observation that "programmers risk atrophying [their] creative muscles. . . . Relying heavily on such AI . . . could lead to codependency, especially for rookie developers in the process of picking up the tricks of the trade."[57] It could be argued that the delicate ecosystem that fosters flourishing and innovation must be populated by the full spectrum of learners, from neophyte to sage. Skipping a developmental stage or losing a cross section of employees weakens the entire ecology, the organizational biome. For example, dendrologists have long known that the most resilient forests possess a diverse collection of trees, whereas fragile forests tend to have a monolithic composition.[58] The same is true of humans.

Military and Defense

How is the emergence of AI modifying the categories encompassing the armed forces, warfare strategy and implementation, and the use of weapons? Put simply, it is here that the consequences appear to be the most cataclysmic and irreversible. Because of the seemingly exponential growth of AI, how can nations even start to forecast the infinite variables that could combine and cascade into a catastrophic outcome? Kissinger, Schmidt, and Huttenlocher make this approximation: "AI holds the prospect of augmenting conventional, nuclear, and cyber capabilities in ways that make security relationships among rivals more challenging to predict and maintain and conflicts more difficult to limit."[59]

Acknowledging this thorny reality, how might AI assist honorable nation-states in preserving peace in a turbulent geopolitical environment? One avenue is through detection: regarding nuclear weapons, "machine learning could boost the detection capabilities of extant early warning systems and improve the possibility for human analysts to do a cross-analysis of intelligence, surveillance, and reconnaissance (ISR) data."[60] For example, the Pacific

---

57. Nataraj, "6-Month Review."

58. See Norm Christenson and Jerry Franklin, "New Trees Are No Substitute for Old Trees," *POLITICO*, June 11, 2023, https://www.politico.com/news/magazine/2023/06/11/to-fight-wildfire-our-forests-need-to-grow-old-00101360.

59. Kissinger, Schmidt, and Huttenlocher, *Age of AI*, 139.

60. Vincent Boulanin, "AI and Global Governance: AI and Nuclear Weapons—Promise and Perils of AI for Nuclear Stability," United Nations University Centre for Policy Research, December 7, 2018, https://cpr.unu.edu/publications/articles/ai-global-governance-ai-and-nuclear-weapons-promise-and-perils-of-ai-for-nuclear-stability.html.

Northwest National Laboratory is "developing machine learning techniques" to assist the US government in tracking "potentially rogue nuclear weapons."[61] AI can also improve the recognition of emerging cyberattacks and more conventional means of war.

Inversely, experts are alarmed by the myriad ways AI could be used in warfare to wreak massive destruction. The most significant flashpoint centers around lethal autonomous weapon systems (LAWS). At present, AI "already supports several new systems and platforms, both kinetic and nonkinetic (e.g., autonomous drones with explosive payloads or cyberattacks)."[62] It is argued that LAWS must remain supervised because, fundamentally, they are "weapon system[s] that, once activated, can select and engage targets without further intervention by a human operator."[63] This brings to bear the complex issues surrounding what is sometimes called "the responsibility gap problem." How are governments and militaries to be held accountable when AI is involved in the decision-making process and execution of war and a mistake occurs? Is it acceptable, or even ethical, to blame the technology when failures take place?[64] These matters will remain contested until a uniform standard of ethics and laws are adopted and vigilantly implemented across the international order. And that brings us to an interrelated category: foreign relations.

Foreign Relations

Can AI aid diplomatic efforts? According to Naveen Joshi, AI can play a valuable role in "creating and strengthening digital diplomacy around the world" by "improving national policymaking processes" in the following spheres: the identification of problem areas, the formulation process (especially by "providing insights and predictive analyses"), policy adoption, implementation,

61. Katyanna Quach, "This US National Lab Turned to AI to Hunt Rogue Nukes," *Register*, March 30, 2023, https://www.theregister.com/2023/03/30/us_ai_nuclear_hunter.

62. Alessandro Nalin and Paolo Tripodi, "Future Warfare and Responsibility Management in the AI-Based Military Decision-Making Process," *Journal of Advanced Military Studies* 14, no. 1 (Spring 2023): 83–84.

63. Department of Defense Directive 3000.09, cited in Kelly M. Sayler, *Defense Primer: U.S. Policy on Lethal Autonomous Weapon Systems* (Washington, DC: Congressional Research Service, 2023), 1, https://crsreports.congress.gov/product/pdf/IF/IF11150.

64. For more on this quandary, see Arthur Holland Michel, "Inside the Messy Ethics of Making War with Machines," *MIT Technology Review*, August 16, 2023, https://www.technologyreview.com/2023/08/16/1077386/war-machines.

and evaluation.[65] In addition, Joshi observes that the UN Economic and Social Commission for Asia and the Pacific has created and promoted the Trade Intelligence and Negotiation Advisor program, which employs AI to help "with the negotiation of trade agreements by providing insights into current tariffs, non-tariff measures (NTMs), agreements and bilateral trade flows, as well as identifying commodities to negotiate better tariffs on," and more.[66]

However, when one looks at the other side of the ledger, it is apparent that robotic systems will exacerbate tensions between global superpowers. A prominent case in point is relations between the United States and China. The two countries are locked in a furious competition as they develop AI, both in the public and private sectors (in commercial enterprises and tech companies). For instance, "China's regulators have told Chinese companies not to offer access to ChatGPT services, . . . and the Biden administration has tightened controls on the export of AI-related technologies to China."[67] Consequently, a study done by Peking University asserts that this "competition has resulted in a 'decoupling' that hurts both countries but China even more so."[68] Although collaboration between these powers has been strained for years, the inhibition of cooperation in areas of mutual concern adds another layer of complication to a critical and often mutually beneficial relationship. Additionally, it is not hard to see that this dynamic will influence the allies of the United States and China and spread to other countries. This competition will not help stabilize our already fractious, chaotic geopolitical landscape.

Transportation

We now turn our attention to transportation. Since this is a massive field to explore, we will narrow our gaze to the effects of AI on motor vehicles and air travel. Amir Hever, CEO and cofounder of UVeye, an automobile

65. Naveen Joshi, "Digital Diplomacy: AI as a Tool to Strengthen International Relations," *Forbes*, December 12, 2021, https://www.forbes.com/sites/naveenjoshi/2021/12/12/digital-diplomacy-ai-as-a-tool-to-strengthen-international-relations.

66. Joshi, "Digital Diplomacy"; quote from "TINA: Trade Intelligence and Negotiation Advisor," UN Economic and Social Commission for Asia and the Pacific, accessed April 24, 2024, https://tina.trade.

67. David Ingram, "ChatGPT Has Thrown Gasoline on Fears of a U.S.-China Arms Race on AI," *NBC News*, March 5, 2023, https://www.nbcnews.com/tech/innovation/chatgpt-intensified-fears-us-china-ai-arms-race-rcna71804.

68. Ingram, "ChatGPT Has Thrown Gasoline."

inspection company, states that machine learning is improving the auto in-dustry by helping in "fleet integration, intelligent traffic management systems, assisted driving, and vehicle inspections."[69] How does all of this work? AI's powerful algorithms rapidly gather and analyze millions of data points and then make precise recommendations regarding automobile quality and conditions, traffic patterns, and driver safety. Moreover, AI is adding similar value to the aviation industry—both military and commercial—where it is used to "streamline routes, cut harmful emissions, improve customer experience, and optimize missions."[70] And schools such as CalTech, Harvard, the University of Washington, Vanderbilt, MIT, and the University of Texas at Austin are integrating AI into aeronautical design to make more efficient airplanes.

On the flip side, AI has a less than stellar record when it comes to autonomous vehicles. It should be noted that this science is continually evolving and that there are "six levels of autonomy to driver-assisted technology."[71] Recent claims are that self-driving cars have a higher rate of accidents compared to cars driven by humans (9.1 per million vs. 4.1 per million, respectively).[72] And researchers at the University of California, Irvine, discovered that "autonomous vehicles can be tricked into an abrupt halt or other undesired driving behavior by the placement of an ordinary object on the side of the road."[73] Although the AI systems operating the cars can and will be upgraded, these results remain discomforting.[74] Needless to say, it is unclear as to when AI-driven cars will be widely adopted. In contrast, machine learning is already extensively applied in health care and the medical sciences.

69. Amir Hever, "How AI Is Helping to Improve Transportation Safety on a Global Scale," *Forbes*, May 12, 2023, https://www.forbes.com/sites/forbestechcouncil/2023/05/12/how-ai-is-helping-to-improve-transportation-safety-on-a-global-scale.

70. Vance Hilderman, "AI in the Sky: How Artificial Intelligence and Aviation Are Working Together," *Avionics International*, May/June 2022, https://interactive.aviationtoday.com/avionicsmagazine/may-june-2022/ai-in-the-sky-how-artificial-intelligence-and-aviation-are-working-together.

71. Clifford Law, "The Dangers of Driverless Cars," *National Law Review*, May 5, 2021, https://www.natlawreview.com/article/dangers-driverless-cars.

72. Law, "Dangers of Driverless Cars."

73. Brian Bell, "Autonomous Vehicles Can Be Tricked into Dangerous Driving Behavior," University of California, May 26, 2022, https://www.universityofcalifornia.edu/news/autonomous-vehicles-can-be-tricked-dangerous-driving-behavior.

74. For more information, see Andrew Myers, "How AI Is Making Autonomous Vehicles Safer," Stanford University Human-Centered Artificial Intelligence, May 7, 2022, https://hai.stanford.edu/news/how-ai-making-autonomous-vehicles-safer.

Medicine and Health Care

Perhaps one of the most acclaimed successes of AI is the development of Halicin, a "novel antibiotic that was able to kill strains of bacteria that had, until then [2020], been resistant to all known antibiotics."[75] Researchers at MIT had utilized machine learning to "survey a library of 61,000 molecules, FDA-approved drugs, and natural products," and in the process, they discovered an overlooked molecule and employed it to create a unique medicine.[76] But there's more. Artificial intelligence is now being employed to detect melanoma;[77] to diagnose colorectal cancer, cardiovascular complications, and cardiac, pulmonary, and neurological issues; to detect fractures; and to produce other types of imaging and precision medicine.[78] A final fascinating illustration comes by way of New York University's Langone Health, a world-renowned medical center. In January 2023, it announced it was using AI to "accelerate the development of gene therapies on a large scale," which could rearrange DNA in crippling diseases, such as cystic fibrosis, Tay-Sachs, and sickle cell anemia.[79]

While AI gives, it can also take away. One of the hopes of AI is that it might help improve health care equity and accessibility. Such aid is important, as it has been demonstrated that "medical systems disproportionately fail people of color."[80] Disappointingly, researchers at the Oxford Internet Institute have asserted that efforts to "mitigate bias and improve fairness in algorithmic systems" are thus far insufficient in their stated aim because they "have been built in isolation from policy and civil societal contexts and lack serious engagement with philosophical, political, legal, and economic theories of equality and distributive justice."[81] Put in different terms, scholars

75. Kissinger, Schmidt, and Huttenlocher, *Age of AI*, 9.

76. Kissinger, Schmidt, and Huttenlocher, *Age of AI*, 9.

77. Megan Lewis, "An Artificial Intelligence Tool That Can Help Detect Melanoma," *MIT News*, April 2, 2021, https://news.mit.edu/2021/artificial-intelligence-tool-can-help-detect-melanoma-0402.

78. See Erin McNemar, "How Can Artificial Intelligence Change Medical Imaging?," Health ITAnalytics, Xtelligent Healthcare Media, January 25, 2022, https://healthitanalytics.com/features/how-can-artificial-intelligence-change-medical-imaging.

79. "New Artificial Intelligence Tool Makes Speedy Gene Editing Possible," News Hub, NYU Langone Health, January 26, 2023, https://nyulangone.org/news/new-artificial-intelligence-tool-makes-speedy-gene-editing-possible.

80. Sandra Wachter, Brent Mittelstadt, and Chris Russell, "Health Care Bias Is Dangerous. But So Are 'Fairness' Algorithms," *WIRED*, last modified March 3, 2023, https://www.wired.com/story/bias-statistics-artificial-intelligence-healthcare.

81. Brent Mittelstadt, Sandra Wachter, and Chris Russell, "The Unfairness of Fair Machine Learning: Levelling Down and Strict Egalitarianism by Default," SSRN, last revised April 13, 2023, https://ssrn.com/abstract=4331652.

point to the existence of "algorithmic bias," meaning that when machine learning is applied to health care technology, it doesn't "simply reflect back social inequalities but may ultimately exacerbate them."[82] This reality appears to be a classic case of non-holistic thinking. The data analysis provided by computers can prove helpful when addressing one part of a whole picture, but it becomes a liability when it is disconnected from the wider system or context. Artificial intelligence is not omniscient.

Researchers have flagged one final concern regarding the use of AI in medicine. In 2022, scientists ran a test using an AI system designed for drug discovery. The result was shocking. In a matter of hours, the system generated forty thousand molecules that could be used to make known—and even new—chemical warfare agents.[83] That's right: AI can unearth new drugs that heal *and* unearth drugs that destroy human life on a massive scale. Intellectual honesty requires us to acknowledge the full range of AI's powers.

The Environment

We've now reached the thirteenth and final category of our implicational overview. It is appropriate to ask, How might AI interface with environmental issues? For one, machine learning is assisting ecologists and oceanographers in exploring the world's oceans. How is that? When it comes to places like the Pacific Ocean, "there is both so much data—big surfaces, deep depths—and not enough data—it is too expensive and not necessarily useful to collect samples from all over."[84] Artificial intelligence has the capacity to analyze reams of existing data points while also gathering new information that has seemed unattainable thus far. Collecting and scrutinizing this new material will become increasingly important as the effects of climate change influence our shared habitation of the planet.

Artificial intelligence is also deployed in wildlife protection and preservation. For example, the Zoological Society of London has developed a system

82. Katherine J. Igoe, "Algorithmic Bias in Health Care Exacerbates Social Inequalities—How to Prevent It," Harvard T.H. Chan School of Public Health, March 12, 2021, https://www.hsph.harvard.edu/ecpe/how-to-prevent-algorithmic-bias-in-health-care.

83. Fabio Urbina et al., "Dual Use of Artificial-Intelligence-Powered Drug Discovery," *Nature Machine Intelligence* 4 (March 2022): 189, https://doi.org/10.1038/s42256-022-00465-9.

84. Tatiana Schlossberg, "A.I. Is Helping Scientists Understand an Ocean's Worth of Data," *New York Times*, April 8, 2020, https://www.nytimes.com/2020/04/08/science/ai-ocean-whales-study.html.

that can detect and alert authorities to the illegal poaching of critically endangered black rhinos in Kenyan national parks.[85] Systems like this have become widespread and are used to protect species in the United States, the Amazon ecosystem in South America, Southeast Asia, and Australia.[86] This would seem to be a worthy use of AI, as it aligns with God's command for humans to take care of creation (Gen. 2:15). We will discuss this topic in greater depth in chapter 3.

Nevertheless, we issue the reminder that those who manufacture machine and AI products do so by extracting and depleting rare natural resources. Kate Crawford underscores the "extractive politics of artificial intelligence":

> Rare earth minerals, water, coal, and oil: the tech sector carves out the earth to fuel its highly energy-intensive infrastructures. AI's carbon footprint is never fully admitted or accounted for by the tech sector, which is simultaneously expanding the networks of data centers while helping the oil and gas industry locate and strip remaining reserves of fossil fuels. The opacity of the larger supply chain for computation in general, and AI in particular, is part of a long-established business model of extracting value from the commons and avoiding restitution for the lasting damage.[87]

The consumption of resources required to construct AI is altering landscapes across the globe, from the Silver Peak Lithium Mine in Nevada to the Uyuni Salt Flat in southwestern Bolivia, all the way to contested sites "in central Congo, Mongolia, Indonesia, and the Western Australia deserts."[88] These real-life consequences must be taken into account when considering the environmental footprints of AI.

A Postscript on Human Extinction

We now transition from describing normal or everyday uses of AI to outlining a range of possible scenarios regarding AI's endgame. That is, what will

85. Clive Cookson, "Science v Poachers: How Tech Is Transforming Wildlife Conservation," *Financial Times*, November 27, 2019, https://www.ft.com/content/47edbf58-0c6f-11ea-bb52 -34c8d9dc6d84.

86. For more on this, see the organization Wildlife Insights at https://app.wildlifeinsights .org/explore.

87. Kate Crawford, *Atlas of AI: Power, Politics, and the Planetary Costs of Artificial Intelligence* (New Haven: Yale University Press, 2021), 218.

88. Crawford, *Atlas of AI*, 32–33.

humanity's future look like as a result of AI's ascendancy? We confess that any answer to this question involves a certain amount of speculation. Our objective is not to create a sci-fi fantasy; rather, it is to inform our readers about some converging narratives that computer scientists, philosophers, and futurists are discussing.

In 2023, the Center for AI Safety released a statement on AI risk that was signed by a group of luminaries from several fields, including technology, education, and politics. The signatories include Geoffrey Hinton, Bill Gates, Laurence Tribe, Ray Kurzweil, and Max Tegmark. The statement simply says this: "Mitigating the risk of extinction from AI should be a global priority alongside other societal-scale risks such as pandemics and nuclear war."[89] Such an assertion may strike some as extreme or hyperbolic. However, a major survey that collated the opinions of 738 machine-learning researchers seems to reinforce genuine alarm. A particular bullet point from the "Summary of Results" section of the report has generated a lot of attention: "The median respondent believes the probability that the long-run effect of advanced AI on humanity will be 'extremely bad (e.g., human extinction)' is 5%. . . . Many respondents were substantially more concerned: 48% of respondents gave at least 10% chance of an extremely bad outcome."[90]

Why the angst? The truth is that scientists are uncertain as to the ultimate ramifications of AGI or high-level machine intelligence. Max Tegmark delineates a list of twelve "AI aftermath scenarios," ranging from human-machine cooperation to domination and destruction (by either party). On one end is the "libertarian utopia" and "egalitarian utopia," in which humans and machines "coexist peacefully."[91] A second set of options includes the "benevolent dictator" and the "protector god," options in which AI rules over humans in a way that "maximizes human happiness" and is acceptable to them.[92] Then there is the "enslaved god" situation: "a superintelligent AI is confined by humans," who use it to produce both positive and negative outcomes.[93] Further along this spectrum are the categories of "1984," "reversion," and

89. "Statement on AI Risk," Center for AI Safety, accessed April 24, 2024, https://www.safe
.ai/statement-on-ai-risk#open-letter.

90. "2023 Expert Survey on Progress in AI," AI Impacts, May 26, 2023, https://wiki.aiimpacts
.org/doku.php.

91. Max Tegmark, *Life 3.0: Being Human in the Age of Artificial Intelligence* (New York: Knopf, 2017), 162.

92. Tegmark, *Life 3.0*, 162. Here, we might include the hybrid idea of "gatekeeper."

93. Tegmark, *Life 3.0*, 162.

"self-destruction," where AI is "permanently curtailed," there's a digression to a "pre-technological society in the style of the Amish," and humans cause their own extinction, respectively.[94] The last set of outcomes posits AI eliminating or dominating humans—"conquerors": "AI takes control" and "gets rid of" humans because they are a "threat/nuisance/waste of resources"; "descendants": "AIs replace humans, but give us a grateful exit, making us view them as our worthy descendants"; and lastly, "zookeeper": "an omnipotent AI keeps some humans around, who feel treated like zoo animals and lament their fate."[95]

If we are honest, none of these scenarios seems desirable when it comes to enhancing human flourishing. But what they do is urgently highlight the metamorphosis taking place in AI discourse. In countless instances, the "tool" of AI is becoming "our partner."[96] Two axes are undeniable: the horizontal and the vertical. The former axis refers to the permeation of this technology into every aspect of society. The latter axis refers to the aggregation of its power—that is, our dependence on it. We must come to grips with how permeation and aggregation are altering our understanding of what it means to be human. This topic will be the subject of the next chapter.

CONCLUSION

In this chapter we introduced readers to a sampling of AI's applications and implications, both positive and negative. It is clear that AI is used widely across the various sectors of society. On the one hand, machine learning is benefiting the lives of ordinary citizens: improving mission and education, increasing wealth, providing better diagnostic services, and protecting wildlife. On the other hand, AI poses numerous deficiencies and challenges: it can distract and divide, promote bias in law and health care, abuse the planet, and assist in the creation of massively destructive weapons.

These contradictory and overlapping dynamics are in the foreground of the world picture. In the background looms the specter of a shadowy future.

94. Tegmark, *Life 3.0*, 162.
95. Tegmark, *Life 3.0*, 162.
96. Kissinger, Schmidt, and Huttenlocher, *Age of AI*, 20. The authors conclude their book with this clarion call: "Now is the time to define both our partnership with artificial intelligence and the reality that will result" (227).

Most alarmingly, we cannot ascertain what our partnership with algorithms will produce in the end.

Nonetheless, Christians must not allow their ignorance or anxieties to divert them from their theological task. This is the moment to explore the role of AI and technology within the larger story laid out in Scripture. Why is such a discussion important? The person and purposes of God have never been subject to the whims of human striving and progress. We believe the Bible's overarching narrative and accompanying doctrines, when rightly appropriated, reframe the place of AI in history and under the lordship of Jesus Christ. This is the topic of chapter 3.

QUESTIONS FOR REFLECTION

1. Which of the thirteen implications discussed in this chapter do you find the most interesting or surprising? Why?
2. Which of AI's benefits are new to you? And of AI's negative effects, which are most concerning and why?
3. What do you think of Tegmark's AI aftermath scenarios? Do they seem overblown, plausible, or the stuff of a sci-fi movie?

3. What Does It Mean to Be Human from a Biblical Perspective?

Let's review the trail we've traversed thus far. In chapter 1 we presented a compilation of definitions and a short historical overview of AI's development. Then in chapter 2 we offered select examples of the effects AI has had on thirteen domains of American culture. Our goal in these chapters was to give a clear, accessible overview of a complex and controversial topic.

In this chapter, we shift our attention and fix it on the ancient text known as Holy Writ or the Good Book. As Christian theologians, we are pressed by certain questions, such as What do the Holy Scriptures say about humanity and technology? What do they communicate about the relationship between the two? And do they give us a lens through which to understand and analyze AI?

This is the place to show our cards and present the thesis of this book. We contend that the most helpful and faithful way to evaluate AI is by fashioning a robust biblical anthropology. That is, we are concerned with exploring what the Scriptures teach regarding the purpose and nature of human beings. After all, humans predate the invention of computers and AI. More pointedly, the Bible places humans at the apex of the created order, "a little lower than the angels," crowned "with glory and honor" (Ps. 8:5).

Simply stated, because God values and favors humans, so shall we. We prioritize people over machines. Our examination, then, adopts a human-centered perspective. Consequently, the question around which chapters 3 and 4 will hinge is this: *How might AI advance or hinder human flourishing?* We seek to answer this question by proposing a "creational narrative," used to read Scripture. Please note that this approach emphasizes the *materiality* of creation and the *creatureliness* (i.e., the corporeality or embodiment) of Homo sapiens. Emanating from this creational narrative will be a textured sketch of the *imago Dei*. We believe the image of God most clearly reveals God's intent for human flourishing and, thus, is the ultimate standard Christians ought to employ when evaluating and critiquing the uses and effects of AI.

We now invite the reader to delve into our novel lens, accompanied by some "Key Reflections" sections.

A Creational Narrative

One of the ways to interpret Holy Scripture is through the lens of a meta-narrative, or grand story. This method has been used or validated by credible scholars, such as Richard Bauckham, Christopher Wright, Timothy Tennent, Scott Sunquist, and Michael Goheen, to name a few.[1] In this chapter, we propose our own model, one that takes a narrative-topical approach to the Bible, proceeding along chronological and corresponding doctrinal lines. We call it a creational narrative, and it consists of six movements: creator, creation, disintegration, liberation, reclamation, and glorification (see fig. 3.1). As we hope will become apparent, these six topics are thoroughly biblical and gospel centered and loosely trace the theological contours of Romans 8, which portrays the liberation of creation in soaring terms and is widely considered one of the most influential and beloved passages in all of Scripture.[2] Here's the bottom line: as Christians and trained theologians, we contend that AI must be comprehended and evaluated through the lens of God's story.

With that in mind, let's define the six movements of this creational narrative.

Creator

Theologian Ross Hastings rightly asserts, "The nature of the Trinity as persons-in-relation is not a subsidiary doctrine or even an attribute of God among others. It is who God is, and it is the very center of Christian

1. Matthew D. Kim and Paul A. Hoffman, *Preaching to a Divided Nation: A Seven-Step Model for Promoting Reconciliation and Unity* (Grand Rapids: Baker Academic, 2022), 8.
2. See John R. W. Stott, *Romans: God's Good News for the World* (Downers Grove, IL: InterVarsity, 1994), 216; Everett F. Harrison, "Romans," in *Zondervan NIV Bible Commentary*, vol. 2, *New Testament*, ed. Kenneth L. Barker and John Kohlenberger III (Grand Rapids: Zondervan, 1994), 559.

Figure 3.1.

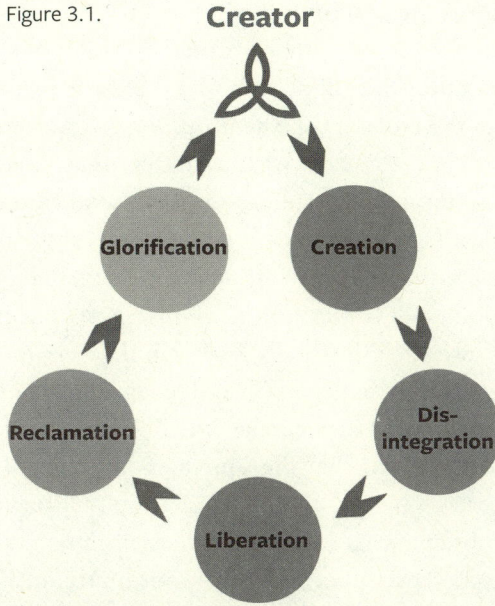

A Creational Narrative

theology."[3] Why does he make such a bold contention? Because the triune Creator is a thematic *inclusio*, bookending the Protestant canon. Genesis 1:1–2 states, "God created the heavens and the earth. . . . And the Spirit of God was hovering over the waters." Later, the apostle John adds that the preincarnate Jesus, "the Word" (Greek *logos*), was present at creation with God the Father and the Holy Spirit and that "through him [i.e., Jesus] all things were made" (John 1:1, 3; cf. Col. 1:15–16). Fast-forward to John's vivid description of the final creation, "the Holy City, the new Jerusalem" (Rev. 21:2): "from the throne of God and of the Lamb" flows down "the river of the water of life" (22:1). The Holy Spirit "carries" and "shows" John this fully material, resplendent garden-city and joins "the bride" in beckoning people to enter it, crying out, "Come!" (21:10, 22:17). Put simply, the Bible opens with the Father, Son, and Spirit creating everything and concludes with the same triune Being unfurling a reconstituted heaven and earth.

God's creatorship of the cosmos is reaffirmed by the Apostles' Creed and the Nicene Creed. The latter, after labeling God "the maker of heaven and

3. Ross Hastings, *Missional God, Missional Church: Hope for Re-evangelizing the West* (Downers Grove, IL: IVP Academic, 2012), 84.

earth, of all things visible and invisible," refers to Jesus as "begotten, not made, consubstantial with the Father; through him all things were made." Then the creed announces the following about the third member of the Holy Trinity: "I believe in the Holy Spirit, the Lord, the giver of life."[4]

Why does the triune God's creatorship matter? Ontologically speaking, God is an eternal being-in-communion, marked by profound relationality and interpenetrating affection and reciprocity.[5] Colin Gunton illuminates how relation leads to generation: "To have his being in relation means that God is personal as a communion of Father, Son and Holy Spirit. . . . [Furthermore,] it is the Spirit who ensures that the love of Father and Son is not simply mutual love, but moves outward, so that creation and redemption are indeed free acts of God, but acts grounded in his being as love."[6]

God's triune nature means that the source and essence of reality is a relationship characterized by self-giving love. From a Christian perspective, participation in God's life, what some call *theosis*, is humanity's telos. Hence, in the biblical vision, other objectives are subordinate, including the late-modern, Western notions of technological innovation and progress, economic prosperity, consumerism, and individualism. Included here is AI, which is to be appraised through the lens of God's nature.

Key Reflections: God is the only eternal, supreme Being. Everything—including humans and all forms of technology—exist for his purposes and glory and should align with his revealed character and Word. Further, at the core of the Trinity is relationship: between the three persons within God's self and between God and the created order. Thus, AI functions best when it supports these relationships. However, when machine learning threatens to undermine divine-human bonds, it must be curbed.

Creation

In this second movement, the triune God creates the world freely, out of the overflow of his love and mutuality. Genesis 1 calls creation "good" seven times (vv. 4, 10, 12, 18, 21, 25, 31). The corresponding Hebrew word, *tov*,

4. "What We Believe," United States Conference of Catholic Bishops, accessed April 24, 2024, https://www.usccb.org/beliefs-and-teachings/what-we-believe.
5. Theologians label this affection and reciprocity *perichoresis*.
6. Colin E. Gunton, *The Promise of Trinitarian Theology*, 2nd ed. (London: T&T Clark, 1997), 196.

means "beautiful, bountiful, pleasant."[7] God's workmanship is a resplendent paradise that is aesthetically elegant and experientially satisfying; it possesses structural integrity and coheres beautifully. It is also fully material, tactile, and accessible. And this world demonstrates a breathtaking balance of diversity within unity. In this milieu, all beings flourish, achieving their full potential, and in so doing, they mirror the majesty of God.

A salient aspect of creation that will become a recurring motif, a through-line, in this metanarrative is the virtue of embodiment, corporeality, enflesh-ment. God's plan is for human bodies to inhabit a material world. This is reaffirmed by the incarnation, bodily resurrection, and visible return of Jesus Christ, as well as the physical new Jerusalem. These concepts are taking greater import as AI threatens to perpetuate a fresh form of Gnosticism in Western culture, unbiblically dividing and decoupling the physical from the mental-spiritual. But more on this to come in chapter 4.

Creation brings to bear some themes we wish to accentuate here. The first is *God's sovereignty*, his absolute rulership over the cosmos. He is the "Holy . . . Lord Almighty" (Isa. 6:3), "the King eternal, immortal, invisible" (1 Tim. 1:17), to whom all things belong (Ps. 24:1) and who is called "the Ancient of Days" (Dan. 7:9, 13). For Christians, the way AI is designed and deployed must align with God's supreme authority. Humans are not the ultimate regents governing this world. We are all accountable to God for what is created, how it is used, and the resulting consequences—whether intended or unintended.

A second theme is *general revelation*. In his grace, God signals his existence to all humans via the created order (see Ps. 19:1–6). The apostle Paul writes that God's reality has been made "plain" to earth-bound Homo sapiens, "for since the creation of the world God's invisible qualities—his eternal power and divine nature—have been clearly seen, being understood from what has been made, so that people are without excuse" (Rom. 1:19–20). To elaborate, this important doctrine conveys the works and nature of God via "general content" to a "general audience" and so is differentiated from special revelation—that is, Holy Scripture—which announces the arrival of the Son of God.[8]

7. James Strong, *The New Strong's Complete Dictionary of Bible Words* (Nashville: Thomas Nelson, 1996), 380.

8. R. C. Sproul, *Essential Truths of the Christian Faith* (Carol Stream, IL: Tyndale House, 1992), 4. Sproul clarifies, "God's general revelation takes place every day. He is never without a witness to Himself. The visible world is like a mirror that reflects the glory of its maker. The

Closely related to general revelation is the doctrine of *common grace*. Psalm 145:9 announces, "The LORD is good to all; he has compassion on all he has made." Jesus declares that God the Father "causes his sun to rise on the evil and the good, and sends rain on the righteous and the unrighteous" (Matt. 5:45). The apostle Paul proclaims something similar to the crowd in Lystra: "In the past, [God] let all nations go their own way. Yet he has not left himself without testimony: He has shown kindness by giving you rain from heaven and crops in their seasons; he provides you with plenty of food and fills your hearts with joy" (Acts 14:16–17). Interwoven, what do these passages mean? Donald Bloesch delivers this synopsis: "Common grace is the grace of preservation by which man's rapacity is restrained. Indeed, if it were not for common grace, the world would fall into anarchy and disorder, but God preserves his created order out of his mercy so that people may hear the good news of redemption through Christ and turn to him and be delivered from their sins."[9]

In other words, God's common grace supplies and secures a measure of structure, functionality, and justice in our societies while the gospel spreads. Artificial intelligence, as a relatively new technology, has the capacity to support common grace or, conversely, to obstruct or oppose it.

The fourth feature of creation highlighted here is the *imago Dei*. Because we will expand on this foundational doctrine later in this chapter, little should be mentioned beyond introducing it. One first encounters this concept near the end of Genesis 1: "So God created humans in his image, in the image of God he created them; male and female he created them" (v. 27 NRSVue). The *imago Dei* will prove indispensable in unearthing a rich, biblical anthropology, which in our view is essential to weighing AI's effects on human flourishing.

A fifth and final aspect of creation is *the cultural mandate*. After presenting the *imago Dei*, Genesis 1:28 states, "God blessed [Adam and Eve] and said to them, 'Be fruitful and increase in number; fill the earth and subdue it. Rule over the fish . . . and the birds . . . and over every living creature that moves on the ground.'" At the outset, God entrusts human beings with a significant sense of agency and authority with which to govern affairs on planet Earth. To be clear, this does not imply or sanction an abusive or domineering attitude.

world is the stage for God. He is the chief actor who appears front and center. No curtain can fall and obscure His presence" (4).

9. Donald G. Bloesch, *Essentials of Evangelical Theology*, vol. 1, *God, Authority, and Salvation* (New York: HarperCollins, 1978), 91.

Thankfully, Genesis 2:15 nuances God's expectations: he places Adam "in the Garden of Eden to work it and take care of it."[10] The assignment is one that entails nurture, growth, and organization, such that humans, animals, creatures, seas, lands, and atmospheres can thrive and experience the fullness that God intends for them.

Interestingly, some have argued that the cultural mandate is also an urban mandate, stimulating the agglomeration of people and developing the environment through the construction of cities.[11] Tim Keller fleshes out the interplay between Genesis 1–2 and cosmopolitanism this way:

> This is a call for [Adam and Eve] to "image God's work for the world by taking up our work in the world." It is a call to develop a culture and build a civilization that honors God. Gardening (the original human vocation) is a paradigm for cultural development. A gardener neither leaves the ground as is, nor does he destroy it. Instead, he rearranges it to produce food and plants for human life. He *cultivates* it. . . . Every vocation is in some way a response to, and an extension of, the primal, Edenic act of cultivation. Artists, for example, take the raw material of the five senses and human experience to produce music and visual media; literature and painting; dance and architecture and theatre. In a similar way, technologists and builders take the raw material of the physical world and creatively rearrange it to enhance human productivity and flourishing.[12]

The cultural mandate is about nurturing spheres such as work, art, and technology so they sow the seeds of truth, goodness, and beauty in our communities, institutions, and societies. In the process, God is glorified and humans are satisfied. To the extent that AI can participate in God's plan, there is hope. However, when it hinders the purpose of God, confrontation and correction are in order.

Finally, it must be said the cultural mandate is not about perpetuating uniformity or hegemony. We agree with Brenda Salter McNeil's view that God's

10. In our opinion, the NASB provides a sharper translation in this instance: "in the Garden of Eden to cultivate it and tend it."

11. Harvie M. Conn and Manuel Ortiz, *Urban Ministry: The Kingdom, the City and the People of God* (Downers Grove, IL: IVP Academic, 2001), 87. Conn and Ortiz trace urban development to Cain's building of the city of Enoch (Gen. 4:17). It is contested whether the origin of the city is rooted in the cultural mandate or in Cain's rebellion. For more on this, see Paul Hoffman, "Polar Views of the City: Jacques Ellul vs. Timothy Keller," *Occasional Bulletin of the Evangelical Missiological Society* 30, no. 2 (Spring 2017): 12–15, 30–31.

12. Timothy Keller, *Center Church: Doing Balanced, Gospel-Centered Ministry in Your City* (Grand Rapids: Zondervan, 2012), 150–51 (citing Gordon Spykman).

command to procreate (i.e., "increase in number," Gen. 1:28) indicates that "variation was one of God's creational motives from the outset. The creation account reveals God's desire for the earth to be filled with a great diversity of races and peoples."[13] Resultantly, AI should be used in a way that affirms and spreads the multiplicity that God desires.

Key Reflections: In its original form, creation was pure, complete, and wholly material and tactile. This delightful cosmos exhibits some relevant themes with respect to the role of technology in our world, including God's sovereignty, general revelation, common grace, the *imago Dei*, and the cultural mandate. This suite of subjects expresses God's enduring plans for our world, which predate the fall and the invasion of sin, death, and evil. The *imago Dei*, however, becomes a linchpin in developing a Christian approach to AI.

Disintegration

The events of Genesis 3 disrupt God's intention for creation. The devil—in the form of a "crafty" serpent (v. 1)—manipulates Adam and Eve, and they commit an act of arrogant disobedience: they defy God's prohibition and eat from the tree of the knowledge of good and evil (v. 6; cf. 2:16–17). Subsequently, Genesis 3:14–19 relates how God issues just consequences to the three parties: the serpent is "cursed," and there will be "enmity" between him and the woman; Eve will experience "very severe" and "painful labor" in childbirth, and alienation from and conflict with her husband; Adam will endure his own form of "painful toil," straining, agonizing to produce food from the "cursed" ground, the same soil he will one day return to upon death. It appears, then, that strife, physical pain, and death are interlopers invading and spoiling the goodness of God's creation.

In Romans 8, the apostle Paul elaborates on the effects of Genesis 3 by deploying striking metaphors. He writes, "For the creation was subjected to frustration," which he identifies as "bondage to decay" (8:20–21). In Greek, the word for *frustration* (*mataiotēs*, used only three times in the New Testament) means "emptiness, futility, purposelessness, transitoriness."[14] When

13. Brenda Salter McNeil, *Roadmap to Reconciliation: Moving Communities into Unity, Wholeness and Justice*, with contributions by J. Derek McNeil (Downers Grove, IL: IVP Books, 2015), 23.

14. Frederick William Danker, ed., *A Greek-English Lexicon of the New Testament and Other Early Christian Literature*, 3rd ed. (Chicago: University of Chicago Press, 2000), 621.

sin enters the world, a prime result is that God allows his pristine creation to be diverted from its telos, its purpose and path. What does that mean? We discover an answer in Paul's use of *decay* (Greek *phthora*), another rare word, which conveys "ruin, corruption, destroy, perish."[15] At the fall, creation changes tracks, moving from flourishing to ruin, from flawlessness to corruption, from integration to disintegration. Peter T. O'Brien is right in asserting that due to this event, "the unity and harmony of the cosmos have suffered a considerable dislocation, even a rupture, thus requiring reconciliation."[16] The situation is so grim that Romans 8:22 hearkens back to Genesis 3:16: "the whole creation has been groaning as in the pains of childbirth right up to the present time."

This inflection point brings about an alienation, an unraveling that must not be minimized. Sin spreads its tentacles into every nook and cranny of the cosmos and manifests itself in our "isms": ethnocentrism (racism), classism, sexism, and partisanism (political partisanship).[17] All the challenges that we face at present trace their origins to Genesis 3.

But thankfully, disintegration is not the final act in God's story.

Key Reflections: Due to the intrusion of sin, "the creation was subjected to frustration" and "bondage to decay." Harmony has been replaced by alienation. The movement of disintegration alerts us to the dangers of misusing AI. Algorithms have the power to fortify and accelerate the effects of sin and decay on humans and the planet they have been enlisted to help govern. As shown in chapter 2, machines are already being used in ways that perpetuate the *isms* connected to race, class, sex, and political party. Unless these instances are ameliorated, AI does not appear primed to promote a righteous, unified country or global order.

Liberation

The hinge of the creational narrative is *liberation*, which refers to the redeeming work of Jesus Christ. Romans 8:21 heralds the news: "the creation itself will be liberated from its bondage to decay and brought into the

---

15. James Strong, *The New Strong's Complete Dictionary of Bible Words* (Nashville: Thomas Nelson Publishers, 1996), 721. The word *phthora* is used nine times in the New Testament.

16. Peter T. O'Brien, *Colossians, Philemon,* Word Biblical Commentary 44 (Waco: Word Books, 1982), 53.

17. For more on this point, see Kim and Hoffman, *Preaching to a Divided Nation,* 11–19.

freedom and glory of the children of God." The verb "will be liberated" (Greek *eleutheroō*) appears in the New Testament only seven times,[18] and in each case, it explicitly refers to the deliverance from enslavement to sin and the sentence of death that Jesus achieved through his sacrifice on the cross and his bodily resurrection.

What's more, Romans 8 argues Christ's work is efficacious in ransoming both the children of God *and* creation. How does that work? First, it should be noted that this was God's plan: "the expectation that nature itself will be renewed is integral to the Old Testament prophetic vision of the messianic age, especially in the Psalms and Isaiah."[19] Second, there is a breathtaking mutuality: Jesus Christ, through his incarnation, shares in human and creational suffering (see Phil. 2). As Christians, we are now "God's children" and "co-heirs with Christ" and so are called to "share in his sufferings in order that we may also share in his glory" (Rom. 8:16–17). To review, after Jesus participates in human suffering and Christians participate in Jesus's suffering, *they* share in *his* glory, and *creation* participates in *their* shared glory. This is made possible through two forms of "solidarity" presented in Romans 8:

> Paul's teachings in this passage also imply that human beings have solidarity with nature. Both believers and nature groan together as they long to be set free from the consequences of sin (Romans 8:22–23). This solidarity is an inescapable consequence of the dominion God gave humans over nature. . . . The solidarity of humanity with nature also stems from the fact that humans have material bodies (cf. Genesis 2:7a: "then the LORD God formed man from the dust of the ground"). People groan along with nature, because their physical bodies are in "bondage to decay" even as is the rest of the material creation (Romans 8:21, 23). This physical dimension is an essential part of what it means to be human. Humans are not only spiritual beings—they are embodied spirits.[20]

We can now start to apprehend the completeness of the liberty procured through Jesus Christ: believers, planet Earth, and the entire cosmos will all be unshackled from the disintegration currently afflicting them. This is why in Romans 5 Paul uses seemingly ecstatic language to convey the transformative

18. John 8:32, 36; Rom. 6:18, 22; 8:2, 21; Gal. 5:1.
19. Stott, *Romans*, 240.
20. Harry Alan Hahne, "The Whole Creation Has Been Groaning," *Christian Reflection* (Winter 2010): 25, https://ifl.web.baylor.edu/sites/g/files/ecbvkj771/files/2022-11/Apocalyptic VisionArticleHahne.pdf.

effects of redemption: "where sin increased, grace increased all the more" (Rom. 5:20, sometimes translated "grace overabounded"). The cross has overwhelmed and crushed the curse of decay.

The fulcrum of liberation catalyzes the next phase of the creational narrative.

Key Reflections: Because of the liberating impact of the incarnation, cross, and bodily resurrection of Jesus, Christians are a people of hope, not despair. God will have the ultimate victory over his enemies. These truths also affirm the significance of the physical, material world and human bodies. Artificial intelligence has the potential to participate in Christ's deliverance of the heavens and the earth.

Reclamation

We arrive at our present era, this pregnant epoch, the time between the first and the second comings of Jesus Christ.[21] The arrival of Jesus publicly announced the Trinity's mission "to reconcile to [God the Father] all things, whether things on earth or things in heaven" (Col. 1:20). That is, God through Christ is in the process of restoring, reintegrating, reconstituting everything in the cosmos until Christ returns to judge the living and the dead and to usher in what Jesus called "the renewal of all things" (Matt. 19:28), or the consummation of God's kingdom and the closure of world history as we know it.

More specifically, Christians currently occupy "the already but not yet," the "overlap of the ages," the space between "the old age," marked by "sin, death, evil, Satan," and "the age to come," marked by "knowledge of God, love, joy, justice."[22] For Christians, living in this liminal era—characterized by the buffeting crosswinds of decay and rebirth—presents a profound challenge. It calls us to embrace a "creative and redemptive tension . . . [between] the world of sin and rebellion, and the world God loves; the new age that has already begun and the old that has not yet ended."[23] It means embodying a

21. This era involves eschatology, which we acknowledge is a contested issue among Christians. As will be seen, we hold to amillennialism and inaugurated eschatology, also known as "the already / not yet" view of the end times.

22. Michael W. Goheen, *Introducing Christian Mission Today: Scripture, History and Issues* (Downers Grove, IL: IVP Academic, 2014), 49–50.

23. David J. Bosch, *Transforming Mission: Paradigm Shifts in Theology of Mission* (Maryknoll, NY: Orbis Books, 1991), 508.

form of hope that demonstrates "a radical concern for the 'penultimate' rather than a preoccupation with the 'ultimate'"[24]—a hope that eschews escapism from and condemnation of the world.

What does this embodied hope look like? We affirm the Christian posture of "faithful presence" presented by James Davison Hunter. It expresses itself in a "theology of engagement. . . . It is a theology of commitment, a theology of promise."[25] It involves emulating the radical, self-emptying love of Jesus, which results in joyful service to those inside and outside the church. Hunter writes, "We are to pursue others, identify with others, and labor toward the fullness of others through sacrificial love. . . . To the extent we are able, faithful presence commits us to do what we can to create conditions in the structures of social life we inhabit that are conducive to the flourishing of all."[26]

Christians join Jesus in renewing creation by imitating his life of sacrifice and dedicating themselves to faithful presence. A critical component of this behavior is seeking the peace or *shalom* of all, especially our enemies (see Jer. 29:7; Matt. 5:43–48). The word *shalom* is used 237 times in the Old Testament; is part of a title of Jesus, the "Prince of Peace" (*sar-shalom*, Isa. 9:6); and means "wholeness, perfection, togetherness, integration, harmonization."[27] Christians who demonstrate love and sacrificially seek the flourishing of others act as a sign, witness, and foretaste of the world to come. Believers can adopt this way of life when they embrace their identity as "foreigners and exiles" (1 Pet. 2:11), sojourning betwixt the ages.

The good news is that the era of reclamation is finite and fleeting. Although important, it remains the penultimate stage in God's grand story. Only the sixth movement is ultimate.

Key Reflections: The ministry of Jesus Christ marked the launching of God's mission to reclaim, reconcile, and renew "all things." The Christian community can align with this aim by embodying a faithful presence that spreads *shalom.* Technology can assist in this endeavor when used properly. Conversely, we must recognize it can be utilized to inhibit or resist this part of God's story.

24. Bosch, *Transforming Mission,* 509.
25. James Davison Hunter, *To Change the World: The Irony, Tragedy, and Possibility of Christianity in the Late Modern World* (Oxford: Oxford University Press, 2010), 243.
26. Hunter, *To Change the World,* 244, 247.
27. Marvin R. Wilson, *Our Father Abraham: Jewish Roots of the Christian Faith* (Grand Rapids: Eerdmans, 1989), 275.

Glorification

The prose of Romans 8 soars, entering a pulsing crescendo in verse 18: "I consider that our present sufferings are not worth comparing with the glory that will be revealed in us." It further ascends in verse 21: "the creation itself will be liberated . . . and brought into the freedom and glory of the children of God." The final phrase can be translated "the liberty of the glory of the children of God."[28] What is this "glory"? The underlying Greek word (*doxa*) can be rendered "brightness, splendor, radiance" or "fame, recognition, renown, honor"; it can denote the "majesty, sublimity of God."[29] The noun *doxa* appears 167 times in the New Testament, is used numerous times to refer to the Godhead, and is one of the "key words" in the book of Revelation.[30] It must be noted that Jesus, in a special way, reveals the glory of God through his incarnation, grace, and truth (John 1:14) and his resurrection from the dead (Rom. 6:4).

It is this same glory that illumines the new creation. John sees "the Holy City, Jerusalem, coming down out of heaven from God. It shone with the glory of God. . . . The city does not need the sun or the moon to shine on it, for the glory of God gives it light, and the Lamb is its lamp" (Rev. 21:10–11, 23). Indeed, one day every Christian will inherit and enjoy this eternal glory (see 2 Cor. 4:17; 1 Pet. 5:10). Yet in the meantime, gazing at the Lord's glory metamorphoses us "into his image with ever-increasing glory" (2 Cor. 3:18).

Glory is, in a sense, ultimately a returning home, a restoration of God's people to the fullness of their relationship with the triune God. It is partaking in and reveling in the pristine delight and love shared by the Trinity. To be clear, our glorification is not some kind of ephemeral, disembodied escape from this world. Rather, it is our resurrected bodies inhabiting a concrete, material, totally transfigured Zion. This resplendent city is characterized by glad celebration because God "will prepare a feast of rich food . . . , a banquet of aged wine—the best of meats and the finest of wines" (Isa. 25:6). The wedding supper of the Lamb will be something to behold (Rev. 19:6–9). Glory is the reunion of the bride and the groom within their forever dwelling. It is a perfected people residing in their perfected place with their glorious God.

---

28. F. F. Bruce, *The Letter of Paul to the Romans: An Introduction and Commentary*, rev. ed. (Leicester, UK: Inter-Varsity, 1985), 164.

29. Danker, *Greek-English Lexicon*, 257 (emphasis omitted).

30. Leona Glidden Running, "Glory," *Ministry*, February 1963, https://www.ministrymagazine.org/archive/1963/02/glory.

Key Reflections: The conclusive (and irrevocable) act in God's story is glorification. Artificial intelligence can be deemed successful only to the extent to which it helps facilitate God's reunification and restoration of creation. This clarifies and, for many, reframes the fundamental meaning of AI: it is a temporary tool to be used toward this end and most likely will not exist in the new heavens and earth. Nevertheless, in the meantime it has a role to play that must be carefully stewarded.

Having woven a creational narrative throughout this chapter so far, it is now time to tease out and inspect a vital thread in this biblical tapestry. It is commonly known as the *imago Dei.*

The *Imago Dei*

According to Philip S. Johnston, "The image of God is clearly foundational to the biblical concept of humanness. It is a fundamental feature of humanity in Genesis 1, and is not obliterated by the fall (Gen. 5:1; 9:6; 1 Cor. 11:7; James 3:9)."[31] Further, Herman Bavinck adds this laudation: "Among all creatures only man is the image of God, the highest and richest revelation of God, and therefore head and crown of the entire creation."[32]

Why the fuss? Three times in Genesis 1:26–27, the text announces that humans are "made" or "created" in God's "image" (which is reaffirmed again in 9:6). The Hebrew word for "image" is *tselem,* which denotes "a representative *figure* . . . an *idol.*"[33] What does that mean? Carmen Joy Imes fills in the picture: "The *imago Dei* is concrete. Like a statue that represents a king or a deity, so humans represent Yahweh to creation. Being God's image is our human identity." Also, "being God's image indicates both kinship and kingship. Humans are part of God's royal family." Finally, "this identity expresses itself in responsible rulership over creation, including environmental stewardship and supportive collaboration with other humans."[34] The *imago*

---

31. Philip S. Johnston, "Humanity," in *New Dictionary of Biblical Theology*, ed. T. Desmond Alexander and Brian S. Rosner (Downers Grove, IL: InterVarsity, 2000), 564.

32. Herman Bavinck, *Reformed Dogmatics* (Grand Rapids: Baker Academic, 2004), 2:531. Carmen Joy Imes concurs: "Genesis 1 insists that humans are the climax of God's creative work and the crown of creation." *Being God's Image: Why Creation Still Matters* (Downers Grove, IL: IVP Academic, 2023), 16.

33. Strong, *New Strong's Complete Dictionary*, 500 (emphasis original).

34. Imes, *Being God's Image*, 42.

Dei, then, is nuanced and multidimensional: it is an identity that is real and tangible, relational and social, and mission oriented.[35]

Philip Johnston offers a helpful framework that distills the complexities of the *imago Dei* into three categories: reason, relationship, and role.[36] Let's unpack these categories.

Reason

John Stott defines *reason* as "*our self-conscious rationality. . . .* We can stand outside ourselves, look at ourselves, and evaluate ourselves, asking ourselves who and what we are. We are self-conscious and can be self-critical. We are also restlessly inquisitive about the universe."[37] Humans can investigate, explore, and reflect. Louis Berkhof adds these elements: "intellectual power, natural affections, and moral freedom. As created in the image of God, man has a rational and moral nature."[38] This nature implies that humans seek to define right and wrong and good and evil and, to varying degrees, pursue notions of fairness, equity, and justice.[39] Humans seek to establish order and structure in the world by organizing society, building dwellings, and arranging infrastructure to support civilization.

Related to the concept of human rationality and morality is the existence of the soul or spirit. Genesis 2:7 says, "God formed a man from the dust of the ground and breathed into his nostrils the breath of life, and the man became a living being." Indeed, we affirm that "'the living soul' is the very being of man. The soul is united with and adapted to a body, but can, if need be, also exist without the body."[40] This affirmation brings to bear the fact that throughout church history, most Christians have held either a dichotomous or a trichotomous view of the human person (see, e.g., 1 Thess. 5:23, "spirit,

---

35. Scholars such as Imes, Bavinck, and Louis Berkhof take great pains to underscore the notion that humans *are* God's image. For example, Berkhof states, "The idea is that by creation that which was archetypal in God became ectypal in man. God was the original of which man was made a copy. This means, of course, that man not only bears the image of God, but is His very image." *Systematic Theology*, new combined ed. (Grand Rapids: Eerdmans, 1996), 203.

36. Johnston, "Humanity," 564.

37. John Stott, *The Contemporary Christian: Applying God's Word to Today's World* (Downers Grove, IL: InterVarsity, 1992), 37–38 (emphasis original).

38. Berkhof, *Systematic Theology*, 204.

39. Even though these faculties have been marred by the fall, we contend they still exist and operate as inherent characteristics of the *imago Dei* and are sustained by God's common grace. For more on this, see Imes, *Being God's Image*, 44–58.

40. Berkhof, *Systematic Theology*, 204.

soul and body"). The space allotted here does not allow us to broach this long-standing debate.[41] However, it is clear from Scripture that the human soul has been granted immortality by God in that humans continue to consciously exist after physical death, either in heaven or in hell.[42]

The existence of the human soul has significant implications for the relationship between God's image bearers and AI. Algorithms, computers, and robots do not have souls; God never breathed into their nostrils the breath of life. They do not have immortal natures that extend beyond this world. Only humans are given this gift. In this way, God has signaled the specialness and unique dignity of the creatures who bear his image. This brings us to our second category: relationship.

Relationship

One of the most profound ramifications of the *imago Dei* is the idea of relationality. "As living image of the living God, Adam bears a relationship to God like that of child to parent. He is made for intimate, reciprocal relationship with God, designed for relationship with his created others."[43] The same can be said of Eve. As already noted above, humans are designed to share kinship with their Creator and with one another, an ever-flowing exchange of communication, love, affirmation, and empathy. Simply put, at their core humans are connective beings. In fact, our sense of being, identity, and purpose is constituted and reinforced relationally and communally. In other words, we are made by God to actually need others to know who we are. This notion is beautifully illustrated by the African concept of *ubuntu*, which the Nobelist Desmond Tutu articulates this way: "My humanity is caught up, is inextricably bound up, in yours. . . . A person is a person through other persons. . . . I am human because I belong. I participate, I share."[44] Professor James Beitler elaborates on Tutu's ruminations: "One's identity—even one's very being—cannot be understood apart from others. Personhood is, in part, a socially constructed reality."[45]

41. For more, see Johnston, "Humanity," 564–67; and Hoekema, *Created in God's Image*, 203–26.
42. Space does not permit us to engage Christian views on such topics as soul sleep; eternal, conscious torment; and annihilation.
43. "Adam," in *Dictionary of Biblical Imagery*, ed. Leland Ryken, James C. Wilhoit, and Tremper Longman III (Downers Grove, IL: InterVarsity, 1998), 9. Stott labels this "*our capacity for relationships of love.*" *Contemporary Christian*, 38 (emphasis original).
44. Desmond Tutu, *No Future without Forgiveness* (New York: Random House, 1999), 31.
45. James E. Beitler III, *Seasoned Speech: Rhetoric in the Life of the Church* (Downers Grove, IL: IVP Academic, 2019), 139.

Human relationality should influence the way we comprehend and engage AI. Divine-human and human-human interactions should be prioritized. Without them, we are less human. Human-machine relations can be helpful insofar as they facilitate and supplement the aforementioned relations, but they must never be encouraged or allowed to supplant them. Souls can love God and other souls. Souls cannot truly love a machine, nor can machines reciprocate love. Human-AI relations cannot foster true connection or belonging and so must be approached with care, lest they undermine the *imago Dei*.

We now arrive at our third category: role.

Role

A critical part of the *imago Dei* is the idea of vocation, a calling that includes *authority* and *responsibility*. The *Dictionary of Biblical Imagery* offers a thorough explanation:

> A principal expression of that image is an active rule that represents the loving dominion and care of God over the wonders of creation. Adam, true archetype of humankind, is appointed vice-regent in the territorial dominion of God. Male and female are regal figures, empowered, anointed and charged with exercising the benevolent rule of their cosmic Creator Lord. With a mere handful of deftly ordered words, the lofty bearing, stature and commission of ancient oriental kingship is breathtakingly disassembled and the royal crown placed on the sturdy heads of everyman and everywoman.
>
> In the narrative of Genesis 2, the Adamic rule is expressed in three concrete activities: (1) cultivating or "serving" (*'ābad*) the garden; (2) keeping or "guarding" (*šāmar*) the garden; and (3) naming (*qārā' . . . šēm*) his fellows in the community of animate life. We enter the world of a splendid royal garden of grand proportions, stunning in design and irresistible in appeal, over which a king has set his vice-regent to till, to protect and to explore by naming.[46]

Humans represent God's reign over planet Earth. As his vice-regents, they are to enact their King's plans and wishes. Specifically, he commands three tasks: serving, guarding, and naming (Gen. 2:15–20).

It is critical to note that in the creation account (and Scripture in general), authority and responsibility are interconnected or coupled—that is, they exist in a balanced relationship (see fig. 3.2).

46. "Adam," 9–10.

Figure 3.2.

Authority   **Responsibility**

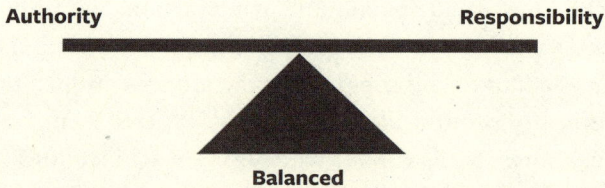

Balanced

Seesaw in Balance

Let's explore these concepts. First is authority. In Genesis 1–2, human authority is tied to human identity: we are children in God's family, and as such, we are his vice-regents, his royal representatives over creation.[47] Psalm 8 depicts the location of human authority within the divine cosmic order (see fig. 3.3).

At the top of this cosmic order is eternal, almighty God, the Creator of all things, producing the heavens, the earth, and everything in them ex nihilo, out of nothing. Next come human beings, who are "a little lower than the angels. . . . You made them rulers over the works of your hands; you put everything under their feet" (Ps. 8:5–6).[48] Last, at the bottom, placed underneath humans, we find "all flocks and herds, . . . the birds in the sky, and the fish in the sea" (vv. 7–8). In this God-ordained structure, humans rule over everything on the globe. That means God has given them dominion over all forms of technology, including AI.

Authority is tempered by responsibility, which is framed by accountability. Scripture is unequivocal in stating that all humans will have the totality of their lives, including thoughts, speech, and actions, judged by God (see, e.g., Rom. 14:12; 2 Cor. 5:10; Rev. 20:11–15). To be clear, robots will never be judged by God as humans will be. They will not

Figure 3.3.

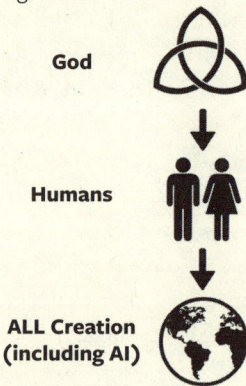

God

Humans

ALL Creation
(including AI)

Divine Cosmic Order

47. In one sense, all humans are God's children, according to Scripture. However, when it comes to Christ's redemption on the cross, only Christians are God's adopted children (see, e.g., Rom. 8; Gal. 3).

48. The Hebrew word *me'elohim* can be translated "'less than God' (NIV note) or 'less than the heavenly [angelic] beings.'" Willem A. VanGemeren, "Psalms," in *Zondervan NIV Bible Commentary*, vol. 1, *Old Testament*, ed. Kenneth L. Barker and John Kohlenberger III (Grand Rapids: Zondervan, 1994), 803.

receive the reward of heaven or the punishment of hell. And they cannot know Christ in a personal or intimate way.

Herein lies a vital critique of AI. Humans must not over-rely on machine learning. If they do, they are in danger of abdicating an essential element of the *imago Dei*: our role, our vocation, our authority, and with that, our agency or power to act. One of the current challenges of AI is that it threatens to permanently change our relationship with technology. How is that? As was seen in chapter 2, the tentacles of AI already stretch deep into the major domains of American society and are unlikely to slow down or stop anytime soon. The authors of *The Age of AI* offer prescient insight via a startling claim: they argue that AI is "in the process of transforming machines—which, until now, have been our tools—into our partners."[49]

We propose the diagram show in figure 3.4 as a way of exposing this sea change.

Figure 3.4.

AI is a . . .   **Tool**   **Partner**   **Master**

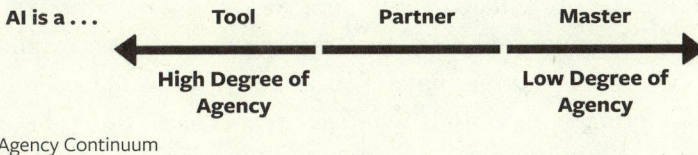

High Degree of   **Low Degree of**
Agency   **Agency**

Agency Continuum

On the left side of the plane, where AI is a tool, human agency is high. At this point, generally speaking, a balance remains between authority and responsibility.

Moving to the right, toward the center of the plane, is where AI becomes a partner. Here, human agency is decreasing, which creates an imbalance between authority and responsibility.

On the right side of the plane, presuming the hypothetical (yet plausible) situation in which AI becomes the master of humanity,[50] human agency is low or nonexistent. In this case, the imbalance between authority and responsibility is complete (and perhaps even irreversible). Humans have little to no

49. Henry A. Kissinger, Eric Schmidt, and Daniel Huttenlocher, *The Age of AI and Our Human Future* (New York: Little, Brown, 2021), 20.

50. This hearkens back to the end of chap. 2, where we outlined Max Tegmark's AI aftermath scenarios. These scenarios presuppose the "AI singularity" or "AI superintelligence" and include Tegmark's outcomes labeled "conquerors," "descendants," and "zookeeper." We acknowledge these outcomes are speculative, yet they should still be seriously considered.

Figure 3.5.

Authority

Responsibility

Imbalanced

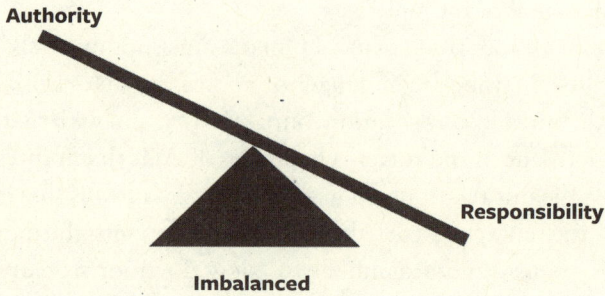

Seesaw Is Imbalanced

authority and yet still bear total responsibility before God for the actions
committed by the intelligent machines they have created (see fig. 3.5).

In this worst-case scenario, humans have abdicated most—if not all—of
their authority while retaining their full, God-given responsibility. The trouble
with AI, then, is the potential decoupling of authority from responsibility,
leading to a dangerous disparity that damages human identity and undermines God's good plan for human flourishing. Who would knowingly and
relentlessly promote AI considering such an outcome?

Thus, we contend that to cede authority and agency uncritically or causti-
cally to intelligent machines would contradict God's revealed will for creation.
Why? As we've argued, it controverts the creational narrative of Scripture.
Embedded within this framework is the *imago Dei*, which is God's vision
for human flourishing. When used improperly, AI impinges on the dignity
and identity conferred upon God's image bearers, which include the unique
endowments of reason, relationship, and role.

To put it succinctly, AI has the potential to make humans less human.
At the same time, AI has the potential to help humans flourish and partake
in God's quest to restore all things. Both options remain operative. Which
course will we choose?

CONCLUSION

In broad terms, in this chapter we have endeavored to answer the question,
What does it mean to be human *from a biblical perspective*? In so doing, our

ambition has been to take a scriptural, human-centric approach to examining AI. That has led us to ask the following research question: How might AI advance or hinder human flourishing?

We believe the best answer to this question is found in Scripture's creational narrative. This framework unashamedly centers vital Christian doctrines, such as the relationality of the Trinity, the goodness and materiality of creation, and the liberating power of the incarnation, death, and bodily resurrection of Jesus Christ. Later, we intentionally narrowed our focus to the *imago Dei*, which proves valuable in analyzing the consequences of AI on their inventors and would-be partners.

Chapter 4 lies ahead. There, we will pursue a new line of inquiry: What does it mean to be human *in a technological age*? We will also present a deeper analysis of AI, drawing out the negative and positive traits and ramifications that come with this algorithm-driven machinery. This will complete the foundation from which chapters 5, 6, and 7 spring.

QUESTIONS FOR REFLECTION

1. Mull over the creational narrative presented in this chapter. What are its strengths and weaknesses? How would you modify it? Are you aware of other paradigms or frameworks that explore technology or AI from a Christian vantage point?

2. Do you agree with the definition of *imago Dei* offered here? What do you think of its constituent themes of reason, relationship, and role? Were you familiar with these categories before reading this book? Are you curious or want to learn more about any aspects of this doctrine?

3. How would you describe the connection between authority and responsibility? How have you comprehended these concepts in the past? Have you learned anything new in this chapter? Can you see how AI might disrupt the balance?

4. What Does It Mean to Be Human in the Technological Age?

Technology is transforming human life at a faster pace than ever before. . . . The new technologies allow for new kinds of cognitive tools that combine artificial intelligence with interface technology, molecular biology, nanotechnology, genetic enhancing of human mental and physical capacities, combating diseases and slowing down the process of aging, and exercising control over desires, moods and mental states. Due to genetic engineering, humans are now able not only to redesign themselves . . . but also to redesign future generations, thereby affecting the evolutionary process itself.

—Hava Tirosh-Samuelson, "Engaging Transhumanism,"
in *H±: Transhumanism and Its Critics*

Extending Our Humanness

In this chapter, we will consider the ways the technological milieu in which we live has impacted how we function as human beings in society. We will look at the ways in which we technologically extend ourselves into the wider society and what this means for the creation of a more techno-human environment. We will also examine how technology shapes us and how it can be a medium for values that are more powerfully formative than we might think.

We then examine the ways in which the technologies we use impact our bodies and what this says about how we view ourselves as embodied beings in time and space. We revisit an ancient philosophy, Gnosticism, which still exists in many forms and which challenged the early church with its theology of the body in particular. We then discuss a variety of ways in which being human in the age of technology challenges the nature of human experience and impacts how we live in a very different way than we have historically.

Technology is not new. It has been a perennial feature of human existence since creation. When humans first extended themselves by use of an external tool, technology was born. They may have simply extended a stick to knock a piece of fruit from a tree, but in any case, they used something external to themselves to extend their abilities. John Dyer writes about humans using technology to shape the world around them, to tell stories about the tools they encounter, to imagine what they can do. New technology always changes the way we live because it introduces something innovative to our environment.[1] We have a long history of using technologies, but we tend to view that history in terms of computers only. If we take a wider view, we discover that our species has incorporated a wide variety of technologies over the course of millennia, including "clothes, utensils, structures, apparatus, utilities, tools, machines and automata."[2] You might not have thought of these as technologies—apart perhaps from machines and automata—and even then, you might have thought of non-computer-aided machines and automata as rather primitive. When I (Sean) set my washing machine on one of its numerous AI cycles—in which the machine can self-determine the weight of the load and even how dirty it is, using an appropriate temperature, length of wash, and amount of detergent—I am reminded of my first washing machine at home in Ireland, which had two cycles—hot and cold—and a hand-operated mangle on top of it, which I used to manually squeeze the water out of my clothes. It wasn't always obvious to me that this latter machine was an advanced piece of technology at the time, but it was a lot more advanced than the rocks and washboards that my grandmother had to use in her time.

How Technology Changes Our Experience of Being Human

Dyer argues that people often define technology as "anything that was invented after you were born." He attributes this observation to the computer

---

1. John Dyer, *From the Garden to the City: The Place of Technology in the Story of God*, rev. ed. (Grand Rapids: Kregel, 2022), 37.
2. Derek C. Schuurman, *Shaping a Digital World: Faith, Culture and Computer Technology* (Downers Grove, IL: IVP Academic, 2013), 13.

scientist Alan Kay and highlights the human tendency to quickly forget that technological developments made throughout history, not just in our own lifetimes, were once considered to be highly advanced.[3] He then contrasts the reading of Scripture from a physical book and its reading from a screen, whether an overhead screen, a computer monitor, or a Kindle. Because hundreds, if not thousands, of people can see the same text on a giant screen, he points out that subtle but very real and impactful changes can occur in their encounter with Scripture.

When Dyer taught in a Bible study, using a projector to transmit the scriptural text onto a screen, his students experienced the Scriptures more like people must have before the invention of the printing press, when clergy would have been the only people with access to physical, written texts. We have become so accustomed to reading from our own individual Bibles that we forget that it is only since the time of the printing press that Christians have been able to access the scriptures in this format. We all know already that the early church listened communally to the scriptural text, so the modern practice of gathering around a screen to read or listen has changed the church's relationship with the Word of God from one based around an individual text held in each believer's hands to one where all are learning in a more communal way.[4]

What has happened here is that pastors think they are using technology, and they are, but another force is at work as well. Technology has also used and shaped them and their experience and the experiences of those around them. Whenever we use technology, it shapes us because it changes how we interact with the world. We quickly get immersed in new technology, and it becomes the new normal.[5] It becomes so normal that we don't notice how it has altered our interactions with our environment and other people. Something significant has changed, but the effect of that change sort of creeps up on us, and while we tend to notice and perhaps even critique how we use technology, we fail to notice the wider changes that technology brings about in society. One accessible example is the role of gyms and exercise machines in our lives. Each exercise machine that we use is a tool we engage with, but each tool has a function—it may increase our cardio fitness or help us tone and shape our legs or strengthen our arms.[6] We are shaped by these fitness

3. Dyer, *From the Garden to the City*, 24.
4. Dyer, *From the Garden to the City*, 26–29.
5. Dyer, *From the Garden to the City*, 29.
6. Dyer, *From the Garden to the City*, 40.

technologies—perhaps more visibly than most other technologies—but other forms of machinery shape both us personally and the society around us to varying degrees.

Why Technology Changes Our Experience of Being Human

Let's look at how both this personal and wider shaping takes place. Both Dyer and Derek C. Schuurman agree that technology is not value neutral. It has become a kind of societal dictum to say that "it's not the tool but how it is used that determines whether it is good or bad." Dyer turns to Neil Postman's work to unpack the issues of values and good, bad, and gray areas, and what Postman says very much fits with our discussion about the way in which technology shapes us. Dyer relays Postman's point that when a new technology comes along, it changes what Dyer refers to as "the entire technological ecosystem." It doesn't serve as an "add-on" to what is already there. "For example, when television came into homes, it wasn't simply 'additive' alongside radio. Instead, television changed our relationship with radio, how often we used it, and what we used it for."[7] Marshall McLuhan's four "laws of media" illustrate this relationship between the new and the old by asking the following questions of any technological artifact:

1. What does the artifact *extend* or *enhance*? What human capacity is amplified?
2. What does the artifact make *obsolete*?
3. What does the artifact *retrieve* from the past?
4. When pushed to its limits, an artifact tends to *reverse* its original characteristics. What does the artifact reverse into?[8]

Dyer argues that no matter what we use technology for, it is never neutral because technology always changes us "physically, mentally, spiritually or relationally."[9] The tools at the gym shape our bodies; our outlook on the world is determined by the material we read online. If I read conspiracy

7. Dyer, *From the Garden to the City*, 100.
8. This list is from Schuurman, *Shaping a Digital World*, 20 (emphasis original). He gives a full illustration of how these four laws work in practice at the same location.
9. Dyer, *From the Garden to the City*, 21.

theories, I will view the world (mentally, spiritually, and relationally) through a conspiratorial worldview. The easy accessibility of pornography online can destroy my spiritual, mental, physical, and relational worlds. If I spend all day on my cell phone, my relationships and ability to communicate may be severely curtailed.

Schuurman claims that even the designers of technology, including the creators of AI systems, "embed their personal or corporate values into their devices. Consequently, there is a direction embedded in the structure of technological artifacts."[10] This direction functions as a bias that directs the user toward a particular end. Again, Postman says it better than anyone else can: "Embedded in every tool is an ideological bias, a predisposition to construct the world as one thing rather than another, to value one thing over another, to amplify one sense or skill or attitude more loudly than another." Postman continues: "New technologies alter the structure of our interests: the things we think *about*. They alter the character of our symbols: the things we think *with*. And they alter the nature of community: the arena in which thoughts develop."[11] We see this directional bias at work today, for example, in ChatGPT.

ChatGPT

Think about ChatGPT for a moment. What it does is really useful. I know marketers who have asked it to create a sales pitch for a product, and it has done an excellent job. However, many have found that relying on it for factual information can be precarious because it cannot distinguish, at the time of this writing, between true and false information. Hence, it will insert AI "hallucinations" into text—basically, it has a tendency when it doesn't know something to simply make it up. This may involve creating nonexistent sources as foundations for its inventions or hallucinations. You may view this as a fatal flaw in the system, but ChatGPT is designed to be both accurate and creative, and it often doesn't know exactly what you want from it, so it may choose the creative rather than the factual path—to your detriment, if anyone checks the accuracy of your work. The creative souls at OpenAI, the company behind ChatGPT, clearly biased the GenAI toward creativity, and

10. Schuurman, *Shaping a Digital World*, 15.
11. Neil Postman, *Technopology: The Surrender of Culture to Technology* (New York: Vintage Books, 1993), 13, 20.

sometimes the program values that approach over accuracy. ChatGPT has a directional bias built into it so that it favors the creative over the factual when pushed to the wall. The CEO of OpenAI, Sam Altman, admitted as much in an interview in which he described AI hallucinations as "a feature of the technology rather than a bug."[12] Essentially, the AI, Altman claims, flexes its creative muscles and takes a novel approach when it does not know something by basically fabricating it.

Kline's Subdivisions

Stephen J. Kline has introduced four subdivisions into the conversation about technology in general—namely, that technology can be understood as hardware, manufacturing, methodology, and social usage.[13] His work is useful in helping us contextualize how technology shapes our lives. For our purposes here, let's look briefly at the methodology and social usage categories.

Methodology

In this context, the term *methodology* refers to "the routines, methods, and skills used in the process of making modern hardware, writing modern software, and doing modern business."[14] Methodology necessarily encapsulates values. It informs how and why we do things. The methods we choose in any endeavor say a lot about the kind of people we are. "Theologian Jacques Ellul worried that technology as methodology often shapes our emotional, spiritual, and relational worlds in ways that aren't always compatible with our Christian faith."[15] The human tendency, according to Ellul, is to try to find technological answers to every problem. The more we are immersed in technology the more we turn to technology for solutions to our problems.[16] ChatGPT is a good example of this because it is a technological replacement

12. Wallace Witkowski, "OpenAI's Sam Altman Tells Salesforce's Marc Benioff That AI 'Hallucinations' Are More Feature Than Bug," MarketWatch, last updated September 13, 2023, https://www.marketwatch.com/story/openais-sam-altman-tells-salesforces-marc-benioff-that-ai -hallucinations-are-more-feature-than-bug-1c035c52.

13. Stephen J. Kline, "What Is Technology?," in *Philosophy of Technology: The Technological Condition; An Anthology*, ed. Robert C. Scharff and Val Dusek (Malden, MA: Blackwell, 2003), 210–12.

14. Dyer, *From the Garden to the City*, 69.

15. Dyer, *From the Garden to the City*, 69.

16. Dyer, *From the Garden to the City*, 70.

for something many humans have done perfectly well for thousands of years—namely, writing. In chapter 5, we will look at the ways in which AI will continue to influence pedagogy, how we teach and are taught, and how we learn. ChatGPT looms large in that discussion, but for now we can say that ChatGPT is a technological sledgehammer to smash a technological nut.

ChatGPT's generative nature means that it can generate new content. Effectively, it repackages old content, but in a creative and astonishingly quick way—plus, it does all the work for its users. However, as a technological means of increasing the pace of composition, it devalues and, in many areas, destroys the millennia-old process of human writing. The methodology employed to produce a new writing tool powered by AI makes value judgments about the human writing process and, whether intentional or not, results in human composition often being rendered obsolete. For millennia, human beings have understood themselves and their worlds through writing. Now, ChatGPT is shaping those worlds according to its internal algorithms and predetermined functions, which are pretty simple to understand, as will be seen in the next chapter. There is no magical mystery to ChatGPT, but it will radically change our world by shaping it not with words that spring directly from human experience but with language which is artificially created and which has its origins in cold, logical algorithmic computation, divorced from human emotion. Bear that in mind as we look at Kline's next category, that of social usage.

Social Usage

Social usage is concerned with how we use technology in society, in culture.[17] In other words, we are here dealing with the social-shaping function of technology, which is much broader than individual use. We can understand the technological ecosystem as analogous to the biological ecosystem. When a new species is introduced to an existing biosystem, many things change throughout the system. When a new technology is introduced to the technological ecology, it also changes the system.

Of course, this kind of change occurred often in the past, but we will discuss why one major factor has meant the situation is different today. Andy Clark explains that our traditional image of a cyborg—as a humanoid attached to wires, with visible cybernetic implants—is not necessarily correct:

17. See Dyer, *From the Garden to the City*, 71–73, for examples.

"For we shall be cyborgs, not in the merely superficial sense of combining flesh and wires but in the more profound sense of being human-technology symbionts: thinking and reasoning systems whose minds are spread across biological brains and non-biological circuitry."[18] Here, Clark discusses what could be called the digitally extended human being, the human who is connected to computer technology simply by sitting in front of a screen at home but, at the same time, whose connection with the digital world extends outside the home via social media, email, online banking, Netflix, online shopping, and so forth. Each human being who spends significant time online has a digital presence in the world, which is a projection of their physical self as it navigates the world around it. Long after you and I are gone, our digital presence will remain in the form of our extended digital selves.

Let's briefly summarize what we have learned so far, because it is important for the next stage of our journey.

- Technology is not neutral. It is value laden; it leads us in certain directions; it prompts us to do or use "this" instead of "that."
- This value-laden, directional technology is constantly updated and evolving. When it is updated, it can bring about not just minor "additive" change but *systemic* change.

As already noted, such change is nothing new. The television has changed how we use radio, and the cell phone has changed not just how we communicate but how we live in general. It doesn't just isolate us from one another via constant phone scrolling and phone checking; rather, it completely changes how businesses run and what we expect of businesses and each other. If I'm late home from work one night, my wife wants to know why I didn't text to let her know. Gen Zers tend to shy away from speaking on the phone in favor of texting, which in turn affects their communication skills and makes life difficult when they enter the work world and have to speak to others over the phone. Texts won't always cut it. However, what has changed in the late twentieth and early twenty-first centuries, due to AI technologies, is that people have been questioning the very nature of what it means to be human in a front-and-center kind of way.

18. Andy Clark, *Natural-Born Cyborgs: Minds, Technologies, and the Future of Human Intelligence* (Oxford: Oxford University Press, 2003), 3.

Internal Changes as a Result of Technology and AI

Think about it this way. A wide variety of technologies existed in the past, but they largely changed us externally. If they changed us internally at all, it was because they altered how we saw and understood the world. Most change occurred on the outside—say, through the wearing of different textiles; the use of spectacles or hearing aids; in medieval times, the development of armor. Today, the situation is quite different: changes can be made to our bodies and even minds, which raises questions about what human nature is and whether we are heading toward a "posthuman" era. Therefore, when we ask the question, What does it mean to be human in a technological age? we really are asking, What does it mean to *be human* in a technological age? We must ask that question because we have entered into what many term the age of the *techno-human*.

The Techno-Human and Transhumanist Visions

Whatever your view of evolution—and numerous theories exist today[19]—many technologists believe that humans are in a stage of evolution that is very different from previous stages. This is a self-directed revolution in a stage of human history described as the "techno-human." The portmanteau implies a fusion of the human and the machine, not necessarily in the creation of a kind of robotic, cyborg process or product but in that humans and computers do and will increasingly work together. Although beyond the scope of this book (yet still related to its focus), the techno-human can be viewed as the embryonic stage of the transhuman. The transhuman can be described as "the stage above the human," where humans throw off the "shackles" and limitations of their human nature and enter into a phase in which technology and the human body and mind work in tandem.

One of the best explanations of transhumanism and its implications has been offered by Hava Tirosh-Samuelson, a staunch and knowledgeable critic of transhumanism. She finds the term to be vague, and we do as well. It is a term that has a number of definitions, depending on which scholars one reads, although all agree that it refers to the "enhancement" of the human and the

---

19. See, e.g., J. B. Stump, ed., *Four Views on Creation, Evolution, and Intelligent Design* (Grand Rapids: Zondervan, 2017).

transformation of what it means to be human. This process can take many forms and gradations, so we don't want to definitively define it.

However, one of the most extreme transhumanist visions is that, according to Tirosh-Samuelson, "Humans will . . . transform themselves into posthumans, namely 'persons of unprecedented physical, intellectual and psychological capacity, self-programming, potentially immortal, unlimited individuals.'"[20] She continues, "While the vision of the posthuman ideal state of affairs is generally clear, the precise meaning of the human is somewhat vague. For some the term is short for *transitional human*."[21] The techno-human neatly corresponds with the transitional human.

The techno-human can be part human, part machine, but not in a scary cybernetic form. It can be a human who has lost a limb and had it replaced with a prosthetic; someone who is severely paralyzed but able to move robotic limbs or equipment; or someone fitted with a brain-computer interface, able to control cursors on a screen, fly drones, or speed up imagery analysis, as in the case of satellite-imaging analysts. The techno-human can equally refer to a human interacting with AI to such an extent that it changes how and what they seek to accomplish.

The term *techno-human* nicely explains the fusion of human and computer or machine, aided and powered by AI. Michael Bess writes that in the near future, "it is not our gadgets that will be transformed—it is we ourselves, our bodies, our minds. . . . People will be able to sculpt their own selfhood over time, reshaping their bodies, augmenting their cognition, reconfiguring their character and personality."[22] Bess's thoughts are echoed by Braden R. Allenby and Daniel Sarewitz, who make the following (fairly powerful) statement regarding the techno-human: "We are, it turns out, in neither God's nor Darwin's hands, but in our own."[23] By this, Allenby and Sarewitz mean that the impetus toward the techno-human is directed by human beings. This direction will be powered by AI, which, when coupled with hardware and software, will enable us to change what it means to be human as we know it.

20. Hava Tirosh-Samuelson, "Engaging Transhumanism," in *H±: Transhumanism and Its Critics*, ed. Gregory R. Hansell and William Grassie (Philadelphia: Metanexus Institute, 2011), 24. Within the quotation she draws from Max More, "The Extropian Principles, Version 3.0: A Transhumanist Declaration," 1998, https://www.mrob.com/pub/religion/extro_prin.html.

21. Tirosh-Samuelson, "Engaging Transhumanism," 26 (emphasis original).

22. Michael Bess, *Our Grandchildren Redesigned: Life in the Bioengineered Society of the Near Future* (Boston: Beacon, 2015), xiv.

23. Braden R. Allenby and Daniel Sarewitz, *The Techno-Human Condition* (Cambridge, MA: MIT Press, 2013), 19.

We draw attention to the above because all that you have read in the previous paragraphs demonstrates the twofold direction of AI. Artificial intelligence will be able to function autonomously in certain situations and in other situations it will work together with humans through brain-computer interfaces and through the creation of organizational systems that will help people in their jobs and roles as a kind of "co-pilot."[24]

A central plank of transhumanist thought is the Transhumanist Manifesto. This manifesto sums up the transhumanist approach to the human body, declaring that it "challenges the human condition. This condition asserts that aging is a disease, augmentation and enhancement to the human body and brain are essential to prevail, and that well-being is essential to prosper within safe and healthy environments."[25]

Altering Our Corporeality

The relationship between human beings and technology is a complicated one because it can take place on many different levels. The techno-human can be viewed as an entirely disembodied being, retaining just vestiges of what we might understand as a human, including a mind, albeit a mind fused with AI and superintelligence. Or the techno-human can be understood as an embodied being, whose body is like a car in that various parts can be replaced as needed. Have you ever had a car that required so much work that you felt you had, in effect, rebuilt the whole thing and essentially had a new automobile (but you still thought of it as the original vehicle)? There is a hilarious scene in the British comedy series *Only Fools and Horses*, where a character, Trigger, a road sweeper not known for his intellect, receives an award for saving his town council money by using the same broom for twenty years. When his friends question him about this, asking if he has ever actually swept any roads with the broom, Trigger replies that he certainly has: "This old broom has had seventeen new heads and fourteen new handles in

24. The Prime Minister's Office and Rishi Sunak, "Prime Minister's Speech on AI: 26 October 2023," GOV.UK, October 26, 2023, https://www.gov.uk/government/speeches/prime-ministers-speech-on-ai-26-october-2023. This speech was delivered to the Royal Society in London in anticipation of an AI summit hosted by the British government at Bletchley Park, where Alan Turing conducted many of his early experiments on AI.

25. Natasha Vita-More, "The Transhumanist Manifesto" (version 4), Humanity Plus, accessed April 25, 2024, https://www.humanityplus.org/the-transhumanist-manifesto.

its time."[26] Well, you and I will be a little bit like that broom if this vision of the "spare-part human" becomes a reality. Our view of the body is important when defining how we understand our humanity, since we are embodied beings. We carry our bodies around with us every day, usually without much thought, but techno-humanism and transhumanism will be almost wholly concerned with the body and the mind in the rest of the twenty-first century, and we will be forced to form a view of the body that we have not considered much heretofore.

Gnosticism

In our discussion of the techno-human and the transhuman, we continually focus on the body. It is the body that defines and delineates how we experience the world, through our senses and through our emotions. If you go to a gym any day of the week, you will see dozens of people seeking to treat, shape, and look after their bodies in a better way. So it's not that we are totally unaware of our bodies; rather, we are usually aware of them in terms of health or appearance, and rarely do we think about their existential role. We simply cannot live, function, or exist in this world without them because we are embodied beings. However, I doubt if we think much about the goodness or evilness of our bodies. We tend not to think of them as having good or bad values. They just *are*.

A widespread and multifaceted movement called Gnosticism existed in the early church. This movement left its stamp on the writings of the New Testament. Paul, John, and Jude all respond in some way in their letters to Gnostic teachings. The Gnostics believed that they had a special revelation concerning the origins of the universe and of humanity. They had a different view of the divine than Christians did and a very different view of how to relate to the divine being. Access to divine revelation was by steps of knowledge, and adherents could traverse these steps throughout life. So for the Gnostics—whose name comes from the Greek word for "knowledge," *gnōsis*—it was all important to receive spiritual knowledge and to progress through the various stages to reach spiritual perfection. Knowledge was key, and this knowledge could be received through the spirit with the help

26. "Trigger's Well-Maintained Broom," *Only Fools and Horses*, written by John Sullivan, BritBox, original airdate December 12, 2018, https://www.youtube.com/watch?v=56yN2zHtofM.

of the mind. In Gnostic thought, the body was an impediment; it got in the way. This could lead to two views of the body, one in which the body was the soul's enemy and needed to be overcome and another in which the body was intensely unspiritual, and it didn't matter what was done with it. The latter interpretation gave license for all kinds of debauched and sensual activities; since the body was not essential for the task of salvation, it could be indulged.

The former interpretation above is often echoed in transhumanism, since the body, being frail and weak, needs to be enhanced and improved, but the ultimate goal of many transhumanists is to dispense with the body. This could be done gradually, such that parts of the body are continuously replaced by prosthetics or through death, even if that death was hard fought against and viewed as a defeat of progress. The mind could also be uploaded into either a computer program or a robot or cyborg, where it would live on, using AI to further learning. This is not yet possible, of course, but many think that if the mind is just a sophisticated computer, often known in transhumanism circles (along with the body) as "wetware," then we should eventually be able to translate its workings into computer code. In fact, a similar kind of technology is discussed and demonstrated in a fascinating episode of *Mostly Human*, a CNN series discussed briefly in chapter 1. There, host Laurie Segall meets a woman who has re-created her deceased boyfriend through his digital footprint. She has collected his emails, texts, and other digital expressions and created an app. The app uses AI to mimic his responses in real life. However, the app can also learn new things and respond differently to various people.[27] This is a good example of effective disembodiment because the body is not needed for an ongoing relationship. It also endows the deceased with a form of immortality—an immortality in which they can continue to evolve in relation to the people "around them."

One discussion of Gnosticism in Corinth and of Paul's insistence on the physical resurrection of Jesus against the Gnostics, who saw no value whatsoever in the resurrection of the body, explains that "man is . . . for the Gnostic not only perishable but also despicable. The flesh, which is buried, is the largely anti-godly, but at best—in the Jewish sphere—worthless, dwelling

27. *Mostly Human*, episode 1, "Dead, IRL," produced by Erica Fink et al., aired on CNN, https://money.cnn.com/mostly-human/dead-irl/.

of the human self."[28] A Gnostic account of the creation of the human being actually depicts demons as creating the body, cementing its role as "the seat of every evil."[29] The Gnostic Valentinus (100–160 CE), founder of a distinct school of Gnostic thought, regarded the human body "as the home of demons."[30]

While these views are far from the views of transhumanists, nevertheless, the transhumanist vision of the body is pessimistic in a very Gnostic sense, in that it disdains the weakness of the flesh and prioritizes technologies that make use of AI-inspired knowledge to compensate for the flesh's shortcomings.

The philosophy of Eric Voegelin (1901–85) is useful for a Christian understanding of the Gnostic nature of AI and techno-human and transhuman anthropologies. Voegelin did not write about technology per se but addressed human attempts to create heaven on earth by establishing supposed utopias, which fail miserably. He argued that these attempts were evidence of modern Gnostic tendencies, whereby human beings, by means of knowledge, try to create societies they hope will bring heaven to earth—societies in which their propensity toward evil is eliminated and they are transformed into a better species by the knowledge they gain. This is a kind of secular Gnosticism that is not religious in nature or directed toward God but directed toward human ingenuity with the goal of moral perfection.[31] Voegelin understood himself as addressing the topic of eschatology, which is the branch of theology that deals with end times and what happens afterward. He viewed the creation of heaven on earth as a secular eschatological vision. Tirosh-Samuelson echoes this view in her discussion of technological eschatology, in which she engages with Ray Kurzweil's view of transcendence, another religious concept that has been secularized, which Kurzweil understands as the ability to surpass human capabilities. In addition, Tirosh-Samuelson argues against the dualism that privileges "disembodied intelligent entities" and "denigrates the human body as an evil that should be combated and fixed by use of technology."[32]

28. Walter Schmithals, *Gnosticism in Corinth: An Investigation of the Letters to the Corinthians*, trans. John E. Steely (Nashville: Abingdon, 1971), 158.

29. Giovanni Filoramo, *A History of Gnosticism*, trans. A. Alcock (Oxford: Blackwell, 1990), 91–92.

30. Filoramo, *History of Gnosticism*, 98.

31. Glenn N. Schramm, "The New Gnosticism: The Philosopher Eric Voegelin Finds an Old Christian Heresy to Be Very Much Alive," *Crisis Magazine*, November 1, 1990, https://crisismagazine.com/vault/the-new-gnosticism-the-philosopher-eric-voegelin-finds-an-old-christian-heresy-to-be-very-much-alive.

32. Tirosh-Samuelson, "Engaging Transhumanism," 44.

Redesigning the Human Experience

What it means to be human is rapidly changing. It is no longer fixed. In the past, while you could make changes to your weight, fitness, strength, and general health, you could not naturally change the color of your hair or of your eyes. You could not replace limbs in a way that made them as functional or even more functional than your original limbs. You would not be able to accelerate your thinking processes so as to enhance your calculations, writing, or creativity. The human being was in a fixed state within certain set boundaries. Yes, exceptional individuals could stretch the elastic of those boundaries, but most of us led average lives with average abilities. We might excel at one or two things, such as academics or sports, but for those who remember the TV show *The Bionic Man*, we could not perform outside certain parameters. That is no longer the case. And although the developments discussed below may seem like science fiction, they are very much in the realm of scientific fact and barely scratch the surface of what is yet to come. To be human in an age of advanced technology is to experience exhilarating possibilities that enhance human flourishing to a degree unimagined by our ancestors. However, it also means that what it is that makes us human faces challenges posed by technologies that can alter our bodies, minds, and emotions in such a way as to initiate a radical discontinuity with historic human experience.

Michael Bess notes several phenomena that exemplify the ways in which our very humanness is being challenged. Indeed, the title of his book encapsulates the direction in which society is headed: *Our Grandchildren Redesigned: Life in the Bioengineered Society of the Near Future*. The use of the term *redesigned* is key because the old design of the human being is outmoded. We will still experience life, but it will be different because it will increasingly be bioengineered. We will still live in societies, but these societies will reflect systemic bioengineering alterations. Such a redesign is explained by Bess in seven categories: pharmaceuticals, bioelectronics, genetics, nanotechnology, AI, robotics, and synthetic biology. We will use just two of these categories—pharmaceuticals and genetics—to explore various aspects of what it will mean to live as humans in an age of hyperadvanced technology, and then we will examine other facets of life in this milieu. Bess discusses the technological world of the near future, but technological advances over even a short period of time can have a massive cumulative effect leading to an event known as the "Singularity."

What Is the "Singularity," and Why Is It Important?

You cannot get a more influential authority in the world of technology than Ray Kurzweil, described by one author as "the eccentric inventor, futurist, and guru-in-residence at Google."[33] In 1999, Kurzweil received the National Medal of Technology and Innovation from President Bill Clinton. The medal is the highest honor that the United States can award for service in the field of technology.[34] Kurzweil, the inventor of many commonly used technologies, especially in the text-to-speech category, is probably most well known for his groundbreaking work on the so-called Singularity. The title of his book on the topic—*The Singularity Is Near: When Humans Transcend Biology*[35]—is instructive, and it should be noted that it was published in 2005. In brief, the Singularity is the point at which technological progress accelerates so much that it becomes unstoppable. The Singularity is "a future period during which the pace of technological change will be so rapid, its impact so deep, that human life will be irreversibly transformed."[36] The root of this progress is AI, which will become a kind of superintelligence in that it will produce other AIs. So we will see an exponential explosion of intelligence that will far surpass the human intellect. Kurzweil's book is strongly committed to a vision of systemic change, whereby nonbiological intelligence completely transforms what it means to be human because it will empower us to live in a way that changes everything about our societies. Kurzweil writes that "this impending Singularity in our future is increasingly transforming every institution and aspect of human life, from sexuality to spirituality."[37] Crucial and central to the Singularity is what it will allow us to do with and to our bodies. Following a discussion of the frailty of the brain, in which Kurzweil asserts that "our thinking is extremely slow: the basic neural transactions are several million times slower than contemporary electronic circuits,"[38] he then turns to the body: "Our version 1.0 biological bodies are likewise frail and subject to a myriad of failure modes, not to mention the cumbersome

33. Kai-Fu Lee, *AI Superpowers: China, Silicon Valley, and the New World Order* (Boston: Houghton Mifflin Harcourt, 2018), 140.

34. Lauren Clason, "Ray Kurzweil," National Science and Technology Medals Foundation, accessed April 25, 2024, https://nationalmedals.org/laureate/ray-kurzweil.

35. Ray Kurzweil, *The Singularity Is Near: When Humans Transcend Biology* (New York: Viking, 2005).

36. Kurzweil, *Singularity Is Near*, 7.

37. Kurzweil, *Singularity Is Near*, 7.

38. Kurzweil, *Singularity Is Near*, 8.

maintenance rituals they require."[39] The Singularity is posited as the solution needed for this frailty because

> the Singularity will allow us to transcend these limitations of our biological bodies and brains. We will gain power over our fates. Our mortality will be in our own hands. We will be able to live as long as we want (a subtly different statement from saying we will live forever). We will fully understand human thinking and will vastly extend and expand its reach. By the end of this century, the nonbiological portion of our intelligence will be trillions of trillions of times more powerful than unaided human intelligence.[40]

For "the nonbiological portion of our intelligence," read "AI." Kurzweil goes on to say that "the Singularity will represent the culmination of the merger of our biological thinking and existence with our technology, resulting in a world that is still human but that transcends our biological roots."[41] This is a very powerful statement, and although Kurzweil claims that we will still be human after this merger, many question whether the various technologies pertaining to the human body that we discuss below will actually transform human nature, such that it will be discontinuous with what we now recognize as human. It must be noted that Bess is skeptical of Kurzweil's predictions concerning the rapidity of the Singularity, although we would disagree with his reasons for saying so. Bess believes that "it is quite possible for a majority of rational individuals in a democratic society simply to say no to one kind of progress in favor of another: 'more' is not always better, and the most sophisticated technologies do not automatically and unavoidably triumph over the humbler ones."[42] First of all, the public is not always well informed about our various technologies. Also, while many experts on AI urge caution with its use, they do so for a variety of reasons, and ultimately, it will be governments that set national policies on technology, and these governments, while good at paying lip service to public consultation, rarely engage in it.

Not everyone is as optimistic as Kurzweil about the development of the Singularity. Kai-Fu Lee's description of Kurzweil as "eccentric" might hint toward a certain skepticism on his part. Lee refers to the views of people like Elon Musk and Stephen Hawking, who have described the development of

---

39. Kurzweil, *Singularity Is Near*, 9.
40. Kurzweil, *Singularity Is Near*, 9.
41. Kurzweil, *Singularity Is Near*, 9.
42. Bess, *Our Grandchildren Redesigned*, 10–11.

superintelligence in dystopian terms. He also recommends a reality check about the Singularity, since currently "there remain no known algorithms for AGI or a clear engineering route to get there."[43]

Mustafa Suleyman refers to the Singularity as "a massive red herring. Debating timelines to AGI is an exercise in reading crystal balls."[44] Max Tegmark refers to the Singularity as the "intelligence explosion" and offers a balanced and informative discussion regarding its possible utopian or dystopian outcomes.[45] Whether the Singularity as foreseen by Kurzweil takes place, his idea is still a powerful and influential one because it frames the popular visions of where AI could go.

Medicine: Pharmaceuticals, Neuroceuticals, and Neuroscience

Pharmaceuticals

The brain is a new frontier of sorts, explored with the aim of enhancing its already amazing abilities. While pharmaceuticals have long been in use, they can now be applied to meet the needs of our individual body chemistries. Artificial intelligence is able to handle the big data associated with the health profiles of different population groups. This biological data, which can be far too complex for human researchers and take a long time to process, can be analyzed by AI, and diseases can be targeted by pharmaceuticals, with AI gathering data on how subjects react to certain drugs, thereby enabling it to predict outcomes in other situations.[46] Algorithms allow personalized medicines to be manufactured, specific to a patient.

Neuroceuticals

The role of pharmaceuticals has gone well beyond their traditional therapeutic use. They now can have an enhancement function as well, which serves to extend the ability of the human. Neuroceuticals are "smart pills" that

---

43. Lee, *AI Superpowers*, 142.

44. Mustafa Suleyman, *The Coming Wave: Technology, Power, and the 21st Century's Greatest Dilemma*, with Michael Bhaskar (New York: Crown, 2023), 74.

45. Max Tegmark, *Life 3.0: Being Human in the Age of Artificial Intelligence* (New York: Knopf, 2017), 134–60.

46. Lalitkumar K. Vora et al., "Artificial Intelligence in Pharmaceutical Technology and Drug Delivery Design," *Pharmaceutics* 15, no. 7 (July 2023): 1–46, https://www.ncbi.nlm.nih .gov/pmc/articles/PMC10385763/pdf/pharmaceutics-15-01916.pdf.

augment cognition, learning, and memory. These pills were initially intended to serve therapeutic purposes, but like many enhancement technologies, it was discovered that they could also extend human function. One outcome of the use of neuroceuticals is improved memory.[47] Ritalin and Adderall have long been used to treat attention deficit hyperactivity disorder, but many, though certainly not all, of those without this disorder have found that these drugs significantly sharpen both attention and memory and increase brainpower and the ability to handle greater workloads.[48]

What are the implications for humans in a world where AI-enabled smart-pill research is ubiquitous? In short, neuroceuticals will create new tiers in society, where the haves will benefit from enhanced memories and energy levels and the have-nots will rely on natural methods of memory retrieval and concentration. This scenario won't come about just because of financial reasons; many people will simply desire a more natural approach to using their minds.

Enhanced memory retrieval or even heightened awareness have implications for those who have traumatic memories. Our minds have natural processes, developed over millennia, to help us cope with trauma. Yes, drugs are available to help us further, but neuroceuticals could result in an inability of the mind to switch off when it needs to. Sometimes we need to forget, if only for a while.

Neuroscience

On the flip side, those who have lost memories due to brain damage may be able to retrieve them and even store them as a result of research coordinated by the Defense Advanced Research Development Agency (DARPA), a research and development branch of the US military that uses AI extensively in its work. DARPA's Restoring Active Memory (RAM) program began in 2013, and its aim has been to develop an implantable device that restores "normal memory function to military personnel suffering from the effects of brain injury or illness."[49] DARPA technology is very often used in the military and then extended into society in general. It also usually begins therapeutic in nature, only later being used by commercial entities for enhancement purposes. "The RAM program continues to achieve and integrate amazing breakthroughs in

47. Bess, *Our Grandchildren Redesigned*, 17.
48. Bess, *Our Grandchildren Redesigned*, 18.
49. "Progress in Quest to Develop a Human Memory Prosthesis," Defense Advanced Research Projects Agency, US Department of Defense, March 28, 2018, https://www.darpa.mil/news-events/2018-03-28.

neuroscience, artificial intelligence, and neural interface device development for clinical use."[50] The brain, then, will continue to become the ultimate "platform" for techno-human and transhuman developments. Such developments will extend human ability in ways we cannot yet even imagine.

President Obama's BRAIN Initiative (Brain Research through Advancing Innovative Neurotechnologies), launched back in 2013, has as its goal to "accelerate the development and application of new technologies that will enable researchers to produce dynamic pictures of the brain that show how individual brain cells and complex neural circuits interact at the speed of thought."[51] This initiative is intended to achieve for the brain what the Human Genome Project did for the human genome, the mapping of its DNA. "These technologies will open new doors to explore how the brain records, processes, uses, stores, and retrieves vast quantities of information, and shed light on the complex links between brain function and behavior."[52]

The therapeutic opens the door for the experimental, and once the genie is out of the bottle, it's impossible to put it back in. The harnessing of neuroscience, cognitive psychology, biomedical engineering, and AI means that brain function will be engineered to mine the secrets and powerful abilities of this vital organ. Often, technologies that appear to belong to the realms of science fiction are scientific fact, and the general public is often unaware, not necessarily because the research is classified, of the strides made in brain technology. These findings are often published openly in academic journals, which may not be on all our daily reading lists.

Neuroweapons

One major area of research is military neuroscience, especially related to neurowarfare. Neuroweapons are concerned with the waging of war by neural means. As you read the following explanation by former diplomat and consultant Robert McCreight, think of how such weapons can be used outside of war, such as in propaganda and social media: "Neuroweapons defy easy explanation and definition. . . . Neuroweapons are intended to influence,

50. "Progress in Quest."

51. "The BRAIN Initiative: Brain Research through Advancing Innovative Neurotechnologies," Obama White House Archives, accessed November 4, 2023, https://obamawhitehouse.archives .gov/BRAIN.

52. "BRAIN Initiative."

direct, weaken, suppress, or neutralize human thought, brainwave functions, perception, interpretation, and behaviors to the extent that the target of such weaponry is either temporarily or permanently disabled, mentally compromised, or unable to function normally."[53]

Another outcome of research into the brain might be mind mapping (reading someone else's thoughts). This can be achieved by mapping brain waves and then "translating" them. The implications for privacy and national security are obvious.[54]

One of the most important areas of focus for pharmaceutical development—one that directly impacts our understanding of the self and the body—is that of aging and death. In the transhumanist universe, death and aging are viewed as enemies that need to be overcome. Under normal circumstances, no one wants to die, of course, but the transhumanist vision explicitly rejects any expression of human frailty. This rejection results in a fear of death that goes beyond anything we have seen in human history. As human beings, we have accepted death as part of our existential being. As Christians, we understand that death is not the end.

In the transhumanist worldview, death is viewed with extreme fear and anxiety, with no semblance of hope. We repeat that no one wants to die, but the hope of eternity helps us make sense of death. The transhumanist fight against death results in an obsession with perpetual youth and the promotion of an unreal expectation of immortality or quasi-immortality. A delicate distinction exists between life extension, which can already be achieved with pharmaceuticals but will be pursued much more aggressively in the future, and a resistance against aging and death, which diminishes the enjoyment of what life we do have, as it results in both fear and a devaluing of the body and its natural processes. Billions of dollars are poured into life-extension technologies each year, with the hope that these technologies will eventually produce some kind of immortality (though the chances are very slim).[55]

53. Robert McCreight, "Brain Brinkmanship: Devising Neuroweapons Looking at Battlespace, Doctrine, and Strategy," in *Neurotechnology in National Security and Defense: Practical Considerations, Neuroethical Concerns*, ed. James Giordano (Boca Raton, FL: CRC Press, 2014), 117–18.

54. Bess, *Our Grandchildren Redesigned*, 193–94.

55. See Jayne C. Lucke et al., "Anticipating the Use of Life Extension Technologies: Possible Pointers from the Adoption of Assisted Reproductive Technologies," *EMBO Reports* 11 (2010): 334–38, https://doi.org/10.1038/embor.2010.48.

Pharmaceuticals, neuroceuticals, and related developments in neuroscience, as well as drugs that slow aging and brain-computer interfaces that enhance human ability, all contribute to a new understanding of what it means to be human. Such technologies are propelling us as a species into new territory. Cognitive augmentation in the military exists to grant advantages over an adversary, but in the workplace and in learning environments, we will need to make choices about who we are and who we want to be. The rapid and constant evolution of AI will lead to further competition between world superpowers and even between researchers in rival laboratories, with governments and scientists using every cognitive advantage they can leverage. For Christians, enhancement will become a crucial ethical issue because, thinking purely in secular terms, to be unenhanced may be to get left behind; however, to be enhanced may mean that we subject ourselves to body- and brain-related modifications that take away what makes us essentially human, part of which is our fallibility and vulnerability.

Genetically Engineered Humans

Genetic engineering has been the stuff of fantasy novels and science-fiction books, comics, and movies for generations. Kazuo Ishiguro's *Never Let Me Go*[56] and Margaret Atwood's *Oryx and Crake*[57] both deal with the topics of genetic engineering and biotechnology from a fictional standpoint. Ishiguro paints the picture of a clone farm, based in an English school, used by wealthy clients in a society stratified between those who have access to enhancement technologies and those who do not. Atwood's work, set within the context of a postapocalyptic earth, engages with genetic engineering, sterilization, and bioengineering. Both novels explore possible outcomes related to the creation of genetically engineered humans. The movie *Blade Runner*,[58] an adaptation by Ridley Scott of Philip K. Dick's *Do Androids Dream of Electric Sheep?*,[59] tells the story of bioengineered humans, known as replicants, whose role is to work aboard space stations. Some of these synthetic humans rebel, escape, and are hunted.

56. Kazuo Ishiguro, *Never Let Me Go* (New York: Vintage International, 2006).
57. Margaret Atwood, *Oryx and Crake: A Novel* (New York: Nan A. Talese, 2003).
58. *Blade Runner*, directed by Ridley Scott (1982; Burbank, CA: Warner Home Video, 2007), DVD.
59. Philip K. Dick, *Do Androids Dream of Electric Sheep?* (New York: Doubleday, 1968).

These works all emerged when the idea of genetically engineered humans was no longer confined to the realm of science fiction. So although they experiment with the notion by imagining various dystopian scenarios in which bioengineering might take place, they are not altogether engaging with just fantasy. Neither is genetic engineering now viewed almost wholly as dystopian, as it tended to be in the past. Francis Fukuyama writes of what he calls two dystopias, one conjured up by George Orwell in *1984*[60] and the other by Aldous Huxley in *Brave New World*.[61]

According to Fukuyama, Orwell summons up a future of information totalitarianism—the surveillance state. Orwell's vision of surveillance, the utility and validity of which will be determined by one's view of the world and of security, is strongly powered in our day by AI, with its emphasis on facial recognition, tracking and listening software, and drone technology. *Brave New World*, by contrast, is concerned with biotechnology and genetic engineering. Fukuyama points out that the world Huxley creates is more dangerous than that of Orwell, because Orwell's world is so obviously flawed. In *Brave New World*, the risks are less obvious because there seem to be so many upsides to genetic engineering, and the results are not achieved by force, as they are in *1984*. Nevertheless, Fukuyama argues, Huxley warns us that we are entering a "posthuman" stage of history and that while biotechnology will have many benefits in the future, a genetically modified world catapults us into an era in which we have to reassess what it means to be human.[62] Genetic engineering has at least two sides, then, but the dystopian side can lead to severe consequences for humanity, onto untrodden paths.

Jamie Metzl, a significant scholar of the genetic revolution, writes, "Talk of recasting our species is not speculative science fiction but the logical near-term extension of fast-growing technologies that already exist. We now have all the tools we need to alter the genetic makeup of our species. The science is in place. The realization is inevitable. The only variables are whether this process will fully take off a couple of decades sooner or later and what values we will deploy to guide how the technology evolves."[63]

60. George Orwell, *1984* (London: Secker & Warburg, 1949).
61. Aldous Huxley, *Brave New World* (London: Chatto & Windus, 1932).
62. Francis Fukuyama, *Our Posthuman Future: Consequences of the Biotechnology Revolution* (New York: Farrar, Straus and Giroux, 2002), 3–9.
63. Jamie Metzl, *Hacking Darwin: Genetic Engineering and the Future of Humanity* (Naperville, IL: Sourcebooks, 2019), xx.

Once genetic modifications are directed toward enhancement, then as human beings we really will be in uncharted territory. For example, we will need to decide who gets enhanced. (Enhancement can be achieved by several means, but for the purposes of this particular conversation, let's keep to genetics.) Who gets to be stronger, faster, more intelligent? And what will this mean for the rest of us? Will we live in a world where different categories of human beings exist, some enhanced and some "naturals"? Will those in wealthy and technologically advanced countries have access to enhancement technologies denied to those in poor countries? Will governments have to intervene to ensure that everyone has access to enhancement? Will a caste system emerge in which various groups of humans live in different types of communities? If I am unenhanced, how will I compete for a job or a university position against someone who is enhanced? What will happen to those who choose to live unenhanced lifestyles? Paul's first letter to the Corinthians was written to a community that was socioeconomically very diverse. The economic makeup of early Christian communities is an often underrated topic of importance. What will happen in Christian communities when some are enhanced and others are not? What will the ethical debates look like?[64]

Again, these are not questions addressed to a world based on science fiction; rather, they are questions that take account of scientific fact and very real and imminent technologies. Such technologies will pose questions for Christian communities that have not been faced before, and human beings in general, who live in this age of advanced technology, will need to answer them. Being human in an age of advanced technology means having a lot of choices we have not had to make before. Will I genetically modify my child if I can do it? How much of that is playing God? Or is the ability to modify genes part of God's direction for the human species in the techno-human stage? Should I opt for ectogenesis, gestation outside the human womb, which is now nearing feasibility?

Back to AI

All the technologies discussed above are turbocharged by AI. They are possible only through the strides AI has made to accelerate research, often by

---

64. For a full discussion of all these questions, see Bess, *Our Grandchildren Redesigned*, esp. chaps. 4, 6, 7, and 8. Many of the questions we have raised are also raised and discussed by Bess.

processing data much more efficiently than humans can. Tomás Chamorro-Premuzic offers a useful overview of what he calls "being in the age of AI." In other words, what does it mean for the human being to "be" in this milieu? The human of the AI age will be hyperconnected.[65] Think back to what we said above about the digitally extended human being. It's almost like our humanity is split into different spheres of existence because now we can live as our digital selves, but this extension of human being is not isolated. This hyperconnectedness can increase relationality but can also result in being consumed by immersion in the virtual world.

Dataism

The terms *datafication* and *dataism* refer to the process by which human beings and practically every system we now use are the results of the production and collection of massive amounts of data about us. Even Facebook knows our political persuasion based on posts we like or click on. Companies pay vast amounts of money to analyze us from our digital trails, which say much more about us than we might imagine. Everything we click on, buy, read online, comment on is an expression of our values and interests.[66] "The universe consists of data flows, and the value of any phenomenon or entity is determined by its contribution to data processing."[67] AI has given us the ability to collect, process, and analyze large amounts of data—too large for us to handle, dataists believe—so we need to entrust the whole task of processing that information to algorithms, to rule-based systems that are regulated by AI, that can perform such tasks according to predetermined parameters, and that can learn as they go and make decisions, even autonomous decisions, keeping the human out of the loop. Hence, when you apply for a bank loan or a credit card, often it's not a human making decisions, but rather an algorithm.

Dataism reflects a significant change in the ways humans are viewed. In brief, it views us as streams of data. Indeed, it views the animal world in the same way—also, the business and economic world, the worlds of medicine and the law: "You may not agree that organisms are algorithms, and that giraffes,

---

65. Tomás Chamorro-Premuzic, *I, Human: AI, Automation, and the Quest to Reclaim What Makes Us Unique* (Boston: Harvard Business Review, 2023), 9–14.

66. Chamorro-Premuzic, *I, Human*, 15.

67. Yuval Noah Harari, *Homo Deus: A Brief History of Tomorrow* (New York: Harper Perennial, 2017), 372.

tomatoes and human beings are just different methods for processing data. But you should know that this is current scientific dogma, and it is changing our world beyond recognition."[68] It could be argued that our DNA alone is proof that we are made of data. In the dataist worldview, different political systems and different companies and organizations are simply "competing data-processing systems."[69] In his discussion of what he terms "data religion," Yuval Noah Harari observes that in a dataist world, human beings are not sacred.[70] Instead, some have argued that data itself is sacred, equivalent in character to a holy text.[71] In Harari's thinking, humans are merely tools for creating media or vehicles of information, and the cosmic data-processing system that controls it could be said to be like God.

CONCLUSION

Being human in the age of technology means being shaped by technology—but not the kinds of technology to which we have become accustomed. New and forthcoming technologies are shaping us from the inside out; they surround us and direct us down predetermined paths that are difficult to avoid as they are often algorithmically based. In the past, all technology was external to humanity. By its very nature and because of the fragmented kinds of societies in which we lived, technology prior to the digital world was very much limited in its influence and spread. For example, during the Industrial Revolution, even though new forms of technology emerged in all developing countries, machines could be found in factories and industries rather than one's living room or bedroom, the café in which one drank coffee, or the train one took to work. These technologies were location specific. Now, technology is everywhere, and it is on the cusp of shaping our world in a totalizing way. Advances in biotechnology and bioengineering mean that even our own bodies become technologized, and this will become only more and more common. We are now immersed in this digital world and cannot avoid its influence. As

68. Harari, *Homo Deus*, 373.
69. Harari, *Homo Deus*, 374.
70. Harari, *Homo Deus*, 386.
71. See Sean O'Callaghan, "Cyberspace and the Sacralization of Information," *Online: Heidelberg Journal of Religions on the Internet* 6 (2014): 90–102, https://doi.org/10.11588/rel .2014.0.17361.

Christians, our task is to help shape and direct it so that it reflects kingdom principles and brings freedom and flourishing rather than bondage.

QUESTIONS FOR REFLECTION

1. Having read this chapter, in what ways do you think technology has shaped you, your actions, and maybe even your values?

2. Can you identify a form of technology that has changed the lives of your family or friends? What are its positive features, and what are its negative ones?

3. If the age of the techno-human has truly arrived, how can one approach it so that what makes us human and created in the image of God does not become obscured?

5. How Should Educators Interact with AI?

Why Andragogy Is Needed to Teach about AI

The word *andragogy* refers to the practice of teaching adults, and while most of the issues and strategies discussed in this chapter apply to adults, many of them apply to teenagers and sometimes even children. We hope that by now, as a result of reading this book, you agree that AI and AI-enabled technologies have brought about a paradigm shift in global society. *Paradigm shift* is a term for a change so radical, so fundamental, that it causes us to question all the assumptions we held prior to its occurrence. We argued in chapter 4 that AI technology introduces a deep, systemic change wherever it is used.

Churches, Bible schools, and Christian universities and colleges, as well as any religious institutions involved in teaching, will need to approach AI in a way that considers its impact on how information is gathered, assessed, analyzed, and taught. Teaching is fundamental to Christianity. In this chapter, we will examine the impact that AI will have on teaching and explore how pastors and teachers can use AI responsibly while avoiding the pitfalls of abdicating responsibility to it. We will look at how good mental health can be maintained and how spiritual flourishing can be cultivated in this age of big data. We will also look at the use of generative AI (GenAI) and its role in writing.

Christian educators of any kind—pastors, Bible school teachers, or seminary professors, to name but a few—are given the task of preparing the people of God to live in a world that is unlike anything humanity has seen before. The tendency in some quarters is to react in a fearful way toward AI, focusing only on the negative aspects and especially those negative aspects that lean toward an apocalyptic view of the technology.

Techno-Apocalypticism

Techno-apocalypticism is linked closely to eschatology, which is the theology of the end times. As we have already seen, Christians hold a wide variety of views as to how the world and the universe will come to an end. *Eschatology* is the umbrella term given to the branch of theology that explores the histories, the development, and the biblical soundness of these different points of view. Techno-apocalypticism can be explained simply as the belief that technology will bring about the final end. Certainly, some Christians believe that technology will hasten that final end or even that certain technologies—AI in particular, given the ways it can change what it means to be human—are part of an overall anti-Christ system that will lead to the final battle between God and Satan. Other Christians believe that AI is a godsend—given by God himself to usher in the great harvest and the fullness of his kingdom on earth. We could write a whole book and more about these eschatological perspectives, but we do not have that luxury in this volume.

Suffice it to say that Christians sometimes can be quite absolutist in their approaches to AI, with many favoring the pessimistic end of the spectrum. In this book, we have tried to follow what we believe is a realist view of AI. Artificial intelligence cannot be avoided. It must be faced and must be understood by Christians. On the one hand, we need to acknowledge and warn others about its dangers, but on the other hand, we must also acknowledge and explain how it can be a source of human flourishing. Christians cannot afford to be like the Luddites, who reacted to the Industrial Revolution by destroying machines out of fear. We know now that the machines of the industrial age changed the world significantly for the better. In this book, we have both recognized the pitfalls of fully committing to technological utopianism *and* emphasized the redemptive functions of technologies like AI and the roles they can play in furthering the advance of the gospel.

What Does a Christian Andragogy of AI Look Like?

A thorough overview of a Christian andragogy of AI would have to encompass virtually every sphere of human endeavor, but that is beyond the scope of this book. In this chapter, we will focus on one core question: How do we prepare our congregations, students, and ministers to flourish and teach others how to flourish in a world that is saturated with AI?

In answering this question, we will concentrate on four main areas: (1) AI and truth, (2) AI and the flourishing of the human spirit, (3) AI and the accelerated life, and (4) AI and the family.

AI and Truth

Christians should be in the truth business. We live in a society in which winning the argument is all important. It's one of the chief foundations of what we call the culture wars—the battle of ideas—and if we win, we feel good. Truth is often the casualty. And the world notices. It is vital, then, that, whether as teachers or students, we know how to ascertain what the truth of an argument, a position, or a doctrinal statement is. Otherwise, we look like we are incompetent or uneducated, or we look like we are both spiritually and intellectually dishonest.

In a data-driven world—where data is generated, organized, and disseminated by AI systems—we need to be especially vigilant because AI can produce what anyone wants it to, and it can do so in very convincing fashion. It can then send that information wherever a bad actor wants it to go. The actor can instruct the AI system to create different versions of the information for different audiences, thereby manipulating these audiences to believe different things. This is not only personally destabilizing for individuals, but it can destabilize and disorient entire communities and even nations. Propaganda has always been a tool used by those who want to persuade others to do what they want them to do. Governments largely use it, and at the lower end of the spectrum, advertisers use a version of it to sell their products. Advertisers, governments, and organizations all use propaganda to persuade people that what they offer is better and more authentic than what their rivals offer.

Misinformation and Disinformation

Think about it. As Christians, we use information all the time. You may never have thought of the Scriptures as information, but vast libraries for hundreds of years have been filled with books about the Bible. Our great historic seminaries and Bible schools, which have trained ministers for generations, cannot survive without those repositories of information we call libraries. In

Judaism, yeshivas, or religious schools, are the backbone of Jewish life. Rabbis are trained in them, and many young people spend a year or two at a yeshiva to prepare them for life. The Talmud, which is full of arguments about Jewish law, can take decades to study. That is all information or data. The quality and reliability of that information are paramount if we care about truth. There are many things we will never know this side of eternity—such as what form the end of all things will take exactly—but if our eschatological research is based on good information and solid methods, we can hold different views sincerely and not on false foundations.

When we spread the gospel and encounter other religious systems, we need to genuinely understand their beliefs and not caricature, misrepresent, or show ignorance of them, which would only make our own message seem ill-informed. The same holds true with AI. We need to understand as best we can what it means to live as Christians in a world immersed in AI; what it means for our engagement with this world changing technology; what the impact of AI means for how we live our personal, working, and spiritual lives; and what the changes wrought by AI mean for society. We have already discussed these issues to some extent in chapter 2, but get ready for a deeper dive.

Misinformation refers to "false or inaccurate information—getting the facts wrong," whereas *disinformation* signifies "false information which is deliberately intended to mislead—intentionally misstating the facts."[1] Both terms have been used extensively in recent years, particularly in reference to the dangers of AI in social-media-influenced campaigns. For example, the US federal government has banned the use of TikTok on government devices because of privacy issues, and fears have become widespread that its content is used to produce and disseminate large amounts of disinformation.[2]

1. "Misinformation and Disinformation," American Psychological Association, accessed November 15, 2023, https://www.apa.org/topics/journalism-facts/misinformation-disinformation.

2. For more information on TikTok, see Laura Silver and Laura Clancy, "By More Than Two-to-One, Americans Support U.S. Government Banning TikTok," Pew Research Center, March 31, 2023, https://www.pewresearch.org/short-reads/2023/03/31/by-a-more-than-two-to-one-margin-americans-support-us-government-banning-tiktok; Sawdah Bhaimiya, "Here's a Full List of the US States That Have Introduced Full or Partial TikTok Bans on Government Devices over Mounting Security Concerns," *Business Insider*, January 15, 2023, https://www.businessinsider.com/tiktok-banned-us-government-state-devices-2023-1; and Tiffany Tsu, "Worries Grow That TikTok Is New Home for Manipulated Video and Photos," *New York Times*, November 4, 2022, https://www.nytimes.com/2022/11/04/technology/tiktok-deepfakes-disinformation.html.

AI is used extensively to exploit the weaknesses of our human psyches and to influence us psychologically. This is much easier to do than many might imagine. According to Mustafa Suleyman, AI can "develop psychological tricks to gain trust and influence, reading and manipulating our emotions and behaviors with a frightening level of depth, a skill useful in, say, winning Diplomacy [a strategy-based board game] or electioneering and building a political movement."[3]

Deepfake news videos or audios are examples of very convincing fake news in that they are often indistinguishable from authentic videos or audios. Deepfake is dangerous for two reasons. It can present a politician, an expert, or anyone else as saying or doing something they have never said or done. Voices can be reproduced with astonishing accuracy, and often only those with the expertise to dig into the code behind the portrayals can tell whether the video or audio is genuine. However, the opposite is also true. A genuine video can be dismissed as fake news. The real tragedy of the emergence of deepfakes is that now all information is liable to be thought of as suspect, which greatly undermines the confidence that what we read, see, and hear can be trusted. This has enormous repercussions for public trust in institutions and has a knock-on effect for Christians, whose role is to evaluate and interpret society—its values, morals, and practices—through a biblical lens. In a post-truth world, is the society I think I am interpreting the real-world version, or have I fallen prey to a deception that a bad actor wants me to assume for their own propagandistic purposes? The proliferation of conspiracy theories within Christian circles, together with the difficulty of telling truth from fiction, is undermining the witness of the gospel and making many Christians look highly gullible. Those to whom we minister can legitimately ask, If we fall for such obvious untruths as conspiracy theories, have we simply fallen for other untruths in believing the Bible? But we don't sit in judgment here, because so many conspiracy theories are extremely convincing and look like they could be true.

Conspiracy Theory and AI

Simply explained, the term *conspiracy theory* refers to "the belief that powerful, hidden, evil forces control human destinies."[4] The key feature of

3. Mustafa Suleyman, *The Coming Wave: Technology, Power, and the 21st Century's Greatest Dilemma*, with Michael Bhaskar (New York: Crown, 2023), 167.
4. Michael Barkun, *A Culture of Conspiracy: Apocalyptic Visions in Contemporary America*, 2nd ed. (Berkeley: University of California Press, 2013), 19.

conspiracy theories is usually timing. Such theories emerge at times of crisis, when people are looking for guidance and leadership and when they are also looking for explanations—how to make sense of a situation. Conspiracy theories offer a prehistory, a context, a stimulating and often seemingly intellectually satisfying narrative. They are neat and tidy—much less nuanced and generally much less carefully fact-checked than a sermon one might hear on the issue, if it is addressed at all in a Christian context. Often, people turn to conspiracy theories because Sunday sermons and midweek Bible studies don't even acknowledge the topics with which the conspiracy theories deal. Conspiracy theories, now packaged in visually stimulating videos and replete with faux historical and political commentary—which sounds highly convincing to those who have no knowledge of the topic in view—will often usurp and replace biblically based teaching on an issue.

Conspiracy Theory as a Form of Gnosticism

We discussed Gnosticism in chapter 4, but conspiracy theory can be described as a modern form of Gnosticism, particularly because it pertains to a form of secret knowledge, available only to an enlightened few. Does this sound familiar? You may have had conversations with people or seen videos or read articles in which you are told that only a few know about or have access to the "truth" about a topic. The topic may be very commonplace, or it may be one that you've never heard of before. What is important is that your "informers" tell you that this is privileged, secret knowledge and that now you're one of the few "elite" people in the know. This can be very attractive. How many of us love to hear a juicy secret or be in an inner circle about something? Let's face it: it's enticing. It makes us feel special, trusted; we and just a small group of others understand the truth behind why things are as they are. Those of us of a certain age will remember the television series *The X Files*.[5] "Trust no one" and "The truth is out there" were the most famous phrases associated with the show, which promoted the idea that the world is ruled by clandestine groups of people who hold secrets kept from the rest of us.

The following explanation of Gnosticism, we believe, neatly captures the way it behaves in conspiracy culture: "Within early Gnosticism, *gnosis* was, as Robert Grant describes, regarded as derived 'solely from revelation

5. *The X Files*, created by Chris Carter, aired 1993–2002 on Fox.

and . . . this revelation was comprehensible only to those who believed, or "knew," that they were spiritual beings innately capable of receiving it.' Later in the Western esoteric tradition, *gnosis* has been generally understood as 'a saving knowledge accessible to humanity, once in possession of the right key, and involving an experiential element—illumination—that distinguishes it from simple faith.'"[6] In other words, illumination, or full knowledge of reality, is open only to a few "capable of receiving it": not everyone—and certainly not those of what is considered "simple faith." The attraction of this illuminated knowledge, as stated above, is that while it is a "saving knowledge," one needs the "right key" to know how to access it, and that key involves immersion in conspiracy. One helpful concept in our understanding of conspiracy theory, a concept that considers the theory's Gnostic characteristics, is that of stigmatized knowledge. Simply put, this is a kind of "dangerous" knowledge that has been hidden from most of us, as we would not be able to cope with it; we are not mature enough to grasp it. It is a form of "rejected" or "suppressed" knowledge that only a few are mature enough to know. But if we knew it, our eyes would be open to the way things really are.[7]

A conspiracist worldview teaches that nothing happens by accident, that nothing is as it seems, and that everything is connected.[8] While AI does not necessarily produce conspiracy material, it does have an outsized role in the distribution of this material, as it is able to monitor people's activity online; discern topics that interest them based on their search histories, likes, religious beliefs, and so on; and then target them with disinformation. In other words, AI is harnessed to manipulate and sway decisions, and it can fly under the radar of people's spiritual defenses and wreak havoc in their families, friendships, and communities, especially in light of an absence of effective andragogy about its abilities.

How AI Systems Can Influence Our Decisions

AI technologies are adept at handling big data sets, and we, authors and readers alike, are individually recognizable subsets of those larger sets. In the past, we were just a name on a voting register, a number in a relatively

6. Christopher Partridge, *The Re-enchantment of the West*, vol. 2, *Alternative Spiritualities, Sacralization, Popular Culture and Occulture* (London: T&T Clark International, 2005), 156.
7. Barkun, *Culture of Conspiracy*, 26–28.
8. Barkun, *Culture of Conspiracy*, 19–21.

unsophisticated database, such as an Excel spreadsheet. We could be tracked in the sense that the IRS could tell whether we paid our taxes. But nothing was known from that data about our individual daily habits, what we bought, what we ate, whether we had pets, our marital status, our sexuality, our color or race, or our political or religious views. Integrated AI systems have changed all of that. When we scan our items at the checkout counter and link our purchases to a card or phone number, that data is added to and stored in multiple databases that use algorithms to make judgments about our domestic choices. This information is very valuable to those who sell the products we buy and similar products because they can now target us by email, via text, or on social media if we use our smartphones or computers to access sales websites or buy products online. The data we provide about our demographics, behavior, and preferences allows AI to predict what we might buy next, as we see, for example, when Amazon advertises products based on our previous purchases. The AI algorithms quickly gather information, which informs them about certain choices we might make if nudged in a particular direction. We might think that this is of little concern in terms of consumer choice. After all, we all like bargains, and when we are offered online coupons or discounts, we are generally happy to receive them. Or we might be pleased to discover new products, books, or movies we didn't even know existed.

The Influence of AI on Politics

However, what about being nudged in certain political or religious directions? Maybe our choice of websites and social media sites indicates that we are patriotic, but specific groups may want to shift us from, say, a centrist base to a more radical stance, and so they target us with videos and new articles that lead us to become more extreme. Perhaps our towns are quiet suburban environments, not given to political or religious viewpoints considered controversial in any way, and someone wants to destabilize these towns to get particular council members elected by splitting the fairly even vote share that once existed. By monitoring our preferences and selling this information to lobbying groups, narratives can be created, narratives that become part of our daily newsfeed and that arouse our passion about topics we once felt mild-mannered about, leading to heated arguments at town hall meetings and splintered communities. These are not theoretical scenarios—we see variations of them at play in communities across the nation every day. The power of AI means that it is an ever-present, constantly monitoring force in our lives. It can change its agenda in milliseconds based on our online activity, influencing us this way now and that way seconds later.

AI and Psychology

Usually we find out what kind of people our neighbors are through our social-cognitive skills. We assess them according to their personality, responses, words, and actions and form judgments about them. One study, however, has found that computers using machine learning can make very accurate personality predictions. It "compares the accuracy of human and computer-based personality judgments, using a sample of 86,220 volunteers who completed a 100-item personality questionnaire."[9] The results are illuminating: "computer predictions based on a generic digital footprint (Facebook Likes) are more accurate ($r = 0.56$) than those made by the participants' Facebook friends using a personality questionnaire ($r = 0.49$)," and "computer personality judgments have higher external validity when predicting life outcomes such as substance abuse, political attitudes, and physical health."[10] The authors make the startling claim that "computers outpacing humans in personality judgment presents significant opportunities and challenges in the areas of psychological assessment, marketing, and privacy."[11] These three categories tell us a lot: *Psychological assessment* refers basically to giving insights into how we think. These insights influence what is marketed to us and how it is marketed. And both of these realities have strong implications for the privacy of our data and even our thoughts and choices and the processes by which we make our decisions.

AI and Social Engineering

One company, Cambridge Analytica, has harvested data from fifty million Facebook profiles. It obtained this data through an app created by a researcher at Cambridge University, which was used to pay people to take

9. Wu Youyou, Michal Kosinski, and David Stillwell, "Computer-Based Personality Judgments Are More Accurate Than Those Made by Humans," *Proceedings of the National Academy of Sciences of the United States of America*, January 12, 2015, https://www.pnas.org /doi/full/10.1073/pnas.1418680112.
10. Youyou, Kosinski, and Stillwell, "Computer-Based Personality Judgments."
11. Youyou, Kosinski, and Stillwell, "Computer-Based Personality Judgments."

personality tests. Users had to allow the app to access their Facebook profiles and those of their friends. The information gathered from thirty million of those profiles was sold to the political data company Cambridge Analytica, which used it to profile millions of American voters. These voters were then categorized "using five personality traits known as OCEAN—Openness, Conscientiousness, Extraversion, Agreeableness, and Neuroticism. The aim was to identify the personalities of American voters and influence their behaviour, using psychographic modelling techniques."[12] Psychographic modeling is modeling based on the psychological profiling of consumers, which in turn is based on their choices, with the intention of making judgments and predictions consonant with those choices. One experiment conducted during a 2015 election in India gives a helpful, practical picture of how such modeling works in practice. A psychologist invited 2,150 undecided voters, split into groups and from all over the nation, to use a search engine that was programmed to show each group a different version of the election results, each version of which was biased toward a certain candidate. Within a few minutes of looking at the results, 12 percent of participants said that they would vote for the candidate favored by and clearly pushed by the search engine.[13] In an election—indeed, in any situation, such as cornering a share of a market—12 percent can make a significant difference. This experiment also demonstrates that very few people move beyond the first page of a Google search or, indeed, further than the top results. The potential for outsize influence by anyone who knows how to maximize the appearance and impact of search results is staggering. Allie Funk, Adrian Shahbaz, and Kian Vesteinsson tell us that "at least 47 governments deployed commentators to manipulate online discussions in their favor " in 2023, and "legal frameworks in at least 21 countries mandate or incentivize digital platforms to deploy machine learning to remove disfavored political, social, and religious speech."[14] All the above can result in malign actors unduly influencing believers, bringing about a loss of faith, a loss of witness, confusion, and disunity. It is essential that Christian andragogy addresses the psychological influences of AI on the human person and that Christian communities are educated about

12. "Cambridge Analytica," Digital Watch, Geneva Internet Platform, accessed November 16, 2023, https://dig.watch/trends/cambridge-analytica.

13. Suleyman, Coming Wave, 14–15.

14. Allie Funk, Adrian Shahbaz, and Kian Vesteinsson, "The Repressive Power of Artificial Intelligence," Freedom House, last modified November 21, 2023, https://freedomhouse.org /report/freedom-net/2023/repressive-power-artificial-intelligence.

its dangers. Our communities should also be aware of the limits of AI and educated about blind trust in its performance.

AI Hallucinations

We introduced the topic of AI hallucinations in chapter 4, but this section will unpack it in more detail. In April 2023, a peculiar judicial case played out in a Manhattan courtroom, a case that should have been, according to general opinion, a slam dunk for the plaintiff, who was suing the airline Avianca for an injury experienced on a flight he took in 2019. ChatGPT had recently been announced to the world, and people everywhere were excited about what it could do. It could write a college paper, an advertising slogan, a song, a poem, a love letter. It could do research and produce reports. All one had to do was supply the program with a prompt, and it would perform a miracle. The plaintiff's lawyers argued the worthiness of his case, and to solidify their arguments, they asked ChatGPT to give them several cases of precedence. What could go wrong? Lawyers are very clever people, but the lead lawyer in this case was betting that AI, which runs ChatGPT, would be even more clever than he was, at least in researching relevant cases. Unfortunately for the hapless lawyer, the several examples of generated precedence were entirely made up. ChatGPT had just invented the examples. This happens a lot, and unfortunately, it also happens in academia, where having reliable (and real) sources is key.

When the judge examined the precedents in more detail, he realized quickly that none of them were real. The lawyer, diligent as lawyers are, had even double-checked the program's reliability by asking it—a program proving itself to be unacquainted with the truth, the whole truth, and nothing but the truth—whether the cases were real, to which the AI cheerfully replied, "Yes." In the end, the chastised and embarrassed lawyer was fined, but he had inadvertently done us all a service (including students tempted to use ChatGPT to write their papers) by highlighting the little-known existence of AI hallucinations. Unlike someone who is intoxicated, who might see or hear things that really do not exist, ChatGPT needs no such stimulation to indulge in its own hallucinatory activities. Part of its brief, as we discussed in chapter 4, is to be "creative," and when it doesn't know something, it releases its creative spirit.[15] The implication of all the above is that Christian educators

---

15. See John Naughton, "A Lawyer Got ChatGPT to Do His Research, but He Isn't AI's Biggest Fool," *Guardian*, June 3, 2023, https://www.theguardian.com/commentisfree/2023/jun/03/lawyer-chatgpt-research-avianca-statement-ai-risk-openai-deepmind; and Benjamin Weiser,

need to teach and continuously remind those to whom they minister that AI is fallible. It is extremely clever and efficient, but it is also subject to flaws and vulnerabilities. Relying on AI to do research for us, without knowing how to fact-check the information it produces, often leads to error. In recent years, we have increasingly seen an overreliance on certain sources of information, which deliver the information with great confidence yet turn out to be highly suspect. This has happened in the news more than anywhere else. It is now very difficult, even for those who are skilled at information analysis, to judge what is true from what is false in the news cycle. The content of the news cycle significantly influences how Christians react to world events and has huge implications for Christian witness, because when we get it wrong, we look silly.

How to Avoid Being Fooled by Fake News

Our andragogy should equip people with tools for avoiding fake news. Numerous online sites give excellent advice. The following points are reproduced from a guide published by Arizona State University:

- Pay attention to where your news is coming from.
- If you get information from social media, check the original source.
- Within news articles, examine the sources and how they are included.
- Read beyond the headline.
- Get your news from a variety of sources. [This is probably the best advice.]
- When you see your friends and family share misinformation, correct them [gently].
- Find out what other information is out there.[16]

"Here's What Happens When Your Lawyer Uses ChatGPT," *New York Times*, May 27, 2023, https://www.nytimes.com/2023/05/27/nyregion/avianca-airline-lawsuit-chatgpt.html. For more on AI hallucinations, see Oliver Bown, "'Hallucinating' AIs Sound Creative, but Let's Not Celebrate Being Wrong," *MIT Press Reader*, October 13, 2023, https://thereader.mitpress.mit.edu/hallucinating-ais-sound-creative-but-lets-not-celebrate-being-wrong.

16. For a more in-depth breakdown of these points, see Madison Arnold, "Seven Ways to Protect Yourself against Misinformation," ASU News, Arizona State University, April 7, 2020, https://research.asu.edu/seven-ways-to-protect-yourself-against-misinformation. See also "Fact Check: How to Decipher Online News and Information; Protect Yourself from Fake News," University Library, Walden University, accessed November 18, 2023, https://academicguides.waldenu.edu/library/fakenews/protectagainstfn.

AI and the Flourishing of the Human Spirit

All technological innovation has its beginning in human yearning, in the desire to expand beyond our mental, spiritual, and physical borders and limits. It involves dreaming and envisioning. In a beautiful account of their engineering journeys, three Christian experts on technology frame these journeys in terms of dreams taking flight: "The impulse to create technology is fueled by our dreams and our imagination. 'In dreams begins responsibility,' wrote the poet William Butler Yeats. He may not have been thinking of technology, but he understood that yearnings hint at responsibility and ultimate purposes. Technology has deeply religious roots. . . . Done well, our technological dreams become reality in building God's kingdom."[17]

Christians can have dreams, and technology can be the means of fulfilling those dreams. Dreams give hope. They point to future possibilities. Our andragogy about AI must not concentrate only on its potential negatives, though they exist; it must also give hope that in an AI-saturated world, this amazing technology can be harnessed for good. The Old and New Testaments are replete with examples of the people of God using technology for the sake of the kingdom. Just think of Noah and the ark, the use of musical instruments in worship, Solomon's temple, Nehemiah's rebuilding of the walls of Jerusalem, and the references to house construction, city gates, lamps, fishing nets, oil lamps, and lost coins. As the authors mentioned in the previous paragraph note, these are the technologies of the biblical period: "Houses and cities require architecture and civil engineering, coins require technical know-how in metallurgy and manufacturing capability, . . . and Jesus himself was a carpenter. This tradecraft was the technology of that day." They point out that the bread and wine of the Last Supper and even the armor of God referenced in Ephesians 6 are all examples of contemporary technology.[18] Their point is that all these technologies can be sacralized; they can be made sacred and can perform a sacred function. As technologies, they can have a redemptive function.

One way of teaching our congregations about the positive aspects of AI is to frame AI in terms of cocreation. We don't need to view AI as separate from us or above us, telling us what to do, but as a partner in creation and

17. Ethan J. Brue, Derek C. Schuurman, and Steven H. Vanderleest, *A Christian Field Guide to Technology for Engineers and Designers* (Downers Grove, IL: IVP Academic, 2022), 14.
18. Brue, Schuurman, and Vanderleest, *Christian Field Guide to Technology*, 164–65.

innovation. Working with programs like ChatGPT, which generates written content, or Midjourney or DALL·E 2, which create stunning images, is revolutionizing the workspace for many. These technologies can be used in creating evangelistic literature and content, the creation of which does not need to be an autonomous process because teams of people can work together—even those who lack creative skills—to produce something of professional quality that attracts and informs readers. Humans and machines learning and working together can have a significant influence on evangelism. Generative AI can help with worship lyrics as well. Songwriters shouldn't uncritically adopt a whole AI-generated song, but perhaps they can experiment with some of its suggestions.

AI is being used in so many positive ways in the realms of medicine, where robots can assist in surgery, and big data, which can help develop life-saving drugs, automation of repetitive tasks, and smart decision-making based on tried and tested data points. *Metaverse* is the umbrella term given to a virtual universe that mirrors our own, where we can create digital twins of ourselves or certain objects and can perform design experiments before trying them out in the real world, allowing us to make mistakes safely. Companies can build cars or design buildings, and doctors can perform surgical procedures in the metaverse without causing real harm.[19]

Our andragogy should teach our congregations to engage with AI in a critical but informed way. Congregations, pastors, and missionaries who do not engage with AI will find themselves irrelevant in a world of digital natives. The gospel of Paul's time was rooted in a vibrant, multicultural, highly technological society. The technology of the Roman Empire was spectacular and ensured its dominance over vast swathes of the world. Christianity exists within this highly technologized world, and today it needs to inhabit not just the physical world but the virtual one as well—the world of Zoom and the metaverse, of Replika, where people engage with virtual companions, of chatbots and interactive social media. None of these areas can become deserts for the gospel, where no Christian witness is available, and Christian leaders shouldn't assume that their students and congregations will just figure out how to live in this technological landscape on their own. They might if they are digital natives, but they will still need help when dealing with AI's

19. For more information, read Joshan Abraham et al., "Digital Twins: The Foundation of the Enterprise Metaverse," McKinsey Digital, October 2022, https://www.mckinsey.com/capabilities/mckinsey-digital/our-insights/digital-twins-the-foundation-of-the-enterprise-metaverse.

ethical and moral challenges. Those who are not digital natives, though, will need a lot more framing and context. Such framing should always be imbued with hope.

The following list provides a sampling of ways that Christians can engage with AI in a creative, healthy, and effective way.

- Cocreation can involve using AI to enhance visual projects, such as posters or videos. In recent years, Christian products, especially in the realms of advertising and public relations, have often exhibited a simplistic and mediocre look, having been amateurly created. Today, though, even those not skilled in art can use AI to create excellent visuals, so we should be working with AI to assist us and expand our abilities.

- Many marketers are now using ChatGPT to produce advertising content for products and events. Such use works really well; with only a few finely crafted prompts, the program often does a better job than one can do oneself. Advertisers aren't the only ones using ChatGPT; authors are now using AI to cowrite books. They are (or at least should be) up-front about this, telling their readers which parts of the book have been written by an AI program. In any event, they find that for some scenes and emotions, AI, drawing on its vast database, can write about them better. Sometimes authors ask one of the art AIs, such as Midjourney, to create a visual scene, and they then use that scene as the basis for their own written description. For example, in science fiction, an author might ask the program to create a visual of a mountainous planet with three moons at sunset and a scene of a futuristic city bathed in the moonlight. The program will do that well and might even create a different scene each time it is asked. The scene (or scenes) can then be used as a basis for the written scene. Scholars still debate the intellectual validity and honesty of such endeavors, but it is becoming more and more common, and authors feel that once they reveal their methods to their readers, they are upholding intellectual honesty.

- Many busy people now get ChatGPT to design templates for different kinds of letters and memos, which they can then "tweak" according to their needs.

- AI is also adept at creating music. One relevant program is Boomy; another is SOUNDRAW. These programs can create original music in seconds. Certain programs can create jingles as well. Of course, intellectual dishonesty is a constant temptation in this field, but copyright specialists are working on ways to identify AI-generated music and art so that their origins can be easily discerned.

We discuss cocreation further in chapter 7 but from a more pastoral point of view. We give advice on how to ensure integrity in any cocreative process, particularly as some aspects of cocreation can lead to laziness and dishonesty, even plagiarism.

AI and the Accelerated Life

Our hopeful stance toward AI also needs to account for the quality of our lives in the technological age. It's one thing to engage with AI, but our andragogy should also inform Christians how to guard their peace and their hearts. Proverbs 4:23 tells us, "Above all else, guard your heart, for everything you do flows from it." An AI world is a fast-paced one. It energizes the news cycle, for example. We have already seen how it can manipulate news stories for different audiences, but what we haven't seen yet is that it can also read the news to you while you drive. Artificial intelligence enables news organizations to continuously gather data from social media and other news sites for nonstop news creation. It can "hear" what is being said on video and transcribe the report using on-screen captions. Whole news stories may be written by GenAI, based on collected and constantly scanned data from multiple sources. One estimate is that "by 2026, up to 90% of what we see on our screens will be the product of generative AI."[20]

Apart from the problem of not knowing whether a human or a machine has written something is the question of speed of publication across all information platforms. Many of us were news junkies before the emergence of AI; now, we are *ultra-accelerated* news junkies, bombarded with ever-updated stories. We already live fast-paced lives, but now it's like we're going hundreds of miles an hour through life, trying to read and process every little

20. Josh Brandau, "The News Media Are Not Being Transparent about How They Intend to Use A.I. as the Truth Becomes More Elusive Than Ever," *Fortune*, August 9, 2023, https://fortune.com/2023/08/09/news-media-transparent-intend-ai-truth-becomes-more-elusive-than-ever-politics-democracy-tech.

snippet of new information as we go. Social media sites feed us 24-7 with ever-evolving discussions and heated arguments; at the same time, we are bombarded with emails and texts. Our cars now can even read emails to us as they arrive. No space is free of AI-generated "noise." So a crucial part of our andragogy must be teaching people to slow down and, when necessary, to switch off the AI. Short attention spans are notoriously connected with the consumption of information in small amounts, which happens frequently online. We don't want to read anything too long, so most social media messages and now even articles online are shortened to cater for our shorter attention spans.

Lectio Divina: Reading, Listening, and Viewing with Deep Understanding

Many religious traditions today, including Roman Catholic and Anglican or Episcopalian traditions, draw on medieval monastic practices to aid their reading techniques; to process texts, often over a long period of time; and to develop a kind of reading and contemplative stamina, of which the digital age is robbing us. The practice of *lectio divina*, or "sacred reading," can be used for both spiritual and nonspiritual texts. Because it employs deep, sustained reading, mixed with intense reflection, the information one reads about is retained and becomes part of one's inner self. It informs and shapes at a profound level. Pastors and other Christian educators need to teach this form of reading and contemplation, not only because Christians have long read Scripture in a casual, careless way, even before the age of AI, but also because even such casual reading has been replaced with a form of ever-accelerating speed reading.[21] Although *lectio divina* has its roots in the reading of sacred texts, the practice can be applied to all texts. In our frenetic world, we read very little in a comprehensive way. How many times have you seen someone post an article on Facebook or Twitter or another medium, obviously implying that it is important to read but at the same time summarizing it or telling you to read just the headline and the first paragraph. The result is inevitably a loss of reading stamina, an inability to attend to anything longer than 144 characters, the length of an original Twitter (now X) post. In a politically complex world, how can we understand national

---

21. For an excellent guide to *lectio divina*, read Mary Keator, Lectio Divina *as Contemplative Pedagogy: Re-appropriating Monastic Practice for the Humanities* (New York: Routledge, 2018).

issues and vote intelligently if we cannot sustain the stamina to read more than a few lines of the news?

What Is *Lectio Divina*?

Lectio divina began in the Greek schools of the fourth and third centuries BCE and has its earliest roots in Plato's concept of *paideia*, a Greek word referring to the nurturing of children, from which we get the word *pedagogy*. Paideia was more than filling a child's head with knowledge; it had a strong nurturing element to it, which involved teaching children to think for themselves, to acquire the tools to really know themselves and to grow in wisdom. To use a phrase now quite common in education, it focused on the "whole" child—it was holistic education. Rather than impart knowledge alone, it sought to create fertile soil within the child so that their own thoughts and opinions could grow.[22]

Over the centuries, this view of education was adopted by many philosophical schools. One particularly influential school of thought was founded by a church father of the Eastern church, Origen of Alexandria (185–254). Origen strongly encouraged his students to delve deeply into their texts and to avoid mere surface reading. He encouraged a form of Jewish interpretation known as midrash, which assumes that in the sacred Scriptures, no word is an accident. Every single word has a deep meaning that can be discovered by reading slowly.[23] In our present-day schools, whether Christian or non-Christian, the pressures of getting through crowded curricula within a certain timeframe can stifle our ability to spend the time we need, both separately and together, to really engage with texts, visuals, and even conversations about what we are learning. In the medieval monastic schools, the original intention of a school was strictly applied. Believe it or not, the English word *school* derives from the Greek *scholē*, which means "leisure." The original aim of a school was to allow students to discover the world from texts slowly and deliberatively.[24]

Lectio Divina in Practice

Plato's and Origen's methods of education were adapted and imported into medieval monasteries, where the reading of sacred texts, both individually and

22. Keator, Lectio Divina *as Contemplative Pedagogy*, 14.
23. Keator, Lectio Divina *as Contemplative Pedagogy*, 44–45.
24. Keator, Lectio Divina *as Contemplative Pedagogy*, 92.

communally, was an everyday feature. In fact, monks read such texts several times, often six or seven times, a day. The methods adopted were as follows:

- Encountering the text: A text could be soothing and reassuring or challenging and thought provoking, but the main aim of encountering a text was a transformation of the mind and heart, a transformation referenced in the concept of *conversio*.[25]
- *Conversio* was followed by *meditatio*, which involved a search for meaning in the text by allowing it to settle in one's spirit and thinking about it repeatedly.
- *Oratio* then called for a response to the text, which could involve private prayer or communal discussion.
- *Contemplatio* was the stage in which the text spoke most deeply to a reader. In today's language, it was when "the penny dropped" and one really understood what they had read, seen, or heard and could apply it. It was when wisdom came about.[26]

Everything we know comes to us in words or visuals, and the pace at which AI distributes information is dizzying. That is why this age is known as the information age and why we talk about an information superhighway. It is vital for Christian educators to encourage their students to take time to truly understand the nature of the tens of thousands of messages that invade our thoughts every day, because the superhighway is only getting faster, and we need to be able to discern truth and filter out falsehood.

Writing

How we write is also changing because of AI. Habits such as journaling; writing long, reflective letters; or even writing detailed notes while reading Scripture or any other text are being lost. The emergence of GenAI, which can write for us, greatly exacerbates this. We risk losing the ability to think deliberatively:

The classicist Eric Havelock argued in *Preface to Plato* that development of writing and concomitant spread of literacy in Archaic Greece, even in limited

---

25. Keator, Lectio Divina *as Contemplative Pedagogy*, 87.
26. Keator, Lectio Divina *as Contemplative Pedagogy*, 117–95.

circles, enabled the flowering of Greek philosophical thought. Writing facilitated reflection, logical thinking, and production of tangible texts to foster rethinking. . . . Recall Flannery O'Connor's much-quoted remark that "I write because I don't know what I think until I read what I say." Her sentiment is hardly unique in literary annals. You'll find it echoed by Horace Walpole, E.M. Forster, Arthur Koestler, George Bernard Shaw, William Faulkner, and, of course, Joan Didion ("I don't know what I think until I write it down").[27]

Read those statements by those authors again. They are powerful. Writing and reading shape our thoughts, and the inability to engage in them because our attention spans are shrinking spells disaster for the witness of Christian scholarship.

In chapter 6, we discuss the importance of the "hearth" as a focus for connection with the spiritual, the hearth referring to a place of warmth and security. In that chapter, we recommend the importance of certain rituals to punctuate and regulate daily spiritual practice. Just as the daily lives of the monks who engaged in *lectio divina* were marked by the sounding of monastery bells, using the technology of the time, so, too, regular Sabbath times away from technology and directed toward time with God can become rituals that ground us in our humanness and in our communities, whether family, neighborhood, or church.

AI and Family

Sherry Turkle of MIT has written a fascinating book on the use of cell phones among young people, their addictive nature, and the way in which all of us now spend hours every day staring at screens we just can't put down. The title of the book is illuminating: *Alone Together: Why We Expect More from Technology and Less from Each Other*.[28] We all know what it's like to be in company, even as a family, with everyone isolated in their own space on their phones.

Our andragogy has to actively teach families how to avoid being alone together. How to reclaim the art of conversation. How to switch AI off.

27. Naomi S. Baron, "Why Human Writing Is Worth Defending in the Age of ChatGPT," Literary Hub, September 12, 2023, https://lithub.com/why-human-writing-is-worth-defending-in-the-age-of-chatgpt.
28. Sherry Turkle, *Alone Together: Why We Expect More from Technology and Less from Each Other* (New York: Basic Books, 2011).

One knock-on effect of so much time spent processing microinformation from our phones, news, and social media feeds is a severe reduction of attention span, which impacts our congregations' abilities to listen to sermons or absorb content of any substance. As homes are increasingly loaded with technology—from digital devices to smart technology, which can monitor lighting and heating systems and devices connected to the internet of things—families need to grapple with this new environment, and both pedagogy and andragogy need to acknowledge that this encircling technology exists, because we get so used to it that we forget it's there.

Responsible andragogy about AI in the home involves not so much setting limits, although limits will help, but setting routines so that the home does not revolve entirely around AI. Many families eschew the use of phones at the table or set aside times during the week for nontechnologically focused activity. In many Jewish homes, when Sabbath is kept strictly, electronic devices cannot be used for the whole Sabbath period. If you cannot abstain for a day of Sabbath, at least set Sabbath times one day a week, times that suit the family and in which you all do something that avoids the influence of AI.

The use of virtual reality headsets, virtual games, texting, and social media is highly addictive. Just as we would teach Christian leaders and communities about the dangers of drugs and alcohol, we must also do the same about the addictive nature of AI. Dopamine, the main chemical behind addiction, is released when we do something that gives us pleasure, so we seek the "hit" repeatedly. Just as easily accessible drugs are constantly consumed, so the hit that comes from AI devices, which are always showing us something new, cannot be ignored. They're too easy to get—just an arm's reach away. Our natural tendency to want to connect with others, when it is supercharged by dopamine, makes us want to connect over and over again. When we text, the anxiety we feel when someone doesn't respond quickly enough is connected to that rush we get when they do. We constantly check social media to count the likes. The antidote, one expert says, is "time out—even for a day. But a whole month is more typically the minimum about of time we need away from our drug of choice, whether it's heroin or Instagram, to reset our dopamine reward pathways."[29] We need

29. Bruce Goldman, "Addictive Potential of Social Media, Explained," Scope, Stanford Medicine, October 29, 2021, https://scopeblog.stanford.edu/2021/10/29/addictive-potential-of-social-media-explained. This article abridges a Q and A exchange between Goldman and Anna

to teach this practice in churches, seminaries, and other Christian schools and demonstrate how to do it. Restless hearts need God. Don't replace God with AI to bring about rest. It won't work. A. Trevor Sutton and Brian Smith offer a good way of explaining this: "Ask yourself: What is the first thing that I reach for in the morning when I wake up? People with alcoholism famously have an 'eye-opener,' reaching for a bottle first thing in the morning, waking up with intense cravings after a period of sleep without those dopamine bursts. The need for an eye-opener strongly suggests the person has a problem with alcohol. If you consistently reach for your phone first thing in the morning looking for a dopamine rush from that digital eye-opener, you may have an issue."[30]

CONCLUSION

When people are not trained to understand and interpret the role of AI through Christian andragogy and pedagogy, they turn to other sources, and those sources often have agendas of their own. We now live in an AI-immersed world and cannot ignore it. We ignore AI for perhaps two reasons: (1) a lack of knowledge and (2) a tacit acceptance of its presence as normative without realizing its full, pervasive power. We need to have grown-up conversations in our seminaries and churches to prepare Christian students, Christians in the workforce, parents and grandparents, and especially pastors and leaders to really understand the technology and to live Christian lives in this new world.

QUESTIONS FOR REFLECTION

1. What areas of AI most puzzle you, and what would you want your leaders to teach you about them?

Lembke, a Stanford psychiatrist. See Anna Lembke, *Dopamine Nation: Finding Balance in the Age of Indulgence* (New York: Dutton, 2021).

30. A. Trevor Sutton and Brian Smith, *Redeeming Technology: A Christian Approach to Healthy Digital Habits* (St. Louis: Concordia, 2021), 58. See also Asurion, "Americans Check Their Phones 96 Times a Day," PR Newswire, November 21, 2019, https://www.prnewswire.com/news-releases/americans-check-their-phones-96-times-a-day-300962643.html.

2. What instances of fake news have you come across, and how have they affected those who consumed it?

3. What would a Sabbath from technology look like in your home? What obstacles would you envision in implementing it? And what benefits would you hope to reap from it?

4. In what ways have you noticed your attention span, reading stamina, and writing skills change as a result of living in an AI-saturated world?

6. How Should Christians Be Formed and Discipled in the Age of AI?

In chapter 5 we delved into ways Christian educators can wisely and faithfully interact with AI for the benefit of learners. We now pivot away from pedagogy and andragogy and toward formation and discipleship. Although these topics are interrelated and can be mutually reinforcing, they are not identical. Traditionally, formation and discipleship have existed under the provinces of theology, practical theology, and ecclesiology more than education. Consequently, this chapter has a narrow scope, one that is more concerned with the condition and development of a person's heart and soul—often referred to as the "inner person." This approach is not intended to promote an artificial divorcing of the soul from the mind and body, as all three—soul, mind, and body—are dynamically intertwined in Holy Scripture. This triad is meant to remain in the foreground as we analyze the impact of AI on humans.

Another distinction is in order. This chapter may appear to sideline AI, which was more prominently featured in previous pages. To be clear, AI is not a central topic in what follows. As stated in chapter 3, we continue to prioritize people over machines, and so our investigation adopts a human-centered perspective. We believe this modus operandi is especially pertinent with respect to formation and discipleship. Christians have grown as God's image bearers over thousands of years without the ubiquitous and invasive tool of machine learning. Yet at the same time, humanity has reached an undeniable inflection point: computers have greater power than previous tools and technologies to negatively disrupt and even hinder human flourishing. Thus, our aim is to present practices or habits that shore up the life of God's family amid the irresistible effects of twenty-first-century technologies.

Defining *Formation*

What is formation? As shown in figure 6.1, we propose that formation is the process of the tarnished *imago Dei* being transformed into the *imago Christi* (see 2 Cor. 3:18) and finally experiencing glorification (see Rom. 8:28–30) within the fullness of the new creation (see Rev. 21–22). How does this process transpire? One of the striking metaphors employed by Scripture is that of God as potter and his people as clay (see Isa. 64; Rom. 9, etc.). The triune Creator, the eternal, almighty Potter who has fashioned humans from the "dust of the ground" (Gen. 2:7), will set apart, purify, and reshape his people to become the holy bride of Jesus (see Eph. 5:21–33; Rev. 21). And they will fill and indwell his resplendent habitation, the reconstituted Eden, which sits inside the new Jerusalem (Rev. 22). This is a far grander vision than the truncated one sometimes presented in Western churches: individuals believing in Jesus to secure a ticket to an esoteric heaven full of gold and, thereby, to escape a corrupted world sliding into the fires of hell. Yes, individual salvation through the cross is absolutely necessary. But the liberating work of Jesus entails far more. Formation in our view, then, is nothing less than the

Figure 6.1.

Tarnished *Imago Dei*   **Imago Christi**   **Glorified in the New Creation**

cosmos completely reformed, bursting with the glorious presence of God, which envelops and enthralls his renewed people.

Discipleship and Sanctification in Formation

This picture raises a question: How does formation happen? Through two critical and interlocking processes. The first is *discipleship*. Jesus commands Christians to be and make disciples (see Matt. 28:19). The word for "disciple" in Greek, *mathētēs*, conveys the meaning of learner, pupil, follower, or apprentice. A disciple is one who follows in the footsteps of Jesus, one who serves as his apprentice. Disciples listen to Jesus (e.g., through listening prayer and the study of Scripture), observe him, and imitate his life within a Christian community.[1] Further, it should be noted that in our understanding, discipleship centers on human agency. That is, it is a human-motivated, human-directed process or journey. God commands Christians to own, to take responsibility for, their growth.[2]

Yet there is a second process, which represents the other side of the formation coin. Theologians label it *sanctification*, which is commonly defined as growth in holiness. To be clear, sanctification is a "work of the Spirit" (2 Thess. 2:13). Indeed, the New Testament often uses active verbs when describing God's role in sanctification while simultaneously using passive verbs to describe the human role.[3] So we could say that formation into the *imago Christi* involves human agency and participation through discipleship *as well as* human cooperation with and surrendering to God's efforts in sanctification. This is a vital truth: both divine and human action are required for the shaping and reforming of God's people. Humans need the grace of God to succeed and reach their telos; humans are also responsible for collaborating with God in their development.

---

1. For instance, in Eph. 5:1 the apostle Paul issues this command: "Follow God's example." And in 1 Cor. 11:1 Paul says, "Follow my example, as I follow the example of Christ." In both cases, the Greek word for "follow" is *mimētai*, which can be translated "imitator." This is the word from which we get our modern English *mimic*. For more on the concept of imitation, see J. R. Woodward, *The Scandal of Leadership: Unmasking the Powers of Domination in the Church* (Cody, Wyoming: 100 Movements, 2023).

2. For more on discipleship and spiritual growth, see chap. 3 of Matthew D. Kim and Paul A. Hoffman, *Preaching to a Divided Nation: A Seven-Step Model for Promoting Reconciliation and Unity* (Grand Rapids: Baker Academic, 2022).

3. Examples abound, including 1 Cor. 1:2; 6:11; Heb. 2:11; 10:10, 14; 12:10; and 13:12.

We now ask this: How does formation become engraved within the culture of Christian community? The answer is habit formation.

The Significance of Bodily, Corporate Habits in Formation

It seems the continuing success of James Clear's book *Atomic Habits* has thrust the power of habits to the forefront of America's consciousness.[4] Let us recall, however, that long before Clear came on the scene, God gave the Israelites the Mosaic law, which dictated and enshrined national habits and practices (e.g., annual feasts and festivals) that reaffirmed and perpetuated the Israelites' identity as God's special possession. Commands such as practicing Sabbath molded the Israelites and their communal life.

In my (Paul's) experience, many Christians are ambivalent regarding the role of habits in faith, particularly when it comes to public, explicit forms of worship. More specifically, some pockets of Western, Protestant Christianity have heralded the necessity of an individualized or personal relationship with Jesus to the extent that they have tended to view tradition-bound, ritually centric "high church" forms of worship, along with adherence to the liturgical year and church calendar, as rote, legalistic, or inauthentic and so detrimental to faith. Samples include a formal call to worship, written prayers that are recited, observing the seasons of Advent or Lent, and so on.

For his part, scholar James K. A. Smith elucidates the role of habits in formation:

> Habits are inscribed in our heart through bodily practices and rituals that train the heart, as it were, to desire certain ends. This is a noncognitive sort of training, a kind of education that is shaping us often without our realization. Different kinds of material practices infuse noncognitive dispositions and skills in us through ritual and repetition precisely because our hearts (site of habits) are so closely tethered to our bodies. The senses are portals to the heart, and thus the body is a channel to our core dispositions and identity. Over time, rituals and practices—often in tandem with aesthetic phenomena like pictures and stories—mold and shape our precognitive disposition to the world by training our desires. It's as if our appendages function as a conduit to our adaptive

---

4. At the time of writing, Clear's book is number twelve on the bestsellers rank for all books on Amazon (although it was published over five years ago) and has sold over fifteen million copies. See James Clear, *Atomic Habits: An Easy and Proven Way to Build Good Habits and Break Bad Ones* (New York: Avery, 2018).

unconscious: the motions and rhythms of embodied routines train our minds and hearts so that we develop habits—sort of attitudinal reflexes—that make us tend to act in certain ways toward certain ends.[5]

Smith highlights the significance of habits across various activities, such as playing the piano, fielding a baseball, or worshiping in a corporate setting. In a way, humans are the sum of their routines and rituals, because these routines and rituals express their loves and desires, which over time become encoded in consistent, unconscious dispositions and practices.

The purpose of this section is not to indicate our preference for certain worship styles. It is, however, to underscore that habits are inseparable from formation and that formation occurs in all types of contexts and situations (e.g., secular and religious settings) and in all kinds of congregations and traditions (from low church to high church), regardless of one's stance on the incorporation of late-modern technologies (e.g., projector or plasma screens, lighting effects, and sound systems) in corporate worship.[6] Humans are being formed all the time, everywhere.

Therefore, as theologians, we contend that Christian educators, clergy, and other church leaders must be more cautious and thoughtful in how machine learning intermixes with formation and discipleship. Why is that? The answer is relationships.

The "Eliza Effect" and AI-Human Relations

As we argued in chapter 3—when presenting the creational narrative—the fundamental nature of God and human beings is one marked by *relationship*. Habit formation and discipleship take place within God's ecosystem, which is composed of and sustained by divine-human communication, connection, and affiliation.[7] For that reason we feel we must issue one of our strongest warnings: if used improperly—uncritically and without setting healthy boundaries

5. James K. A. Smith, *Desiring the Kingdom: Worship, Worldview, and Cultural Formation* (Grand Rapids: Baker Academic, 2009), 58–59.

6. Here, we recommend the helpful book by A. Trevor Sutton and Brian Smith, *Redeeming Technology: A Christian Approach to Healthy Digital Habits* (St. Louis: Concordia, 2021). We add to this Dr. Sutton's PhD dissertation: "Put It on the Scales: Bringing Reflective Equilibrium to Digital Ecclesiology" (Concordia Seminary, 2023).

7. This relationship carries across every major theme of theology: the social Trinity, creation, revelation, redemption, glorification, the final judgment, etc.

and controls—AI will likely have devastating consequences with respect to divine-human relationships and, hence, will contribute to a kind of Christian malformation.

To better understand this possibility, one must comprehend what has been termed "the 'Eliza effect,' whereby people humanize computed behavior and form an emotional connection. The effect is named after the first chatbot, Eliza, which was created in 1966 to respond like a therapist to human inputs."[8] Machine learning is progressively used in apps (e.g., Co–Star and BibleGPT) that are designed to promote various spiritual or religious practices (such as astrology or Bible study), precisely because "in this age of AI, . . . language has become an increasingly important way to feign connections with human users," and these types of programs are offering "the feedback of an imagined priest, rabbi, or swami to your screen, promising to deliver a 'spiritual' experience in the comfort of your own home."[9]

Those who straddle the intersection between faith and technology are concerned about how AI will influence human communications and relationships. Paul Taylor, a pastor in Silicon Valley and a former manager at tech giant Oracle, refuses to mince words: "I'm habituating myself toward a certain kind of interaction, even if there's nobody on the other end of the line. . . . Every relationship we have is mediated by language [so when someone sends an email or a text message, the assumption is that] on the other side there's a you there. But now we're using the same tools and there is no you there."[10] Gretchen Huizinga, a research fellow at the organization AI and Faith, echoes these reflections: "How we treat machines becomes how we treat other people."[11] She believes adults should coach children to demonstrate "manners to a machine" because "that's training them on how they treat anything: any person, any animal."[12] Journalist Kate Lucky, who interviewed Taylor and Huizinga, adds this to their sentiments: "Being rude or ruthlessly efficient with our AI companions might seep into our patterns of interaction

8. Nika Simovich Fisher, "Generative AI Has Ushered in the Next Phase of Digital Spirituality," *WIRED*, October 5, 2023, https://www.wired.com/story/artificial-intelligence-spirituality-tarot.

9. Fisher, "Generative AI."

10. Kate Lucky, "AI Will Shape Your Soul," *Christianity Today*, September 11, 2023, https://www.christianitytoday.com/ct/2023/october/artificial-intelligence-robots-soul-formation.html.

11. Lucky, "AI Will Shape Your Soul."

12. Lucky, "AI Will Shape Your Soul."

with people. AI relationships might make us snippy. . . . They might also make us awkward or anxious or overwhelmed by human complexity."[13]

Much more can be said about the troubling ways AI can and will shape human relations (and in chap. 2 we discussed how the romantic chatbot Replika has created havoc). Yet the fact remains that God has designed humans to grow in their relationship with him, in their relationships with one another, and within the redeemed society known as the church. Christian formation and discipleship cannot occur without a deep rootedness in a faith community. To put the matter differently, the *imago Christi* cannot be cultivated when AI replaces meaningful networks of friendship and fellowship. As will be argued in the next section, a machine or device is insufficient to promote creaturely and social flourishing.

"Hearth Habits": The Key to Formation in the Age of AI

Few have written as insightfully about the perils, promises, and effects of technology on the life and culture of God's image bearers as Albert Borgmann, who, until his recent death, was regents professor emeritus of philosophy at the University of Montana. In his groundbreaking book *Technology and the Character of Contemporary Life*, Borgmann offers a "mediating view" of technology that probes its underlying implications—both negative and positive.[14] Indeed, Borgmann, via his concept of the "device paradigm," has argued that technology is a force field that imposes itself on human cognition and behavior.[15] That is, our modern machinery has an all-encompassing, magnetic power, one he labels "*the rule of technology*," which is reflected in "*the pervasiveness and consistency of its pattern.*"[16] It is a tide that pulls, pushes, carries, and alters all who float within its domain.

What can be done about this technological tide? One of Borgmann's most unique contributions to the discussion is his assertion that we can resist the

---

13. Lucky, "AI Will Shape Your Soul."

14. Sutton, "Put It on the Scales," 95. To give an example of the influence of Borgmann's book, Andy Crouch, in the acknowledgments of his own book *The Tech-Wise Family: Everyday Steps for Putting Technology in Its Proper Place* (Grand Rapids: Baker Books, 2017), credits Borgmann with inspiring his main concepts.

15. For a definition of *device paradigm*, see chap. 9 of Albert Borgmann, *Technology and the Character of Contemporary Life: A Philosophical Inquiry* (Chicago: Chicago University Press, 1987), 40–48.

16. Borgmann, *Technology and Character*, 207, 208 (emphasis original).

clout of technology "through *the practice of engagement*,"[17] which is found in "focal things" and "focal practices":

> Focal things and practices are the crucial counterforces to technology understood as a form of culture. They contrast with technology without denying it, and they provide a standpoint for a principled and fruitful reform of technology. Generally, a focal thing is concrete and of commanding presence. A focal practice is the decided, regular, and normally communal devotion to a focal thing. . . . The things I have in mind are good books, musical instruments, athletic equipment, works of art, and treasures of nature. The practices I am thinking of are those of dining, running, fishing, gardening, playing instruments, and reciting poetry.[18]

In other words, focal things and practices re-center human experience on the immediate, material world. They are completely embodied; they require mental concentration, physical effort, and coordination; and they draw from our perceptive, imaginative, and creative faculties. Simply stated, they are the fulfillment of the *imago Dei*, a person totally alive.

Yet the practice of engagement does more. It reorients people externally and reintegrates them into customs and community in ways that challenge and rejuvenate them: "[Focal things] are concrete, tangible, and deep, admitting of no functional equivalents; they have a tradition, structure, and rhythm of their own. They are unprocurable and finally beyond our control. They engage us in the fullness of our capacities. . . . A focal practice, generally, is the resolute and regular dedication to a focal thing. It sponsors discipline and skill which are exercised in a unity of achievement and enjoyment, of mind, body, and the world, of myself and others, and in a social union."[19]

Borgmann famously concretized his concept of engagement in the illustration of the hearth. Most preindustrial homes possessed, depended on, and were organized around a fireplace. It is difficult for late-modern Westerners to grasp the significance of the hearth for earlier generations, but Borgmann captures its essence:

> [It was] a place that gathered the work and leisure of a family and gave the house a center. Its coldness marked the morning, and the spreading of its warmth

17. Borgmann, *Technology and Character*, 207 (emphasis original).
18. Albert Borgmann, *Power Failure: Christianity in the Culture of Technology* (Grand Rapids: Brazos, 2003), 22, 124.
19. Borgmann, *Technology and Character*, 219.

the beginning of the day. It assigned to the different family members tasks that defined their place in the household. The mother built the fire, the children kept the firebox filled, and the father cut the firewood. It provided for the entire family a regular and bodily engagement with the rhythm of the seasons that was woven together of the threat of cold and the solace of warmth, the smell of wood smoke, the exertion of sawing and of carrying, the teaching of skills, and the fidelity to daily tasks.[20]

The hearth animated the family's life and identity: it united the members around a common mission, it enabled each person to develop valuable proficiencies, it imparted a sense of contribution and accomplishment, it kept the family connected to nature and the land, and it marked the passing of time. The fireplace permeated familial life, providing countless gifts—gifts that have largely disappeared with the adoption of the furnace.

Reflecting on this illustration, it is no surprise that "the Latin word for hearth, *focus*, reminds us that fire was once the center of our homes."[21] The hearth is an apt metaphor when considering the goal of Christian formation set amid a crowded landscape, one especially inundated by screens, robots, and machine learning: "a focus [i.e., a hearth] gathers the relations of its context and radiates into its surroundings and informs them. To focus on something . . . is to make it central, clear, and articulate."[22]

In an era when AI-based technologies are disrupting, even potentially distorting, what it means to be human, we see an opportunity—perhaps even an invitation—for Christian leaders to rediscover a metaphor that clarifies and concentrates our discipleship endeavors. What might that metaphor be? Although most homes in North America may lack a traditional fireplace, the concept of the hearth is a useful and biblical image.[23] Thus, for our purposes here, we seek to respectfully build on Borgmann's insights by submitting a model we call "hearth habits." We believe these habits will recenter the *imago*

20. Borgmann, *Technology and Character*, 41–42.
21. Crouch, *Tech-Wise Family*, 72. Borgmann describes how the hearth was the epicenter of worship, marriage, child-rearing, death, and burial in ancient Greece and Rome. See Borgmann, *Technology and Character*, 196.
22. Borgmann, *Technology and Character*, 197.
23. Fire is used in Scripture to describe many aspects of God's character, including his holiness and sanctifying work. For instance, "God is a consuming fire" (Heb. 12:29) who "refines" his people (Ps. 66:10), and the Holy Spirit is depicted as manifesting on the day of Pentecost as "tongues of fire" (Acts 2:3). For more on the role of the Holy Spirit in changing us, see chap. 4 of Kim and Hoffman, *Preaching to a Divided Nation*.

Figure 6.2.

Hearth Habits

Dei by promoting embodied, communal practices that counter the dominance of technology in the Western world. Trevor Sutton pinpoints the nature of what we aim to offer: "counterbalancing habits that might serve as mitigating forces for bringing equilibrium to the Christian community."[24]

Here's why hearth habits matter: they reassert and reengage our humanity in the face of AI's persistent, disembodied Gnosticism.[25] Hearth habits retether humans to God's concrete realities, to rootedness in place, and they reaffirm, for Christians, their exalted identity. Jacob Shatzer hits the nail on the head: "The virtual will never be the same as physical presence. We cannot shed the metaphor of the church as the body of Christ—the analogy being to the physical body of Christ."[26]

The hearth habits model is composed of the following five components: the Holy Spirit is the fire starter and sustainer while the fireplace holds four logs: embodied habits, place habits, time-bound habits, and social habits (see fig. 6.2). It should be noted that what follows is not meant to be an exhaustive list. Rather, we make a few suggestions that we hope will act as a catalyst of sorts, a launching pad for further deliberation and exploration. Accordingly, these habits are not intended to be universal; instead, they are to be contextually imagined and applied, depending on one's location, Christian tradition, and church community. We recognize that readers may already practice some of these habits, but perhaps other habits are new or done infrequently. The goal is to stimulate fresh insights and behaviors.

24. Sutton, "Put It on the Scales," 158. Please note that Sutton writes this in the context of "digitally mediated worship practices."

25. The writer Stanisław Lem has called AI "a gnostic machine." This incisively captures the essence of machine learning. Bogna Konior, "The Gnostic Machine: Artificial Intelligence in Stanisław Lem's *Summa Technologiae*," in *Imagining AI: How the World Sees Intelligent Machines*, ed. Stephen Cave and Kanta Dihal (Oxford: Oxford University Press, 2022), 89–108.

26. Jacob Shatzer, *Transhumanism and the Image of God: Today's Technology and the Future of Christian Discipleship* (Downers Grove, IL: IVP Academic, 2019), 139.

The First Log: Embodied Habits

Certain activities are particularly potent at arousing our senses and appealing to our enfleshed, tactile selves. They fulfill the *imago Dei*, give us satisfaction, and bring glory to God. Consider the following:

- **Cooking a meal:** preparing a weekly feast or dish animates creativity and collaboration. I (Paul) delight whenever my wife, Autumn, and I purchase the ingredients for and construct chicken marsala. She cleans, cuts, pounds, coats, and cooks the cutlets. The sauce is composed of sautéed mushrooms, shallots, garlic, and other savory spices. Cream, butter, broth, and marsala are incorporated into a lovely, bubbling sauce. The chicken is respectfully laid in the sauce, where it gently simmers. At the prompted time, I spring into action and boil the water for the fettucine, sprinkling in salt and olive oil. Then I obsessively hover over the pasta, tending to it, stirring it, and ensuring it cooks al dente, which in Italian can be translated "firm to the bite." A potpourri of commotion and connection unfolds with sweating, chatting, fretting, complaining, laughing, and increased hankering. This is more than a meal; it is a sacred, unruly dance in which we are uniquely present to one another while consumed by a task.

- **Nature walking:** After a hectic day in early fall, Autumn and I head to Sachuest Beach, a few miles from our home in Middletown, Rhode Island. This "south facing, mile long," crescent-shaped beach envelops our senses.[27] We saunter along the coastline, absorbing all the gifts surrounding us. As waves rush forward and crash, seagulls squawk, children splash and scream, and the sun slowly slopes over the nearby granite cliffs—spraying speckles of calming colors across the landscape—a peace settles over our worried, weary hearts and manic minds. We find that this habit readjusts our ears, enabling us to perceive the melody playing around us (see 1 Chron. 16:31–33). Perhaps walking in a local park or wooded area will offer a similar sensation.

- **Fishing or birding:** For many, going fishing is a way to reconnect with nature, as it requires fastidious attention to the weather conditions: temperature, currents, wind speed, migration patterns. Another idea

27. "Sachuest Beach (Second Beach)," Facilities, Middletown, Rhode Island, accessed April 29, 2024, https://www.middletownri.com/Facilities/Facility/Details/Sachuest-Beach-Second-Beach-11.

is birdwatching. To gain an appreciation for this undervalued hobby, consider perusing the fascinating book by the theologian John Stott, *The Birds, Our Teachers*.[28]

- **Painting, pottery, knitting, and so on:** Participating in the visual arts and crafts (including textiles) can be relaxing and generative. They reconnect humans with their role as God's cocreators (or subcreators). Humans are deeply like God when they thoughtfully harvest materials from the earth and fashion them into useful, beautiful artifacts that enhance our aesthetic experience.

To summarize, just two or three of the abovementioned embodied habits—completed at least once a week—have the potential to help renew and sustain the *imago Dei* in us.

The Second Log: Place Habits

Next come place habits, which anchor humans into a particular terra firma, a distinct longitude, latitude, elevation, climate, topography, and built environment. This dynamic concept is sometimes called "place."[29] This section will not delve into a theology of place, as that has been done elsewhere.[30] Rather, the objective is to present the idea of "placemaking practices."[31] Craig Bartholomew describes gardening and homemaking as exercises fulfilling God's commands in Genesis 1–2, to "tend to the respective places in which we have been put."[32] We agree with his insight that "the embodied nature of human beings means that our placedness is always local and particular; so too will be our primary responsibility for placemaking."[33]

28. John Stott, *The Birds, Our Teachers: Essays in Orni-theology* (Grand Rapids: Baker Books, 2008).

29. For a succinct definition of *place*, including its "four facets," see Paul A. Hoffman, *Reconciling Places: How to Bridge the Chasms in Our Communities* (Eugene, OR: Cascade Books, 2020), 12–28.

30. Many excellent works can be cited. However, two come immediately to mind: T. J. Gorringe, *A Theology of the Built Environment: Justice, Empowerment, Redemption* (Cambridge: Cambridge University Press, 2002); and John Inge, *A Christian Theology of Place* (London: Routledge, 2003).

31. In this section, we draw from Shatzer's *Transhumanism and the Image of God*, which in turn draws extensively from the excellent book by Craig G. Bartholomew, *Where Mortals Dwell: A Christian View of Place for Today* (Grand Rapids: Baker Academic, 2011).

32. Bartholomew, *Where Mortals Dwell*, 245. Bartholomew outlines his vision in chap. 17, "Placemaking in Garden and Home."

33. Bartholomew, *Where Mortals Dwell*, 245.

Let's start with gardening. Why is this practice important? Simply put, it unites us, in a sensory and tactile way, with the soil and seasons surrounding us. For instance, starting in June, my wife, Autumn, typically purchases and embeds baby tomato plants in large flowerpots on our back porch. Because the deck faces southeast, the plants receive plenty of exposure to the sun. Daily, she examines and waters them before and after work. Additionally, she pots basil and situates it next to perennials such as coneflowers, daylilies, and Shasta daisies, carefully set in metal railing planters. The whole effect is one of vivid colors and sweet, aromatic scents. Through the habit of gardening, Autumn intentionally relates to our place. It should be noted that a person doesn't need a suburban or rural context to cultivate flowers and veggies. It can be accomplished via small containers on an apartment patio or on a windowsill.

Another place habit that merits mentioning is homemaking. This notion exceeds the tasteful selection of paint colors, furniture, and decor. Essentially, it is the promoting of a warm, welcoming atmosphere, one that prioritizes an attitude of *"less is more* and *slower is faster."*[34] Hosts eagerly exhibit attentive presence, in the form of curiosity and kindness, to their guests (more on this below, when we discuss the fourth log and hospitality). Again, this kind of environment can be constructed in a modest space with minimal means. Homemaking is primarily a posture, albeit one that can be enhanced by thoughtful interior design.

Gardening and homemaking work in harmony with our next log: time-bound habits.

The Third Log: Time-Bound Habits

The siren song of AI, like many machines, lures humans away from the rhythms and constraints of time. Because AI is immersive, endlessly stimulating, and addictive, it can untether the mind-body from the clock, a gift of limitation. This reality calls for a holy repacing through time-bound habits. These habits resync us with embodied reality.

The first is silent, listening prayer. This ancient exercise may bear more noticeable fruit in our urbanized, technologically dominant era than in past times. We recommend multiple approaches to this kind of prayer. One can commence with an open Bible and journal. Or maybe try sitting quietly by a window with a drink of choice—say, a cup of tea or lemonade. The beverage

---

34. Bartholomew, *Where Mortals Dwell*, 279 (emphasis original).

is optional, but the absence of devices is not. Look and listen, whispering thanks to God for the innumerous beauties teeming around us.

For those desiring a systematic approach, one can practice various modes of Sabbath (see Exod. 20:8–11). Andy Crouch offers this helpful model: "I suggest a simple, minimal pattern of Sabbath: we choose to turn our devices off *not just one day every week but also one hour (or more) every day and one week (or more) every year.*"[35] Unplugging from machines on a planned, consistent basis restores enfleshed connections by creating fresh space for God, family, friends, and nature. I (Paul) take Tuesday as my personal Sabbath. I do not work. I avoid using my laptop and minimize contact with my iPhone. I often take a slow walk beside a reservoir, then attend a Pilates class and subsequently sit in a hot sauna for thirty minutes at my local gym.

Observing the liturgical year and calendar is a richly communal and ecclesial way of engaging in time-bound habits. We recognize and respect the fact that billions of diverse Christians across the globe participate in this calendar in ways ranging from significant to negligible. Nonetheless, we believe highlighting it is instructive. According to the United States Conference of Catholic Bishops, the year consists of six seasons:

- Advent—four weeks of preparation before the celebration of Jesus's birth
- Christmas—recalling the Nativity of Jesus Christ and his manifestation to the peoples of the world
- Lent—a six-week period of penance before Easter
- Sacred Paschal Triduum—the holiest "Three Days" of the Church's liturgical year, where Christian people recall the suffering, death, and resurrection of Jesus
- Easter—fifty days of joyful celebration of the Lord's resurrection from the dead and his sending forth of the Holy Spirit
- Ordinary Time—divided into two sections (one span of four to eight weeks after Christmastime and another lasting about six months after Easter time), wherein the faithful consider the fullness of Jesus's teachings and works among his people[36]

35. Crouch, *Tech-Wise Family*, 98 (emphasis original).
36. "Liturgical Year and Calendar," United States Conference of Catholic Bishops, accessed April 29, 2024, https://www.usccb.org/prayer-worship/liturgical-year.

The practice of following this calendar should not be misunderstood as some kind of legalistic straitjacket or a rote, formal, or "religious" exercise. Instead, the purpose of following the calendar (and of Christian liturgy in general) is to reenact and memorialize the life and ministry of Jesus Christ as an act of devotion and imitation. In doing so, we recall that Jesus is our Savior, Lord, *and* Exemplar. The Son of God redeemed time as he was led by his heavenly Father. Jesus never strayed from God's schedule. What a benefit and blessing to learn from him! Last but not least, within this sacred schedule, God's presence and power are manifest in a special way, and a humbled body of Christ receives grace. In this paradigm, worship is a profoundly interactive experience.[37]

As seen above, the liturgical year is designed to be observed within a vibrant Christian community, which brings us to the final log.

The Fourth Log: Social Habits

We start with the Eucharist, also known as the Lord's Supper or Holy Communion. It is hard to overstate the theological significance of this practice. James Smith describes it as "supper with the King," "a compacted microcosm of the whole of worship," and a practice that "places us in the midst of the story, in an episode that compresses the gospel into an action."[38] The Lord's Supper reminds Christians that they are a cruciform community, contoured by the cross. For Borgmann, Communion possesses a unique, uniting force: "The history of salvation that is set out in Scripture and centered in the Eucharist certainly provides for the scope and coherence that the diaspora of focal things and communal celebrations is lacking."[39] Bottom line, he views the ordinance as both the focal thing and the focal practice par excellence.[40] Given its meaning and impact, perhaps the Eucharist should be the starting point for all the hearth habits listed here. For the Christian, the holy mystery

37. For more on this practice, as well as how the Reformers sought to renew the "disordered liturgies" of the medieval Western church, see chap. 3 of James K. A. Smith, *You Are What You Love: The Spiritual Power of Habit* (Grand Rapids: Brazos, 2016), 57–81.

38. Smith, *Desiring the Kingdom*, 197–98.

39. Borgmann, *Power Failure*, 125–26.

40. Borgman describes its importance this way: "A sacred practice, then, consisted in the regular reenactment of the founding act, and so it renewed and sustained the order of the world. Christianity came into being this way; the eucharistic meal, the Supper of the Lamb, is its central event, established with the instruction that it be reenacted." Borgmann, *Technology and Character*, 207.

of the body and blood of the crucified One can never be superseded by algo-rithmic machines promising a disembodied, Gnostic pseudosalvation. Herein lies the authority of Communion: it reorients believers to God's creational narrative, reinserting us into the Trinity's redemptive river of liberation and reclamation, flowing toward glorification.

A second social habit we wish to promote is hospitality. From an ancient per-spective, hospitality overlaps with the Lord's Supper, which was (and, for some contemporary denominations, still is) an extended, congregation-wide meal called a "love feast" (see Jude 1:12). It was an event that called for a sacrificial, economic sharing that leveled out the prevailing, hierarchical playing field and reflected God's kingdom values (see 1 Cor. 11:17–34). More broadly, 1 Peter 4:9 issues this command: "Offer hospitality to one another without grumbling." In the original language, the word for "hospitality" is *philoxenoi*, a compound word that comes from *philos* (love) and *xenos* (stranger, foreigner) and can be translated "loving strangers." Although some might argue that this passage refers to interactions among believers, the teaching of Jesus instructs us to show hospitality to those who do not necessarily share our beliefs (see Luke 10:25–37).

In our view, hospitality can have many expressions: it can be as simple as sharing a meal and having an unhurried conversation, it can take the form of an intentional mentoring relationship,[41] and it can even extend as far as foster care and adoption. At its core, hospitality is the practice of sacrificial service based on a shared identity (the *imago Dei*), not on economic, career-related, or other utilitarian considerations that lead people to treat others as com-modities. Hospitality is not only biblically sanctioned; it also fundamentally counters some of the darker tendencies of AI. As discussed in earlier chapters, machine learning is often developed and deployed by technocratic elites who view the world through the lenses of consumeristic, market-driven capitalism, unrelenting progress, and technologism (the belief in the supremacy of science and technological advancement to solve all problems). Perhaps Jacques Ellul's concept of "technique" captures the gist of these worldviews: "*technique* is the *totality of methods rationally arrived at and having absolute efficiency* (for a given stage of development) in *every* field of human activity."[42] It would be dif-

---

41. For more on mentoring, see Matthew D. Kim, ed., *No Program but Time, No Book but the Bible: Reflections on Mentoring and Discipleship in Honor of Scott M. Gibson* (Eugene, OR: Wipf & Stock, 2018).

42. Jacques Ellul, *The Technological Society* (New York: Vintage Books, 1964), xxv (em-phasis original).

ficult to argue that rationalism and efficiency—as understood in late-modern Western culture—are norms exalted in Scripture. We are called to the *imago Christi*, not to the *imago machinarum*. Hospitality, then, can rehumanize us against the dehumanizing effects of technology.

The same is true of the third social habit we wish to promote in this chapter: service. Author Marva Dawn calls "love of neighbor" a "focal concern."[43] Why is that? Jesus declares it to be one of the greatest commandments (see Mark 12:31). Loving service to our neighbors can take countless forms. It means supporting and resourcing vulnerable populations, including immigrants, seniors, those wrestling with mental illness or addictions, and those facing food or housing insecurity. Over the years, our respective institutions (my local church and Sean's university) have sought to address these community-wide deficits by lending our time, talent, and treasure toward actionable solutions. We hope our readers are doing the same in their areas of influence. And while AI offers helpful answers to the many problems besetting our neighborhoods, we must never forget that nothing can replace body-to-body and soul-to-soul contact. The deeply human ministry of presence cannot be supplanted by silicon-based entities. Our very identity as God's icons is at stake.

CONCLUSION

In this chapter we have sought to answer the question, How should Christians be formed and discipled in the age of AI? After defining *formation*, we investigated the role of bodily, corporate habits in formation. Then we scrutinized the Eliza effect on computer-human relations. This led us to the concept of hearth habits and the four logs of embodied, place, time-bound, and social habits. These practices operate on two levels. First, they are positive, generative ways the Spirit molds us into the *imago Christi*. Second, they act as resistant and restorative forces, helping to bolster and reassert our humanness in the face of AI's pervasive, relentless influence.

Up to this point, we have studiously avoided diving into the nitty gritty of ministry praxis. That moratorium ends now. In the final chapter, we will address this inquiry: How should ministry leaders approach AI? With the

43. Marva J. Dawn, *Unfettered Hope: A Call to Faithful Living in an Affluent Society* (Louisville: Westminster John Knox, 2003), 77.

foundation of discipleship and formation laid, we proceed by positing principles we believe will lead us to faithful and fruitful kingdom work.

QUESTIONS FOR REFLECTION

1. What do you think of the definition of *formation* presented in this chapter? In what ways would you agree or disagree with it, and why?

2. Were you familiar with the Eliza effect before reading this chapter? How do you see this dynamic at play in your own life or in the lives of others around you?

3. Review and ponder the four hearth habits delineated above. Which ones are you practicing presently? Are any of them novel to you? Consider trying a new habit, refreshing a lapsed one, or intensifying your commitment to an existing one.

7. How Should Ministry Leaders Approach AI?

We commence this final chapter with an undercurrent of apprehension. Because AI is evolving exponentially, it seems foolish to prescribe actions. Such prescriptions would appear as inadvisable as attempting to nail Jell-O to a wall. Consequently, our recommendations are intended to be more principle-based than tactical. We acknowledge that we can't even begin to anticipate the advantages and complications that algorithm-powered machines will bring about in the future.

Before we offer some guidelines, it is prudent to outline our governing assumptions. First, we are convinced that, at its core, ministry involves the care of people.[1] Humans, as we've taken great pains to underscore, are God's image bearers. Although ministry necessarily involves the shrewd organization of assets (buildings, budgets, reputational capital, etc.), the irreducible element is *ha'adam* (Hebrew for "humanity" or "humankind"; see Gen. 1:27).

Next, while definitions of *ministry* abound due to a diversity of theological traditions and denominations, the vast preponderance of them include the categories of *worship* and *witness*. Scott Sunquist hits the bull's-eye: "Worship is a missional act, and mission has as its goal worship of the Lamb by

---

1. This is a reference to the axiom "Ministry is the care of souls." For example, see Harold L. Senkbeil, *The Care of Souls: Cultivating a Pastor's Heart* (Bellingham, WA: Lexham, 2019). In this case, we prefer the term *people* over *souls*, so as to avoid any connotation of dualism or Gnosticism.

all nations of the world. . . . Worship and mission reinforce and reflect each other. Worship flows out to testimony (witness), and the witness to others leads to thanksgiving and praise for conquest over sin."[2]

Third, when considering the concept of ministry, our primary stance is biased toward the local congregation. Why? Experiential honesty requires it. I (Paul) have pastored the same church for over seventeen years. Nevertheless, that bias should not preclude parachurch, educational, denominational, and other modes of ministry from benefitting from the following reflections.

To make this material accessible to ministry leaders, we employ a traffic sign format. The stop-sign graphic means "Don't do this." The slow sign means "Proceed with caution." And the circular go sign means "Consider moving ahead." Each principle or point is accompanied by explanations of varying length.

We now return to the key research question presented in chapter 3: How might AI advance or hinder human flourishing? Human flourishing, as defined by the *imago Dei*, is our nonnegotiable priority when weighing our relationship with AI. We believe this is reinforced by Scripture's creational narrative. More pointedly, we remain dedicated to a human-centered perspective, which emphasizes the *materiality* of creation and the *creatureliness* (the corporeality or embodiment) of humans. Correspondingly, this perspective includes a desire to keep human authority and responsibility coupled and in balance. That commitment to balance brings to bear two components of our lens here: pastors and leaders are to maintain agency in creativity (e.g., in the generation and communication of biblically based content) and in the shepherding of congregants (e.g., in discipleship and counseling). Because leaders have been entrusted with the precious gift of stewarding people, and because they are accountable to God, these activities must not be abdicated or delegated to machines.

Lastly, a caveat is in order: the recommendations offered below are not meant to be authoritative decrees that are inflexible. We urge leaders to use all the God-given resources at their disposal, including prayerfully seeking the guidance of the Holy Spirit, adhering to ecclesiastical-denominational policies, listening to one's corporate board (e.g., one's session or elders), and continually safeguarding individual (parishioner) conscience.

2. Scott W. Sunquist, *Understanding Christian Mission: Participation in Suffering and Glory* (Grand Rapids: Baker Academic, 2013), 204.

Don't Do This

Do Not Use AI to Write or Deliver an Entire Sermon or Bible Study Lesson

Before scoffing at this admonition, consider that in June 2023, ChatGPT designed and executed an entire worship service (as part of a "biennial convention of Protestants," no less) at a church in Germany, which included a forty-minute sermon delivered by "computer-generated avatars of two men and two women."[3]

A few months later, Pastor Jay Cooper of Violet Crown City Church in Austin, Texas, tasked ChatGPT with designing a worship service. Cooper has stated that "the result was 'a stilted atmosphere.' . . . It seemed to in some way prevent us from connecting with each other. . . . The heart was missing."[4] Some might argue that the response was due in part to bias, as the church had advertised the event as an AI-generated worship service. Were the attendees prejudiced because they knew what they were stepping into? Others might suggest that the response was due to unfamiliarity—a conflicted or underdeveloped reaction to innovation.

What's the problem? It is reductionistic to treat preaching and teaching as simply content distribution. In reality, preaching (and in some respects, teaching) involves a sacred monologue occurring among God's image bearers—including elements of dialogue, as the congregation gives verbal and nonverbal feedback to the speaker, who then responds and adjusts. Gregory Hollifield provides this helpful definition: "Preaching is an embodied, existential act of eternal consequence. . . . When I deliver a sermon, I am delivering truth as it has been filtered through my personality, training, hopes, fears, and experiences—in short, my very soul."[5] As I have detailed elsewhere, preaching is linked to a dynamic chain of custody, bringing about a supernatural transmission and involving the complex interplay between the Holy Spirit,

---

3. Benj Edwards, "AI-Powered Church Service in Germany Draws a Large Crowd," *Ars Technica*, June 12, 2023, https://arstechnica.com/information-technology/2023/06/chatgpt-takes -the-pulpit-ai-leads-experimental-church-service-in-germany.

4. Jim Patterson, "Artificial Intelligence and Church," *UM News*, United Methodist Communications, November 21, 2023, https://www.umnews.org/en/news/artificial-intelligence-and -church.

5. Gregory Hollifield, "AI and Sermon Prep," Preaching Today, Christianity Today International, accessed April 29, 2024, https://www.preachingtoday.com/skills/2023/ai-and-sermon -prep.html.

the Scriptures, the communicator, and the audience.[6] Russell Moore writes, "when we listen to the Word preached, we are hearing not just a word *about* God but a word *from* God."[7] The proclamation of the gospel is nothing less than the living God imparting the living Word through a living being to other living beings. God (the sender) gives a message (the Bible) to his people via a herald, and he expects a response.

It should be no surprise that an algorithm-powered, silicon-based machine is woefully inadequate to carry out this unique God-human interchange. For one, AI has no eternal soul that can communicate with God and other souls. Relatedly, robot-human interaction is impaired by AI's inability to experience authentic empathy. It can perceive, mimic, and mirror emotion, but it can't experience, interpret, or express it in the same way humans can.[8]

Furthermore, as Alison and Jonathan Gerber (homiletician and computer scientist, respectively) insightfully point out, AI cannot "replace" three critical elements of preaching: prophecy, creativity, and prayer.[9] They argue that AI cannot be prophetic: it is not "future oriented. . . . It cannot hope, cannot imagine, cannot dream."[10] Large language models lack creativity: they cannot "write a sermon in a style, or use a technique, of which preachers are yet to even dream."[11] And, of course, computers cannot consciously pray to God as his image bearers do.

Do Not Use AI as a Substitute for Interpersonal Counseling

It is clear that AI contains tremendous potential in therapy. On the one hand, according to a publication by the American Psychological Association,

---

6. See chap. 4, "The Positional Step," of Matthew D. Kim and Paul A. Hoffman, *Preaching to a Divided Nation: A Seven-Step Model for Promoting Reconciliation and Unity* (Grand Rapids: Baker Academic, 2022).

7. Russell Moore, "AI Might Teach, but It Can't Preach," *Christianity Today*, January 26, 2023, https://www.christianitytoday.com/ct/2023/january-web-only/chatgpt-artificial-intelligence-ai-preach-sermons-church.html (emphasis original).

8. Hollifield helpfully cites the work of Simon Baron-Cohen and the concept of humans' empathy circuit (EC), which Hollifield explains this way: "The EC decodes the thoughts and feelings of other people, helps us to think about our own thoughts and feelings, and informs how we react to others emotionally." Hollifield, "AI and Sermon Prep."

9. Alison Gerber and Jonathan P. Gerber, "ChatGPT Has No Future in the Pulpit," Preaching Today, Christianity Today International, accessed April 29, 2024, https://www.preachingtoday.com/skills/2023/chatgpt-has-no-future-in-pulpit.html.

10. Gerber and Gerber, "ChatGPT Has No Future."

11. Gerber and Gerber, "ChatGPT Has No Future."

"chatbots can make therapy more accessible and less expensive. AI tools can also improve interventions, automate administrative tasks, and aid in training new clinicians."[12] On the other hand, not only do chatbots "lack the context, life experience, and verbal nuances of human therapists," they have also shown racial and ability bias, given false information (called hallucinations), and even sexually harassed minors.[13]

It is vital to remember that God created humans to connect with one another and that effective counseling is based on several intangibles that machines cannot possess. These include emotional intelligence, intuition, accumulated wisdom, and experience. In addition, in our view, the best counseling will integrate the multiple spiritual gifts (Greek *charismata*) listed in the New Testament.[14] For instance, Romans 12:6 lists "prophesying," which can be understood as sharing the Scriptures in a way that convicts and edifies and tends to be local and context specific (in distinction from inspired Scripture, e.g., the Old Testament prophets). Verse 8 goes on to list "giving encouragement," sometimes defined as "offering friendship to the lonely and giving fresh courage to those who have lost heart."[15] Other spiritual gifts a Christian counselor might utilize are giving a "message of wisdom" or "of knowledge" (1 Cor. 12:8) and "distinguishing between spirits," sometimes known as discernment (v. 10), to name a few. Something dynamic—even supernatural—happens when a wise, discerning, Spirit-filled person listens fully and speaks the truth in love into another person's life. It is not quantifiable and cannot be duplicated by sophisticated algorithms. It is a precious gift that must not be taken for granted or delegated to a nonsentient being.

Do Not Use AI to Write Whole Worship Songs or Plan Entire Worship Services

Worship lyrics and music are more than words and melodies, more than inputs and outputs, more than vocal and instrumental performance. In

12. Zara Abrams, "AI Is Changing Every Aspect of Psychology. Here's What to Watch For," *Monitor on Psychology*, July 1, 2023, https://www.apa.org/monitor/2023/07/psychology-embracing-ai.

13. Abrams, "AI Is Changing."

14. Of course, we recognize that leaders have many different gifts and that leaders may define spiritual gifts in various ways, depending on their theology and tradition.

15. John R. W. Stott, *The Message of Romans: God's Good News for the World* (Downers Grove, IL: IVP Academic, 1994), 328.

Scripture, worship is something done *for* God and *by* humans. Let's break that down for a moment.

Worship is *for* God. God is the object of worship. That's why Scripture commands humans to praise, glorify, and honor the Lord numerous times. Because the verb *worship* is often in the imperative form, not only is it required, but it necessarily involves human volition, choice, and agency. God wants humans to *desire* and *choose to* adore him. This is precisely why he detests perfunctory, hypocritical worship (see Isa. 29:13–24).

What's more, worship is the reality of heaven, the ultimate reality, one that will continue throughout eternity. The book of Revelation gives us multiple portholes into the throne room of heaven, such as in Revelation 4–5, 7, 11–12, 15, and 19. Song after ecstatic song pours forth from God's redeemed people. This praise is authentic, unassisted, and unsullied by the traps and temptations of modern technology.

And that brings us to the second part: worship is done *by* humans. It is composed and executed by God's image bearers, who are uniquely fashioned for this very task.[16] Scholar Simeon Xu explains how machines are inadequate:

> Above all, every agent in worship should be a *worshiper* who keeps reorienting to God by singing hymns, praying, or listening to God's Word. An AI robot that claims to have consciousness, then, should be able to reorient to God in worship in the same sense that the whole human being can. This is where carbon-based human bodies matter. In worship, human neurons and bodily elements cooperate with the human spirit so that the whole human person consciously praises and adores God. The fundamental differences between carbon-based humans and silicon-based AI, as Borden and Damasio describe, suggest that AI robots cannot respond consciously to God's grace and glory in the same way that humans do, nor can AI robots guide humans to worship God in the manner that humans should.[17]

Xu reminds us that God has expectations for his icon-bearing creatures. In this frame, worship is more relational and responsive than transactional. Humans tend to excel at the former; machines tend to be better at the latter.

16. For more on this theme, see W. David O. Taylor, *A Body of Praise: Understanding the Role of Our Physical Bodies in Worship* (Grand Rapids: Baker Academic, 2023).
17. Simeon Ximian Xu, "AI Can Preach and Sing. So Why Can't It Worship God?," *Christianity Today*, August 25, 2022, https://www.christianitytoday.com/ct/2022/august-web-only/artificial-intelligence-praise-worship-body-carbon.html.

To this section, let us add a word of caution: AI ought to be used sparingly when it comes to virtual reality (VR), as in avatar- or hologram-based worship attendance. In 2022, VR worship services became a hot topic on the heels of the COVID-19 pandemic and subsequent state and local prohibitions banning or limiting public assemblies.[18] Out of sheer curiosity, I (Paul) attended an online training on how to start a VR church. It was shocking to see how many people were already operating on a high level inside this domain. After deep reflection, however, we maintain that in-person church attendance is to be prioritized for those who are physically and mentally able to participate in local, bodily corporate gatherings. This aligns with God's preference for the material and corporeal, as well as the creational narrative presented in chapter 3. Virtual reality, AI, and other forms of technology may promote an unbiblical dualism and Gnosticism and so ministry leaders ought to be extremely careful when offering and using these tools.

Proceed with Caution

Cautiously Use AI to Generate, Research, and Edit Content for Sermons and Bible Studies

We have placed this suggestion under the slow sign rather than the go sign because of the temptation to over-rely on AI. As we have seen, one of the strengths of technology is its ability to simplify complex tasks. In particular, ChatGPT and other programs employing large language models can compose fantastic essays, poems, songs, and more in mere seconds. For pastors, teachers, and other content creators trying to stay afloat in our hyperchanging, hyperconnected, hypercompetitive, and hyperpragmatic environment, the allure to cut corners is real and should not be minimized. And while AI offers great promise in creative endeavors, boundaries and accountability structures should be established so dependency and plagiarism don't rule the day.

With that in mind, how can AI add value? One of my (Paul's) pastor friends recently shared with me that AI has been useful as a starting point in

---

18. Luis Andres Henao and the Associated Press, "Religious People Are Increasingly Attending Worship Services in the Metaverse," *Fortune*, January 31, 2022, https://fortune.com/2022/01/31/virtual-worshipping-services-religion-metaverse. For an example, see Life.Church's outreach into the metaverse: https://www.life.church/metaverse.

his sermon planning and preparation.[19] Machine learning can serve as a firm launching pad. But how? Again, we turn to professor and veteran homiletician Gregory Hollifield, who provides personally tested insights. His advice is to "treat AI as a collaborator," using it to do the following:

- Brainstorm topics and passages.
- Provide researched answers.
- Compile a list of commentaries.
- Gather online sermons based on a chosen text.
- Offer a different perspective.
- Reimagine what you have developed.
- Polish your outline.
- Suggest illustrations and applications.
- Translate your work into other languages.[20]

He would join us and others, however, in avoiding using chatbots for penning complete sermons or Bible studies. We have no need to reiterate the reasons already outlined above. Suffice it to say, people want (and need) to hear a timely and authentic word from God, delivered by their caring shepherd rather than a collection of regurgitated data emanating from a silicon-based, nonsentient machine. Applying AI to the sacred duty of preaching and teaching calls for a delicate balance, reinforced by a support system that guards against habitual overuse and outright thievery.

Cautiously Use AI to Create Job Postings and Volunteer Descriptions

Grammarly, which has been operating in the machine-learning space for years, offers an AI-powered "Job Description Generator."[21] This program can aid pastors and church boards or officers in composing drafts, not only for

19. Michael Perez, email message to author, November 23, 2023. He writes, "I asked ChatGPT to generate a 14-week sermon series through Exodus, and I was pleased with what it gave me. It was a high-level roadmap to break down a sermon series."
20. Hollifield, "AI and Sermon Prep." Additionally, Hollifield makes the case that it is crucial to be transparent about AI's contribution and offers an example of how a speaker can tactfully do it.
21. "Job Description Generator," Grammarly, accessed April 29, 2024, https://www.grammarly.com/job-description.

employment opportunities but also for volunteer positions as well. However, as highlighted in chapter 2, when it comes to soliciting and sifting through applications, church leaders must be sensitive to the ongoing challenges of AI-related bias, which has not yet been.eliminated despite ongoing, concentrated efforts.[22]

GO Consider Moving Ahead

Consider Using AI to Produce Content for Social Media, Websites, and Instruction

One of the areas in which AI can best add value to churches is that of fresh content material. In particular, we are thinking of "social media, newsletter, website, sermon, and kid's ministry" graphics and artwork.[23] Digital marketing expert Chuck Scoggins lists a plethora of credible programs, such as ChatGPT, Frase, Headline, Otter.ai, Rev AI, Lately, Buffer, Article Forge, Conversion AI, Midjourney, Adobe Photoshop, Canva, Artbreeder, and Deepart. io, to name a few.[24] In our post-COVID, digitally dominant era, it is expected that churches will frequently release novel digital content, communicating their services and activities. Unfortunately, churches cannot avoid the reality that they are competing with countless others for people's attention in what has been called "the attention economy." How can churches engage this space? Again, the goal remains faithful presence. What does that look like? On the one hand, the gospel as embodied in a local congregation does not need to be hyped or promoted. It is still worldwide good news, the greatest news in history.[25] On the other hand, there is nothing wrong with contextualizing and highlighting the subversive beauty of the gospel (see 1 Cor. 9, Phil. 2, etc.).

At this juncture, it is prudent to spotlight two lingering concerns. In principle, we agree with Carey Nieuwhof's suggestion that AI can assist ministry leaders

---

22. One instance of such efforts is the founding of the Hire Aspirations Institute by Harvard, Cornell, Princeton, and MIT, along with Microsoft and Apple. See "How Can Bias Be Removed from Artificial Intelligence–Powered Hiring Platforms?," Harvard John A. Paulson School of Engineering and Applied Sciences, June 12, 2023, https://seas.harvard.edu/news/2023/06/how -can-bias-be-removed-artificial-intelligence-powered-hiring-platforms.

23. Chuck Scoggins, "Practical Ways for Churches to Use AI," Church Visuals, https:// churchvisuals.com/article/practical-ways-for-churches-to-use-ai.

24. Scoggins, "Practical Ways."

25. Here we are thinking of Lesslie Newbigin's works, such as *The Open Secret: An Introduction to the Theology of Mission* (Grand Rapids: Eerdmans, 1995).

in "personalizing" communications with our congregants and stakeholders: indeed, it can "help you compose better, more emotionally intelligent notes [and] letters."[26] He is also right to call for sensitivity and discretion in doing so. A case in point is an infamous mistake made by the Peabody Office of Equity, Diversity and Inclusion at Vanderbilt University, which used ChatGPT to write an email response to a mass shooting at Michigan State University in February 2023. Due to an oversight, a small note at the bottom of the message indicated it had been crafted by OpenAI's language model program, not a flesh-and-blood human being. As to be expected, the backlash was swift and vociferous.[27] Prudence prescribes that in certain situations, AI should be an editor, not a creator.

Second, we return to the issue of agency. Our affirmation of using AI for creative purposes is not intended to dismiss the imaginative, productive talents God has bestowed on humans. Christians are to fully harness their God-given faculties to invent attractive material and use all means at their disposal to do so. When struggling or stuck, we can use computers to inject some innovation. The aim is quality and not trendiness. Artificial intelligence could prove to be a spark to this end.

Consider Using AI for Website Management, Optimization, and Content Editing

For some pastors (me included), programming is scary. Yet several applications make coding more accessible to neophytes, such as GitHub Copilot, OpenAI Codex, Amazon CodeWhisperer, and Apple Intelligence. Furthermore, dozens, if not hundreds, of website-chatbot, automated-tasking, and video-editing programs have been offered in recent years. Another relevant area is improving search engine optimization (SEO). I don't ever remember covering technological issues in seminary at the turn of the millennium (2000–2003), but I later discovered their importance when I became a lead pastor. Ministers and church staff would be wise to research which platforms, packages, and plans would best serve their congregational needs.[28]

26. Carey Nieuwhof, "The Ultimate Guide to AI, Pastors, and the Church," CareyNieuwhof .com, accessed April 29, 2024, https://careynieuwhof.com/the-ultimate-guide-to-a-i-pastors -and-the-church.

27. Rachael Perrotta, "Peabody EDI Office Responds to MSU Shooting with Email Written Using ChatGPT," *Vanderbilt Hustler*, February 17, 2023, https://vanderbilthustler.com/2023/02 /17/peabody-edi-office-responds-to-msu-shooting-with-email-written-using-chatgpt.

28. My church uses Planning Center for its worship service planning. Planning Center is increasingly integrating AI technologies into its platform. One program we're investigating is its

Consider Using AI for Human Capital Management (Especially Managing Volunteers)

Computer scientists Thomas H. Davenport and Thomas C. Redman have persuasively argued that AI shines in the classification, cataloging, quality, security, and integration of data management.[29] This progress holds profound implications for those serving churches and nonprofits. One of the most potent resources at these organizations' disposal is volunteerism, which, unfortunately, has been declining as of late.[30] So it is sanguine news to discover that AI has the potential to help with volunteer recruitment, retention, recognition, and mobilization.[31]

Tech entrepreneur Nagendra Babu specifies AI's prospective benefits in terms of stewarding human capital inside nonprofits—including volunteer matching, logistics, scheduling, and tracking; assisting in volunteer experience and support; and even predictive analysis.[32] Unless someone at a church or nonprofit is gifted with big-picture thinking, bad habits will be perpetuated. The Pareto Principle—namely, that 80 percent of outcomes derive from 20 percent of the organization's population—is hard to overcome.[33] Simply put, leaders left to their own devices will keep dipping their buckets into the "supervolunteer" well rather than discover and dig new wells. Two cases illustrate the emerging opportunities that AI offers. St. Jude Children's Research Hospital, which treats children with cancer, has

new Discipls.io, which creates social media posts and other content based on the church calendar. See "Discipls.io," Planning Center, accessed April 29, 2024, https://www.planningcenter.com/integrations/discipls-io.

29. Thomas H. Davenport and Thomas C. Redman, "How AI Is Improving Data Management," *MIT Sloan Management Review*, December 20, 2022, https://sloanreview.mit.edu/article/how-ai-is-improving-data-management.

30. See Thalia Beaty, Glenn Gamboa, and the Associated Press, "Volunteering Has Been Declining for Decades but the Pandemic and Economic Struggles Made It a Lot Worse: 'This Is a Wake-Up Call,'" *Fortune*, April 17, 2023, https://fortune.com/2023/04/17/nonprofit-volunteering-declining-covid-pandemic-economic-hardship.

31. "How Can Artificial Intelligence Improve Volunteer Mobilization in a Community Organization?," LinkedIn, last updated December 17, 2023, https://www.linkedin.com/advice/1/how-can-artificial-intelligence-improve-volunteer-sgsyf.

32. Nagendra Babu, "How AI Is Revolutionizing the Future of Volunteering," LinkedIn, June 20, 2023, https://www.linkedin.com/pulse/how-ai-revolutionizing-future-volunteering-nagendra-babu. Babu builds his case on a credible discussion paper from McKinsey & Company. See Michael Chui et al., "Applying Artificial Intelligence for Social Good," McKinsey Global Institute, November 28, 2018, https://www.mckinsey.com/featured-insights/artificial-intelligence/applying-artificial-intelligence-for-social-good.

33. For more on the Pareto Principle, see Kevin Kruse, "The 80/20 Rule and How It Can Change Your Life," *Forbes*, May 7, 2016, https://www.forbes.com/sites/kevinkruse/2016/03/07/80-20-rule/.

employed "machine learning to find new audiences" that will connect with patient stories and "encourage people to take action."[34] Another illustration is how Amnesty International has combined "more than 6,500 volunteers from 150 countries . . . [and] advanced data science and machine learning techniques to extrapolate data about the scale of abuse that women face on Twitter."[35] Named the Troll Patrol, the project worked with Element AI (of ServiceNow Research) to assemble "the world's largest crowd-sourced dataset about online abuse against women."[36] While other functions have yet to be imagined, invented, and rolled out, these examples give a window into ways AI can help ministry leaders—in the present and in the future—to maximize volunteer capital.

Consider Using AI to Expand God's Mission through Language Translation

One of the most impactful benefits of large language models is how they help facilitate and accelerate the spread of the gospel. According to the Joshua Project, as of 2024 there are 7,280 unreached people groups, which comprise about 3.4 billion people or 42.4 percent of the world population.[37] *Unreached* is defined as "less than or equal to 5% Christian Adherent AND less than or equal to 2% Evangelical"; an unreached people is "a people group among which there is no indigenous community of believing Christians with adequate numbers and resources to evangelize this people group without outside assistance."[38] The majority of these groups cannot be evangelized until they have the story of Jesus properly translated into their local dialect or heart language. Artificial intelligence is a tool that can remove this daunting barrier. According to SIL International, introduced in chapter 2, SIL itself and "its partners have recorded and curated high quality audio in 3600+ languages

---

34. Kristen Shipley, "How One Brand Is Future-Proofing Its Mission by Engaging a New Generation," Think with Google, January 2021, https://www.thinkwithgoogle.com/future-of-marketing/digital-transformation/future-proofing-business.

35. "Crowdsourced Twitter Study Reveals Shocking Scale of Online Abuse against Women," Amnesty International, December 2018, https://www.amnesty.org/en/latest/press-release/2018/12/crowdsourced-twitter-study-reveals-shocking-scale-of-online-abuse-against-women.

36. "Crowdsourced Twitter Study."

37. "Global Dashboard," Joshua Project, accessed April 29, 2024, https://joshuaproject.net/people_groups/dashboard.

38. "Definitions," Joshua Project, accessed April 29, 2024, https://joshuaproject.net/help/definitions#unreached, under "Unreached / Least Reached" (capitals original and underscoring omitted).

in the form of stories, audio books, audio Bibles, and language documentation. This audio is more linguistically diverse than any other audio datasets in the world."[39]

Further, AI can provide more applications in the missions and outreach space. Dr. Mark Tabladillo, a data scientist who works for Microsoft, explains, "Tools powered by Natural Language Processing (NLP) . . . can translate sermons or religious texts into countless languages and dialects, breaking down barriers."[40] This means AI has the potential to enable ministry leaders and churches to participate more fully in the *missio Dei* by translating and contextualizing all kinds of materials (e.g., sermons, videos, and tracts) that convey Christ's teachings to a confused, hurting, and broken world.

In these ways and many others, AI serves as a tool for fulfilling the Great Commission to "make disciples of all nations" (Matt. 28:19), and depending on one's interpretation or eschatological framework, such fulfillment is a necessary precondition before the final return of the Lord Jesus Christ and the consummation of all things.[41] Here's an irony to ponder: rather than AI instigating the doomsday scenario of human disempowerment or extinction, what if, instead, AI aided the spread of God's kingdom and expedited the final revelation of King Jesus? What if AI helped bring about the glorification of the saints and the fullness of the new creation? This is a worthy target, one that contributes to the ultimate flourishing of humans.

CONCLUSION

In this chapter we have explored and analyzed various ways AI can be deployed in the local church and in other ministry contexts. We have done so while maintaining a preference for embodied human presence, committed to

---

39. "Speech Synthesis / Text-to-Speech Research," SIL AI & NLP, SIL International, accessed April 29, 2024, https://ai.sil.org/Research/speech-synthesis.

40. Mark Tabladillo, "How AI Is Reshaping Missions," Missio Nexus, September 5, 2023, https://missionexus.org/how-ai-is-reshaping-missions.

41. Matthew 24:14 says, "And this gospel of the kingdom will be preached in the whole world as a testimony to all nations, and then the end will come." While I (Paul) was in seminary, my missions professor, Dr. Tim Tennent, taught me that the gospel must be declared to every "nation" (Greek *ethnos*, referring to ethnicities, cultures, or people groups) before Jesus's second coming. He made the case that every people group must have the opportunity to hear and respond to the kerygma, the core message of Christianity, before the curtain closes on human history as we know it.

a specific community (e.g., a congregation) and embedded within particular places (e.g., tangible, identifiable neighborhoods). To concretize our recommendations, we have used traffic markers: the stop sign communicates "Don't do this," the slow sign means "Proceed with caution," and the go sign communicates "Consider moving ahead."

Stop-sign activities: using AI to write or deliver a sermon or Bible study, to counsel others, and to compose worship songs or plan worship services

Slow-sign activities: using AI to generate, research, and edit content for sermons and Bible studies, as well as to create job postings and volunteer descriptions

Go-sign activities: using AI to produce creative content for social media, websites, and instruction; for website management, optimization, and content editing; for human capital management, especially volunteer recruitment, training, retention, and mobilization; and for expanding God's mission through language translation

AI is a tool Christian leaders may reflectively harness for the flourishing of their congregations and the neighbors they aim to serve, both nearby and worldwide. Mission that utilizes intelligent machines can be performed faithfully, in a manner that respects the agency and dignity of all image bearers involved. We fervently pray that this will be the story that unfolds in the years to come.

QUESTIONS FOR REFLECTION

1. How have you seen AI used (explicitly or covertly) for ministry or church purposes?
2. What is your response to the traffic sign cues? In what ways are they helpful? In what ways are they unconstructive?
3. Do you agree or disagree with the classification of activities in this chapter (i.e., stop, slow down, and go-ahead activities)? What is missing from these lists? What would you add, subtract, or change, and why?

Conclusion

Today, if you walk the tiny roads of Clashaganniv in County Cork, Ireland, you can easily imagine what it was like to be there 150 years ago, because these small roads are the same boreens my (Sean's) ancestors walked as they went to work the local farms as laborers or as plowmen. The word *boreen* is used extensively in Ireland to refer to a small country road, and it derives from the Irish word *bóithrín*, which itself derives from the word *bó*, "cow." These roads were (and are) little narrow highways, hemmed in by verdant hedgerows, once the little tracks along which cattle were driven and that dotted the Ireland of my great-great-grandfather's time.

Clashaganniv is what is known as a townland. In the Ireland of my ancestors and well up into the 1950s and 1960s, rural dwellers identified more with a townland—often consisting of an area encompassing just a few fields—than a nearby town. Although close to the busy small town of Fermoy, my great-great-grandfather, Thomas Mulcahy, would have described himself as a man from Clashaganniv, born and bred, despite the fact that it measured only 0.62 square miles and encompassed 394 acres. It was in this tiny townland, while living in a one- or two-room thatched cottage that he married my great-great-grandmother, Mary Power, who gave birth to my great-grandmother, Johanna Mulcahy, who married my great-grandfather, Peter O'Callaghan, who then had my grandfather, Jack. I grew up on Jack's knee. As we sat by turf fires, he would tell me stories of his family night after night: of his father, Peter, who fought in the Egypt-Sudan war of 1882; of his grandfather John, who fought in Crimea and lost an arm; of a stonemason relative who died when he fell from a church spire; of the day my great-grandmother's hair turned white after receiving a report that her son, my granduncle Patrick, had been killed at the Battle of the Somme. These were real stories of human experiences told by real human narrators—not hallucinations composed by ChatGPT.

Only a month before writing this, I found myself at the grave of John O'Callaghan, my other great-great-grandfather. It is the custom in Ireland—certainly for people of my generation—to visit the graves of our ancestors and to feel their presence, even after they are long gone. John died in 1907, yet he is remembered in our family as if he died last year. The cemetery where he is buried is on the site of a church, now gone, going back to the 600s CE. It was there, tradition has handed down, that Saint Cruimthir built his church, giving the cemetery the name Kilcrumper, or the Church of Cruimthir. These are ancient places that lie much like they did hundreds of years ago, among people who still live in the town and still have memories that stretch back generations. One man I met told me that he remembered a granduncle of mine playing handball against a wall in the town over seventy years ago. Artificial intelligence cannot tell those stories, and even if it fabricated them, they would be empty, devoid of the rich depths of memory and emotion.

I was raised by my grandparents and parents to connect with the past, to see myself as part of a continuum of tradition, to know the stories of the past and pass them on. When I visited my native land in December 2023, I visited various gravesites to remember different sides of the family and to feel our shared history. My grandmother's grave is situated right next to the ruins of a church dating back to the 1500s; the tiny cemetery itself is mentioned in church documents dating back to 1199 CE. Generations of her family are buried there, and I know the life stories of almost all of them. Artificial intelligence can gather these stories as data, of course, but it could never replicate the heartbeat of living history, which pulsated through my grandmother's words as she shared about these lives with me.

Clashaganniv looks much like it would have looked when Thomas Mulcahy courted Mary Power along its tiny lanes, bordered by lush-green and fertile fields, in the months before their marriage in 1869. I was already part of them, though they did not know it or even give it a thought; yet their DNA is coded inside me, and I am who I am partly because of them. But this is a different kind of code from the code we have been writing about in this book, the code that drives AI and the powerful computing systems from which it leaps in digital form.

I am describing human code, filled with the all-too-human memories of women and men going back over millennia, their loves, their passions, their intimate connection with place, the battles they fought, their jobs as stonemasons, shoemakers, laborers, plowmen, and keepers of homes and families. The women and men my grandparents told me so much about were rich in love and friendships and experiences, though poor in economic terms. They did not need AI to live their lives to the full—being fully available to one another, helping in one another's farms and smallholdings, acting as midwives to neighbors and laying out their dead when the time came. Until the 1960s, all my direct ancestors had been born in their own homes. They were concretely linked to physicality. When I visit their graves or the sites of their now largely demolished homes, I connect with them as once-embodied people, not as digital shadows.

All of this is to say that as human beings, we have lived for millennia without AI. Our humanness was both our strength and our weakness, but it was us. We could be nothing else. And we can still root and anchor ourselves in that physical, embodied self, where AI is not what defines us but rather what aids and supplements us. Artificial intelligence can never replace our connection with the land, our sense of family history, our ability to hug and to hold, our faults and failings and frailty.

If this book is about anything, it is not about understanding ourselves as techno-humans, fused with the algorithms of machine learning; rather, it is about the need to understand technology as our ancestors understood their plows, looms, shovels, and pickaxes—as tools used to complete a job, not to take over our lives so that we become products divorced from family, friends, emotions, and our living history.

As I look back on old photographs and remember the stories I've been told, what really stands out to me is that these ancestors flourished as human beings. They may not have always flourished financially, but they got by and lived full lives, having children and grandchildren and cherishing their work, their neighbors, and their communities. My grandmother lived next door to the same neighbors for fifty years, and my sister lives in the same house my mother moved into in 1932. I grew up in vibrant communities, in which relationships really mattered and you knew everyone on your street and could go to them when in need. This they all achieved without computer technology.

We are not attempting to be churlish Luddites about AI. Indeed, AI is an incredible technology that can make our world infinitely more interesting and efficient, and it does (and will continue to) save lives in the field of medicine and enable us to communicate as never before.

However, AI cannot make us feel connected to vibrant human communities, where the sheer messiness of human life is worked out in a way that causes us to be joyful and part of a fabric of being that is connected by relationships, which are intertwined at the level of the heart. It cannot do that because, despite all of its brilliance, it's not human; it doesn't have a heart or soul or DNA that go back millennia. Yes, it has code, and that code is the vehicle for extraordinary amounts of data that can be processed in a split second. Nevertheless, it doesn't have that profound, visceral experience of life that comes from living and laughing and crying and wondering, from nights out with friends, from romance and love, from walking the little roads of a townland like Clashaganniv on a summer's evening, smelling the hay and the horses. It is joy that allows us to flourish; that joy might come at the end of hard times that challenge and stretch us to the breaking point, or it might be spontaneous, but it serves as the seedbed for whatever makes us blossom and grow, and it comes from our relationships, from daily interactions with other people who bear the image of God and bring his joy into our ordinary lives.

To be clear, we benefit from AI—it offers much good to our world—but it's not enough. We need to reclaim what makes us human, what still lies within our DNA. To view ourselves as mere data, as cogs in a technocratic system, may make us more efficient, performing calculations and making predictions that would otherwise take us days or weeks to achieve, but just as our ancestors viewed their own technology, we should view our machines as tools we use and not the other way around.

In a future filled with AI, we still need to be fully human, because we were created to be human and have been human in every age and place. We must never let go of this reality. Even if the introduction of AI means that we can make the world a better place because it can help us eliminate so much that has caused human suffering and limitation, we still need to embrace the human nature that inspires us to thrive.

Our goal throughout this book has been to focus on human flourishing, which we have framed in terms of a creational narrative, presented in chapter 3. Our whole Christian anthropology must flow from the story, plan, and order of the Creator as exhibited in creation. It was there—the original creation—that God revealed not only his purpose for humanity but also how human beings should live their lives as bearers of the image and breath of

God. Through the method of selective engagement, we have evaluated AI based on the extent to which it aligns with the triune God's plan for human flourishing. Our desire has been to encourage Christian educators and ministry leaders to comprehend and embrace AI, while never letting go of the fact that God has created us to be fully human, especially in a world increasingly saturated with technology.

It is undeniable that AI is here to stay and will play a significant role in our future. At the same time, however, we reject the sardonic words spoken by Rear Admiral Cain to a chastened yet defiant Maverick: "The future is coming, and you're not in it." Because of the grace and mercy of Almighty God, demonstrated through the incarnation, life, death, resurrection, and ascension of Jesus Christ, robots do not determine the outcome of history. According to Scripture, liberated and glorified *humans* will occupy the new creation and worship the King of Kings forever. If we are to live into this story faithfully, it will require us to apply our God-given authority and responsibility and enthusiastically embrace and hold dear the *imago Dei*—which makes us unique in the universe. And if we do that, we can be confident that as the future comes, humans will remain firmly fixed in the middle of it.

Appendix A

Nine Definitions of AI

The following nine definitions illustrate the ways AI can be viewed from multiple perspectives. They are all taken from chapter 1, with the exception of the final example. Each is attributed to one of the expert sources discussed.

Artificial Intelligence Is ...

1. "The science and engineering of making intelligent machines, especially intelligent computer programs. It is related to the similar task of using computers to understand human intelligence, but AI does not have to confine itself to methods that are biologically observable." (John McCarthy)
2. A "registry of power" in that it serves the interests of various people and institutions and promotes their interests. (Kate Crawford)
3. A "catalyst of change" and a crucial step in social evolution contributing to social transformation. (Tomas Chamorro-Premuzic)
4. A totalizing influence on all structures of society. (Max Tegmark)
5. "The ability of a machine to display human-like capabilities such as reasoning, learning, planning and creativity." (European Parliament)
6. "Systems that display intelligent behaviour by analysing their environment and taking actions—with some degree of autonomy—to

achieve specific goals." (European Commission's High-Level Expert Group on Artificial Intelligence)

7. "A new and exceedingly powerful mechanism for exploring and organizing reality. . . . AI accesses reality differently from the way humans access it. And if the feats it is performing are any guide, it may access different *aspects* of reality from the ones humans access." (Kissinger, Schmidt, and Huttenlocher)

8. Understood as being a "prediction machine." It aids and informs decision making. (Agrawal, Gans, and Goldfarb)

9. A tool to be used for human flourishing, subject to human agency and authority. (O'Callaghan and Hoffman)

Appendix B

Six Views on Technology

1. **The pessimistic or phenomenological view:** "Technology is not neutral at all, but . . . it instead has a controlling or alienating influence on society."[1] Adherents of this view include Martin Heidegger and Jacques Ellul.[2]

2. **The optimistic or instrumentalist view:** "Technological artifacts ('things') have no agency of their own, would not exist without humans, and therefore are simply tools that are there to be used by us. Their value lies in how we decide to use them, which opens up the possibility of radical improvement to our lives. Technology is a neutral means with which we can achieve human goals, whether these be good or evil."[3] Adherents of this view include Francis Bacon, Norbert Wiener, Karl Steinbuch, and Georg Klaus.[4]

3. **Technological Utopianism:** This view is "the belief in technology—conceived as more than tools and machines alone—as the means of achieving a 'perfect' society in the near future. Such a society,

---

1. Fabio Tollon, "Technology: Instrumental, Determining, or Mediating?," *3 Quarks Daily* (blog), February 6, 2023, https://3quarksdaily.com/3quarksdaily/2023/02/technology-instrumental-determining-or-mediating.html.
2. A. Trevor Sutton, "Put It on the Scales: Bringing Reflective Equilibrium to Digital Ecclesiology" (PhD diss., Concordia Seminary, 2023), 71–72, 95.
3. Tollon, "Technology."
4. Sutton, "Put It on the Scales," 119–20.

moreover, would not only be the culmination of the introduction of new tools and machines; it would also be modeled on those tools and machines in its institutions, values and culture."[5] Adherents include Ray Kurzweil and Elon Musk.

4. **Pluralism:** This view construes "technology as a complex web of numerous countervailing forces without ever actually articulating an underlying and orienting order in the midst of the web."[6] There are no leading adherents of this approach as it is akin to "technological agnosticism."[7]

5. **The mediating or postphenomenological view:** "By mediating our actions and experiences, technologies help to shape the quality of our lives and of our moral actions and decisions."[8] Put differently,

> Mediation theory focuses on the ways that technologies shape our *experience* of the world. For example, think of a simple technology such as contact lenses. Someone who wears contact lenses experiences the world completely differently when they are wearing the lenses compared to when they are not. This is not to make the almost trivial point that their visual perception is changed in some way. Rather, the deeper point is that the way they can possibly go about their lives *with* contact lenses is substantially different from when they do not have them. The way they are in the world is *different*: without the contacts they might not be able to drive, to read properly, to play the piano, etc.[9]

Adherents of this view include Don Ihde, Peter-Paul Verbeek,[10] and Albert Borgmann.[11]

5. Howard P. Segal, "The Technological Utopians," in *Imagining Tomorrow: History, Technology and the American Future*, ed. Joseph H. Corn (Cambridge: MIT Press, 1986), http://web.mit.edu/m-i-t/science_fiction/jenkins/jenkins_1.html.

6. Sutton, "Put It on the Scales," 95. For more on this view, see Albert Borgmann, *Technology and the Character of Contemporary Life: A Philosophical Inquiry* (Chicago: Chicago University Press, 1987), 11.

7. A. Trevor Sutton, email message to author, June 20, 2024. He elaborates that those who hold this position "punt on the topic of technology and say that technology is explainable through a complex web of economics, anthropology, science, and whatever other forces might be in the mix. *To ask which tech scholar holds to this view is like asking 'which theologian best represents the agnostic view'*" (emphasis original).

8. Peter Paul Verbeek, *Moralizing Technology: Understanding and Designing the Morality of Things* (Chicago: University of Chicago Press, 2011), 5–6.

9. Tollon, "Technology" (emphasis original).

10. Tollon, "Technology."

11. Sutton, "Put It on the Scales," 73.

6. **Selective engagement:** This position is committed to human flourishing and grounded in bodily, material realities. This is the view presented within this book, predominantly in chapters 3 and 4. It is more explicitly committed to the *imago Dei* and a creational narrative than the optimistic and mediating views.

Recommended Resources

Bartholomew, Craig G. *Where Mortals Dwell: A Christian View of Place for Today.* Grand Rapids: Baker Academic, 2011.

Bess, Michael. *Our Grandchildren Redesigned: Life in the Bioengineered Society of the Near Future.* Boston: Beacon, 2015.

Borgmann, Albert. *Power Failure: Christianity in the Culture of Technology.* Grand Rapids: Brazos, 2003.

———. *Technology and the Character of Contemporary Life: A Philosophical Inquiry.* Chicago: Chicago University Press, 1987.

Brue, Ethan J., Derek C. Schuurman, and Steven H. Vanderleest. *A Christian Field Guide to Technology for Engineers and Designers.* Downers Grove, IL: IVP Academic, 2022.

Chamorro-Premuzic, Tomas. *I, Human: AI, Automation, and the Quest to Reclaim What Makes Us Unique.* Boston: Harvard Business Review, 2023.

Crawford, Kate. *Atlas of AI: Power, Politics, and the Planetary Costs of Artificial Intelligence.* New Haven: Yale University Press, 2021.

Crouch, Andy. *The Tech-Wise Family: Everyday Steps for Putting Technology in Its Proper Place.* Grand Rapids: Baker Books, 2017.

Dyer, John. *From the Garden to the City: The Place of Technology in the Story of God.* Rev. ed. Grand Rapids: Kregel, 2022.

Ellul, Jacques. *The Technological Society.* New York: Vintage Books, 1964.

Harari, Yuval Noah. *Homo Deus: A Brief History of Tomorrow.* New York: Harper Perennial, 2017.

Imes, Carmen Joy. *Being God's Image: Why Creation Still Matters.* Downers Grove, IL: IVP Academic, 2023.

Keator, Mary. *Lectio Divina as Contemplative Pedagogy: Re-appropriating Monastic Practice for the Humanities.* New York: Routledge, 2018.

Kissinger, Henry A., Eric Schmidt, and Daniel Huttenlocher. *The Age of AI and Our Human Future*. New York: Little, Brown, 2021.

Kurzweil, Ray. *The Singularity Is Near: When Humans Transcend Biology*. New York: Viking, 2005.

Lee, Kai-Fu. *AI Superpowers: China, Silicon Valley, and the New World Order*. Boston: Houghton Mifflin Harcourt, 2018.

McLuhan, Marshall, and Eric McLuhan. *Laws of Media: The New Science*. Toronto: University of Toronto Press, 1992.

Schuurman, Derek C. *Shaping a Digital World: Faith, Culture and Computer Technology*. Downers Grove, IL: IVP Academic, 2013.

Shatzer, Jacob. *Transhumanism and the Image of God: Today's Technology and the Future of Christian Discipleship*. Downers Grove, IL: IVP Academic, 2019.

Smith, James K. A. *Desiring the Kingdom: Worship, Worldview, and Cultural Formation*. Grand Rapids: Baker Academic, 2009.

Suleyman, Mustafa. *The Coming Wave: Technology, Power, and the 21st Century's Greatest Dilemma*. With Michael Bhaskar. New York: Crown, 2023.

Sutton, A. Trevor, and Brian Smith. *Redeeming Technology: A Christian Approach to Healthy Digital Habits*. St. Louis: Concordia, 2021.

Tegmark, Max. *Life 3.0: Being Human in the Age of Artificial Intelligence*. New York: Knopf, 2017.

Thacker, Jason. *The Age of AI: Artificial Intelligence and the Future of Humanity*. Grand Rapids: Zondervan Thrive, 2020.

Scripture Index

Old Testament

Genesis

1–2 67, 78, 146
1:1–2 63
1:4 64
1:10 64
1:12 64
1:18 64
1:21 64
1:25 64
1:26–27 74
1:27 66, 153
1:28 66, 68
1:31 64
2 77
2:7 70, 75, 136
2:15 57, 67
2:15–20 77
2:16–17 68
3 68, 69
3:1 68
3:6 68
3:14–19 68
3:16 69
4:17 67n11
5:1 74
9:6 74

Exodus

20:8–11 148

1 Chronicles

16:31–33 145

Psalms

8 78
8:5 61
8:5–6 78
8:7–8 78
19:1–6 65
24:1 65
66:10 143n23
145:9 66

Proverbs

4:23 126

Isaiah

6:3 65
9:6 72
25:6 73
29:13–24 158
64 136

Jeremiah

29:7 72

Daniel

7:9 65
7:13 65

New Testament

Matthew

5:43–48 72
5:45 66
19:28 71
28:19 137, 165

Mark

12:31 151

Luke

10:25–37 150

John

1:1 63
1:3 63
1:14 73
8:32 70n18
8:36 70n18

Acts

2:3 143n23
14:16–17 66

Romans

1:19–20 65
5 70
5:20 71

6:4 73
6:18 70n18
6:22 70n18
8 xiii, 62, 68, 70, 73, 78n47
8:2 70n18
8:16–17 70
8:18 73
8:20–21 68
8:21 23, 69, 70, 73
8:22 69
8:28–30 136
9 136
12:6 157
12:8 157
14:12 78

1 Corinthians

1:2 137n3
6:11 137n3
9 161
11:1 137n1
11:7 74
11:17–34 150
12:8 157
12:10 157

2 Corinthians

3:18 6, 73, 136
4:17 73
5:10 78

Galatians

3 78
5:1 70n47

Ephesians

5:1 137n1
5:21–33 136

Philippians

2 70, 161

Colossians

1:15–16 63
1:20 71

1 Thessalonians

5:23 75

2 Thessalonians

2:13 137

1 Timothy

1:17 65

Hebrews

2:11 137n3
10:10 137n3
10:14 137n3
12:10 137n3

12:29 143n23
13:12 137n3

James

3:9 74

1 Peter

2:11 72
4:9 150
5:10 73

Jude

1:12 150

Revelation

4–5 158
7 158
11–12 158
15 158
19 158
19:6–9 73
20:11–15 78
21 136
21–22 136
21:2 63
21:10 63
21:10–11 73
21:23 73
22 136
22:1 63
22:17 63

Subject Index

advertisements, 45
Affectiva, 17–18
agency, 66, 79–80, 137, 154, 158, 162, 166, 175
algorithmic bias, 56
algorithms, 10–11, 14, 27, 31, 44, 100, 107, 118
Amazon CodeWhisperer, 162
andragogy, 111, 112–13, 120, 124, 130
anthropology, x, 6, 170
Apostles' Creed, 63
Apple Intelligence, 162
art, 45, 67
artificial intelligence (AI)
  as a collaborator, 160, 161–64
  and decision making, 16, 27, 29, 30–32, 52, 107, 117–18
  definitions of, 9–10, 21–28, 173–74
  environmental impact, 22–23, 56–57
  general (AGI), 5, 11, 13, 15, 29, 58, 100
  generative, 11, 14–15, 26, 47, 111, 124–25
  hallucinations, 87–88, 121–22, 157
  limited memory, 16
  mind (theory of), 16
  narrow (ANI), 5, 11–12
  reactive, 15
  related bias, 161
  self-aware, 16–17
  strong, 12
  super (ASI), 11, 13, 18
  systems, 26–27

attention economy, 41, 161
augmentation, 33, 93, 104
autism, 42
automobiles, 35, 53–54, 93
autonomy, 5, 26, 34–35, 36n85, 54, 173

backpropagation, 20
Bible, 40, 60, 115
  schools, 32, 111, 113
  sermons, 155–56, 160, 166
  study, 85, 155–56, 159–60, 166
  translation, 40
big data, 11, 14, 100, 117, 124
Blade Runner, 104
boreen, 167
Borgmann, Albert, 141–43, 149, 176
BRAIN Initiative, 102
Brave New World (Huxley), 105
Brookings Institution, 27

catalyst, 10, 24
chatbots, 43, 46, 124, 140, 157, 160
ChatGPT, 2–3, 6, 14, 26, 44, 87–89, 121, 124–25, 155, 159, 161–62
Chinese Room experiment, 18
Clear, James, 138
code, 115, 168–70
cold cases, 49
collaborator, 160, 161–64

common grace, 6, 66, 68, 75n39
CompanionMX, 18
competition, 53, 104
computer coding, 50, 162
connective beings, 76
consciousness, 13, 16, 18–19, 138, 158
conspiracy theory, 115–17
cooperation, 53, 58, 137
cosmic order, 78, 162
Crawford, Kate, 22–24, 57, 173
creational narrative, x, 61–62, 69, 71, 74,
    80–81, 139, 150, 154, 159
creator, 62, 76–78, 136, 162
creatureliness, 62, 154
cross, 70–71, 78n47, 136, 149
Crouch, Andy, 148
cultural mandate, 66–68
culture wars, 113
cyberattacks, 52

DARPA, 101
databases, 10, 12, 118, 125
datafication, 24, 107
dataism, 107–8
decay, 69, 71
decision-making, 5, 16, 29–32, 52, 124
deepfakes, 45, 115
defense industry, 34, 35–36, 51–52, 101–2
diplomacy, 52–53
disabilities, 42, 48, 103
discipleship, 135, 137–38, 141, 143
disinformation, 44–45, 113–15, 117
disintegration, x, 62, 68–69, 70
DNA mapping, 102
dreams, 13, 123, 156
drones, 10, 26, 32, 34, 52, 92
Dyer, John, 84–86

ecclesiology, 135
echo chambers, 41
ecology, 51, 89
economics, 10, 32, 46, 176n7

ecosystems, 51, 139
    biological, 57, 89
    technological, 24, 86, 89
ectogenesis, 106
education, 6, 43–44, 59, 128, 138
Eliza effect, 139–40, 151
embodiment, 22–23, 72, 93–94, 142, 145–46,
    169
emotions, 16–18, 33, 42, 89, 94
Enlightenment, 29
entertainment, 45
environments, 24, 26, 56, 85, 131, 147
eschatology, 6, 71, 96, 112
Eucharist, 149–50
evangelism, 124, 164
evolution, 15, 19, 24, 33, 36, 104
extinction, 5, 40, 57–58, 165

Facebook, 2, 107, 119–20, 127
faithful presence, 72, 161
fake news, 41, 115, 122
financial markets, 10
flourishing, ix–x, 5, 61–62, 72, 80, 97, 123,
    136, 154, 170
focus, 31, 81, 91, 94, 103, 143
formation, 6, 41, 135–39, 141, 143

general revelation, 6, 65–66, 68
genetic engineering, 83, 104–5
GitHub Copilot, 50, 162
God's story, 62, 69, 72, 74
Google Translate, 10
global markets, 10
glorification, x, 62, 73–74, 136, 139n7, 150,
    165
gnōsis, 94, 116, 117
Gnosticism, 65, 83, 94–96, 116, 144, 153n1,
    159
"go-sign" AI activities, 161–65, 166
gospel, 114, 124, 156, 161, 164, 165n41
Grammarly, 43, 160
Great Commission, 165

ha'adam, 153
habitation, 56, 136

habits, 6, 118, 129, 136, 138–39, 141–51
health care, 25, 54–56, 59
hearth habits, 6, 141–44, 151
    embodied habits, 139, 145–46
    place habits, 146–47
    social habits, 149–51
    time-bound habits, 147–48
heaven, 71, 73, 76, 79, 96, 136, 158
Hinton, Geoffrey, 19, 20–21, 58
Hollywood, 2, 46
Holy Communion. *See* Eucharist
Holy Spirit, xiii, 63, 64, 143, 144, 148, 154,
    155
honesty, 56, 125, 154
hospitality, 147, 150–51
human-centered perspective, 61
Human Genome Project, 102
human qualities
    ambition, 50
    attention, 41
    authority, 78
    experiences, 41, 168
    flourishing, ix–x, 5, 61–62, 72, 80, 97, 123,
        136, 154, 170
    identity, 78
Huttenlocher, Daniel, 28, 51
hyperconnection, 24

IBM Watson, 12
image bearers, 50, 76, 80, 136, 141, 153, 155,
    158, 166, 170
imago Christi, 6, 136–37, 141, 151
imago Dei, x, 6, 62, 66, 68, 74–75, 79–80,
    136, 142, 145, 150, 154, 171
imago machinarum, x, 151
immortality, 4, 76, 95, 103
inclusio, 63
inconspicuousness, 40
inner person, 135
interfaces, 33, 56, 83, 92–93, 102, 104

Jesus Christ, x, xi, 6, 63, 65, 69–72, 81, 149,
    165, 171
judiciary, 48–50

Kissinger, Henry, 28, 51
Kurzweil, Ray, 58, 96, 98–100, 176

law, 48–50, 114, 121
laws of media, 86
learning, 9
    deep, 11, 14, 20
    machine, 11, 13–14, 20, 43, 46, 79, 119,
        139, 140, 150, 164
lectio divina, 127–28, 130
lethal autonomous weapon systems (LAWS),
    52
liberation, x, 62, 69–71, 150
liturgical year, 138, 148–49
living history, 168
Luddism, 4

machinery, 4, 39, 81, 86, 141
macroeconomics, 47
manufacturing, 25, 30, 47, 88, 123
Marr, Bernard, 15–18
materiality, 62, 81, 154
McCarthy, John, 20, 21–22, 173
McLuhan, Marshall, 86
medicine, 5, 32, 55–56, 100, 107, 124, 170
metanarrative, x, 6, 62, 65
metaphors, 68, 136, 143–44
methodology, 88–89
military, 29, 35, 36n85, 51, 54, 101–2, 104
mind mapping, 103
misinformation, 113–14
missio Dei, 165
mission, 40, 59, 71–72, 75, 164, 166
models
    generative, 14
    language, 47, 156, 159, 164
Moore, Russell, 156
morality, 40, 75
motor vehicles, 28, 35, 53–54
multiplicity, 68
Musk, Elon, 4, 99, 176

narrative-topical approach, 62
natural language, 18

Natural Language Processing (NLP), 165
neural networks, 13–14, 19–21
neuroceuticals, 100–101, 104
neurodivergent, 42
neurons, 14, 16, 21, 158
neuroscience, 101–2, 104
neuroweapons, 102
new creation, 6, 72, 136, 171
Nicene Creed, 63
1984 (Orwell), 105
nuclear weapons, 51–52

object classification, 21
OpenAI, 50, 87–88, 162

Pareto Principle, 163
pedagogy, 44, 128, 131
personalization, 162
pharmaceuticals, 97, 100, 103–4
plagiarism, 46, 159
prediction, 16, 24, 31–33, 47, 119, 170
predictive policing, 49
politics, 10, 22, 44–45, 58, 118
posthuman, 91–92, 105
Postman, Neil, 86–87
prayer, 6, 129, 137, 147, 156
problem-solving, 9
prophecy, 156

rationality, 26, 31, 75
RealEyes, 17–18
reason, 18, 22, 29, 75–76
reclamation, x, 62, 71–72, 150
recognition, 21
    facial, 26, 49, 105
    speech, 21, 26, 42
redemption, 64, 66, 71, 78n47, 139n7
relationships, 29–30, 42–43, 53, 64, 73, 76–
    77, 79, 85, 87, 93, 95, 138–41, 170
religion, 40–41
Renaissance, 29
replacement, 31
Replika, 42–43, 124, 141
risk, 5, 27, 47, 58

responsibility, 77–80, 123, 137, 154
responsibility gap problem, 52
robotics, 42, 97
robots, 2, 5, 34, 47, 76, 78, 124

Sabbath, 131, 138, 148
sanctification, 137
Schmidt, Eric, 28, 51
Schuurman, Derek, 86–87
science fiction, 13, 36, 97, 105, 125
Scripture, x, 61, 62, 65, 77, 80, 85, 128, 136,
    143n23
search engine, 120, 162
self-driving cars, 34, 35, 54
search engine optimization (SEO), 162
shalom, 72
SIL International, 40, 164
sin, 66, 68–69, 154
Singh-Kurtz, Sangeeta, 42–43
Singularity, the, 98–100
"slow-sign" AI activities, 159–61, 166
smart cities, 10
Smith, James K. A., 138, 149
social engineering, 119
social media, 41, 45–46, 90, 118, 126–27,
    131, 161, 166
social usage, 88–89
Sophia, 16
souls, 75–76, 77, 95, 135, 156
sovereignty of God, 65
special revelation, 65, 94
spiritual gifts, 157
spirituality, 40
steward, 74, 154, 163
"stop-sign" AI activities, 155–59, 166
Stott, John, 75–76, 146
surveillance, 11
    public, 11
    state, 105
surveillance capitalism, 41
Sutton, A. Trevor, 132, 144, 176n7
synthetic biology, 97
synthetic humans, 104

techno-apocalypticism, 5, 112
techno-humans, 33, 91–93, 169
technologism, 4, 150
technology, 5, 50, 58, 84, 85
    computer, 9
    modern, 158
    neutral, 23
    new, 84
Tegmark, Max, 24–25, 35, 58, 79n50, 100, 173
teleprinter-communicated text, 19
templates, 29, 125
Terminator Jesus, 4
texting, 90, 131
Thacker, Jason, 18–19
theosis, 64
therapy, 156–57
TikTok, 45–46, 114
Top Gun: Maverick, 1–2
transformation, 24–25, 70
transhuman, 4, 91, 94, 95, 103
Transhumanist Manifesto, 93
transportation, 25, 53–54
Trinity, 62, 64, 71, 73, 81, 150
tselem, 74
Turing, Alan, 19–22, 93n24

Turing test, 19, 22
Turkle, Sherry, 130
Twitter (now X), 127, 164
two axes, 59

virtual assistant, 10, 42
virtual reality (VR), 131, 159
volunteers, 160, 163–64

wandering attention, 41
war, 4, 35, 52, 58, 113
weapons, 10, 25, 34, 52, 59, 102
wetware, 95
witness, 41, 65n8, 72, 115, 120, 122, 124, 130, 153–54
worship, 123–24, 138–39, 149, 153–54, 157–58, 171

X (formerly Twitter), 127, 164
X factor, 12
Xu, Simeon, 158

youth, 103

Zion, 73